"Human beings have never had more access to more information through more channels. But all that data is meaningless apart from human trust. In *Untrustworthy*, Bonnie Kristian, a knowledgeable and reliable guide, helps us to consider the causes, consequences, and hopes for working through what is not only an epistemological crisis but also a relational one. Overcoming our current polarization will begin only when trust is built across fractured communities, and this book will help in that work."

—**Karen Swallow Prior**, Southeastern Baptist Theological Seminary; author of *On Reading Well: Finding the Good Life through Great Books*

"In *Untrustworthy*, Bonnie Kristian pulls together a compendium of resources for understanding the media landscape and disrupting its hold on our lives, our relationships, and our politics. Bonnie understands that Christianity has much to do with knowledge, and knowledge much to do with Christianity, and has written a book that will help restore knowledge to its rightful place in the lives of Christians and the church."

—**Michael Wear**, author of *Reclaiming Hope: Lessons Learned in the Obama White House about the Future of Faith in America*

"Our country's epistemological crisis is perhaps the greatest threat to democracy. And while it's tempting to feel hopeless in light of 'fake news' and people who speak 'their truth,' Kristian offers us ways to move forward. *Untrustworthy* is an incisive, deeply researched, and personal analysis of our truth crisis. It should be widely read and discussed."

—**Alan Noble**, Oklahoma Baptist University; author of *You Are Not Your Own*

"Many of us have a sense that all we once took for granted is now up for grabs. We are living through a crisis of knowledge, and the result can be a feeling of suffocating uncertainty. *Untrustworthy* opens a window and lets in a breath of fresh air—and hope. Bonnie Kristian offers a way out of pointless debates and fearmongering conspiracy theories. This book is never condescending and always sympathetic; it is never partisan and always incisive."

—**Jeffrey Bilbro,** author of *Reading the Times*

"We are living in the midst of a truth crisis. Every single day information swamps our social media—popping up on our alerts or forwarded from friends. Not only do we not know what to believe but we also don't know how to believe. This is why this book is so vitally important. Bonnie Kristian is a first-rate journalist who is uniquely able to sift through the layers of today's truth crisis and help guide faithful Christians to know how to pursue knowledge and understand the times in ways that are in obedience to the lordship of Christ. She skillfully gets at the motivations that have caused a sense of distrust and alienation that drives us to extremes. This is a book the American church desperately needs and that pastors have been asking for. I'd urge you to give it a careful read and pass it on to anyone in your sphere of influence."

—**Daniel Darling,** director of The Land Center for Cultural Engagement, Southwestern Baptist Theological Seminary; author of *A Way with Words*

UNTRUSTWORTHY

UNTRUSTWORTHY

The Knowledge Crisis Breaking Our Brains,
Polluting Our Politics, and Corrupting
Christian Community

BONNIE
KRISTIAN

Foreword by David French

BrazosPress

a division of Baker Publishing Group
Grand Rapids, Michigan

© 2022 by Bonnie Kristian

Published by Brazos Press
a division of Baker Publishing Group
PO Box 6287, Grand Rapids, MI 49516-6287
www.brazospress.com

Printed in the United States of America

Library of Congress Cataloging-in-Publication Data
Names: Kristian, Bonnie, author.
Title: Untrustworthy : the knowledge crisis breaking our brains, polluting our
    politics, and corrupting Christian community / Bonnie Kristian.
Description: Grand Rapids, Michigan : Brazos Press, a division of Baker Publishing
    Group, [2022] | Includes bibliographical references.
Identifiers: LCCN 2022004815 | ISBN 9781587435621 (cloth) | ISBN 9781493438549
    (pdf) | ISBN 9781493438532 (ebook)
Subjects: LCSH: Truthfulness and falsehood—Religious aspects—Christianity. |
    Truth—Religious aspects—Christianity. | Common fallacies. | Christianity and
    culture—United States.
Classification: LCC BV4647.T7 K75 2022 | DDC 241/.672—dc23/eng/20220303
LC record available at https://lccn.loc.gov/2022004815

Some of my discussion within this book draws from material that originally appeared in columns for *Christianity Today* and *The Week*. It has been adapted for this format, and the original articles are cited in the endnotes.

The author is represented by WordServe Literary Group, www.wordserveliterary.com.

Baker Publishing Group publications use paper produced from sustainable forestry practices and post-consumer waste whenever possible.

22   23   24   25   26   27   28   7   6   5   4   3   2   1

To our twins,
who aren't allowed on the internet
'til they're thirty

CONTENTS

FOREWORD

David French

If you're in the journalism business, there's a question you've heard a thousand times: "How do I know what's true?" We live in a nation awash in speech yet lacking in knowledge. We live in a nation full of citizens who claim to distrust institutions yet seem to place almost blind faith in those institutions and individuals who reaffirm their worldview.

It is not uncommon to hear someone declare with confidence that others cannot and must not believe the latest report in the *New York Times*. And what's the proof? A "fact check" they found on a fringe outlet on Facebook.

Does that mean that the *Times* is always right, and the fringe outlet is always wrong? Of course not. But it's an example that illustrates a larger truth. We not only don't know what's real, we don't even know how to discover what reality is.

We live in an age of earned distrust. There is no question that key institutions have too often failed in their obligation to report the truth, even if one charitably allows for the fact that it is often impossible to discern the full dimensions of complex events in real time. We're always operating with varying degrees of partial knowledge, and the "fog of war"—the confusion that accompanies crisis—can be very real indeed.

But we also live in an age of manufactured distrust. Partisan news sources amplify and exaggerate the failures of the other side—even as they ignore, minimize, and rationalize their own obvious flaws. There is much money to be made and much fame to be gained by telling partisans exactly what they want to hear and inoculating them against external critique.

This is the cultural and political backdrop that renders this book so vitally important. It's critical to understand not just what is true but also how we discern truth. It's imperative to see America's knowledge crisis as having implications that extend far beyond politics.

In many ways America's knowledge crisis is also a relationship crisis. Our inability to agree on even the most basic facts can destroy friendships and fracture families. Creating communities around conspiracy theories can provide people with a sense of meaning and fellowship they can find nowhere else. How can fact checks be enough to pull a person out of the cause that provides them with a mission and a purpose?

America's knowledge crisis is also a faith crisis. Pastors and parishioners alike speak of painful divisions that are so often rooted in a complete failure to understand or believe a basic set of common facts. That failure invariably leads to friction, to a sense that we share the pew with people who are deeply deluded. How long can churches remain intact when divisions are that profound?

Read Bonnie's book to discern the causes of the crisis. Read her book to understand its effects. And read it to understand the role you can play in solving one of the most pressing issues of our time. To quote *The X-Files*, one of my favorite television shows from the 1990s, "The truth is out there." It's up to us to find it, share it, and solve the knowledge problem that threatens to tear this nation apart.

ACKNOWLEDGMENTS

I owe a debt of gratitude to the many who helped me in this work. Thanks to my agent, Greg Johnson, for shepherding my proposal to a contract, and to my editor, Bob Hosack, for taking me on first as an author and later as a near-neighbor. Thanks to Julie Zahm, Paula Gibson, Kara Day, and everyone else at Brazos who worked on the text, cover, marketing, and more. Thanks to David French for writing the perfect foreword, and to my interviewees—Derek Kubilus, Ben Marsh, James Kendall, Katie Herzog, Dennis Edwards, and David French again—whose willingness to speak with me made this a better book. Thanks to our nannies in Minnesota and Pennsylvania for caring for our twins while I wrote. Thanks to Abby for her unparalleled enthusiasm for this project from the moment I pitched it in the group chat, and to Rachelle for clarifying my inchoate ideas about cover design and reminding Abby and me what's of interest to normal, nonpolitical people. Thanks to my parents and in-laws for their various help with our house, pets, and twins. Thanks to my husband, Peter, for holding down the fort while I sprinted to the end of the book. And thanks to God for pointing out the beginning, directing the progress, and helping in the completion.

INTRODUCTION

American society has a knowledge crisis, and the American church is no exception.

It's a crisis that's difficult to fathom or even name, lurking as it does among the foundations of our minds, the semiconscious corners where we determine what we can know and who we can trust. It's a crisis that concerns me daily because of my work in journalism but also because I see it slinking into the lives of my loved ones and American evangelicalism writ large, reshaping hopes and joys—and fears and rages.

I'm not the only one experiencing that grim advance, because this crisis is increasingly ubiquitous in our public life. We don't know what is true, what is knowable, what is trustworthy. Our information environment is chaotic and overwhelming, rife with conspiracy theories, "fake news," and habit-forming digital manipulation. It is breaking our brains, polluting our politics, and corrupting Christian community. It may be the most pressing and unprecedented challenge of discipleship in the American church.

Picking Up Pieces

I began writing about our knowledge crisis in 2018, though I didn't see it then as a single, coherent phenomenon. I saw

1

pieces—a statistic here, a story there—and explored them in my articles as a political columnist for *Christianity Today* and as an editor at *The Week*.[1] I wrote about traditional media and social media, deception and gullibility, shame and guilt, populist paranoia and elite expertise, unjustified certainty and needless confusion.

Many of these stories drew on my own experiences: the steady stream of political half-truths and hysteria a relative has been emailing me for years; complaints from friends that Facebook and Fox News have turned their parents into angry, obsessive people they barely recognize; conversations with my husband about how to keep our twins' faces off Instagram and their brains off YouTube.

With each piece I explored, it became clearer that the knowledge crisis I was gradually investigating wasn't unique to me and my circles. I wasn't observing isolated incidents. There was reason to think the problem I perceived was national in scale, and our frenetic news cycle seemed to keep whirling back to these same themes. So I started digging deeper, pursuing these stories more intentionally, looking for the right words to label what I saw so I could help others see it too. The more I researched and wrote, the more convinced I became that calling our knowledge problem a "crisis" was not hyperbolic.

Then, in the fall of 2020, a former colleague of mine (I'll call him Jim) wanted to buy a house. He and his wife were planning to move to be near family in a midsize city. They were getting older, and it would likely be their final move. They didn't have a large budget to work with—or, in semiretirement, much regular income—but living near their family's neighborhood in the city would allow them to get something both comfortable and affordable, maybe even a duplex that could bring in passive income when they were fully retired.

All my friends know I love browsing real-estate listings, especially for old houses and fixer-uppers. As Jim and his wife started their hunt, we texted a lot of Zillow links back and forth, and they toured a number of the properties I'd found. It was about a month before the 2020 election, and though I generally steered our conversations clear of politics—it's shop talk for me, and I don't like to do it in my free time—I knew they were both confident their favored candidate, then-president Donald Trump, would win.

But he didn't win. And as it became clearer that Trump's loss was final, Jim began backing away from his own plans. Trump's departure, he was certain, would lead to mass chaos. Supply chains would break down with the Democrats in charge. The economy would crumble as some hybrid of dictatorship and mob rule emerged. Living in a densely populated area without farmland wouldn't be safe.

"I don't want to be in the middle of a million starving people," Jim told me. Afraid of this dystopian fantasy, he didn't buy a house. He spent half of what he'd budgeted for a down payment on a used camper instead.

During that conversation—or rather, several hours later, as in the moment I was too flabbergasted to muster a lucid thought—is when I think I finally realized the significance, scope, and severity of our society's knowledge crisis. Here was a fellow Christian making life-changing choices on the basis of fearmongering falsehoods. I don't know how his financial decisions will shake out, or if he'll decide, as normal life continues, he can live in the city after all. But there's a chance Jim's final decades will be more difficult than they should have been because he mistook lies for truth.

Frothing talk radio, pixelated YouTube videos promising to reveal what "they" don't want you to know, and an endless stream of print and email newsletters (each ending with the inevitable sales or fundraising pitch) had convinced him. He was impervious to pushback, though I share his faith and many of his policy preferences and (I thought) held his respect for my

3

work as a journalist. He was sure he could see this imagined hellscape looming on the horizon. He made tracks.

The Media Piece

Most people affected by our knowledge crisis won't so dramatically alter their lives. But an accumulation of smaller changes matters too. How we handle knowledge and how we assess truth claims are crucial for the development and outworking of our faith as Christians. It's fundamental to everything in the political arena and so much of our private lives as well. The simplest conversations can feel impossible when we can't agree about what is true—or whether and how truth can even be found. And if we can't talk to one another, how do we worship together? How do we govern together? How do we live together?

Around the same time Jim was shopping for a house, three other experiences helped me better grasp the contours of this crisis and start to move beyond the stupefaction and helplessness I felt in that "million starving people" moment.

The first came as I was scrolling through Instagram. I noticed a friend had shared someone else's post raising awareness about child trafficking and pornography. I knew this wasn't mere social media performance. She's not the type to "pray standing in the synagogues and on the street corners to be seen by others" (Matt. 6:5). So I clicked.

The post seemed . . . off, but for a few minutes I couldn't figure out why. Then I looked at the hashtags. Alongside #Save TheChildren was #WWG1WGA, an acronym used in the QAnon conspiracy movement, which alleges (among other things—we'll explore this further in chap. 4) that our government and other major institutions have for decades or even centuries been run by a powerful cabal of Satan-worshipping cannibalistic pedophiles. The post my friend shared mixed truth about modern human trafficking with QAnon delusions.

I privately messaged her to ask if she was getting into QAnon, hoping to warn her away before she was pulled into a movement known to end marriages and estrange families. She replied that she'd never even heard of it. She'd shared this post totally unaware that it was by design an entry point to a false and dysfunctional group that later would be centrally involved in the storming of the US Capitol. She'd unwittingly lent her good name to a pernicious lie.

But where, exactly, had she gone wrong? She's right to deplore the abuse of children, of course, and she had come across this post because she was attempting to accompany her faith with action (James 2:17), both online and off.

Should she have recognized the hashtags? I did because it's my job to research this stuff. But my friend doesn't work in press or politics. Because her consumption of political media is responsibly limited, she was unaware of what was then a little-known conspiracy claim. I could hardly say she should consume more political content. If anything, I should consume less.

Was the problem that she was using Instagram? Social media is an easy, obvious target here, but my friend's Instagram use is about as innocent and justifiable as it gets. There was no glaring failure, no one place I could point to and say, "Ah, *that's* your problem. Make this change and you'll never share political misinformation with hundreds of people again!"

My discussions with Jim had directed my attention toward disordered political engagement, news consumption, and social media use as a means by which our knowledge crisis grows. They're all part of it, yes, and quite a visible part. (Traditional and social media are the subject of chap. 2—I address them early in the book because I suspect most of us already know something has gone wrong there.) But they're just three contributors among many, and each one is as much a symptom as a cause. Ditching Instagram might be wise, but by itself it's not enough to keep the crisis at bay.

The Community Piece

The second experience was a discernment process at my church. We'd heard our denomination was planning to take a vote on gay marriage and ordination at an upcoming national conference, and we wanted to decide how the representative from our congregation should cast his ballot. The trouble was we'd never discussed the topic as a community. A lot of us had simply assumed everyone else shared our views, but when we broached the issue, it became clear we were sharply divided.

The divide was not merely about the question proper, though there was indeed division there. What truly made the process difficult were the differences among us around *how* to discern the issue, differences that cut across our theological lines.

Some members of our congregation wanted to approach this question as a matter of scriptural study: What are the relevant biblical texts? How did their original audiences understand them? How should they apply to Christians today? Are there larger scriptural themes—of love, sexual morality, pastoral care, and so on—that should affect our interpretations and the church policies they inform?

For others, however, it seemed obvious the decision must be far more intuitive and experiential, more about gut instincts, personal relationships, the influence of the Holy Spirit, and what it would feel like to bring friends and family to a church that adopted one policy or another. For many, it was significantly about identity: What will it mean for me to be a covenant member of a congregation that commits to a given stance? What kind of person does that make me? How does it label me?

As I write this, I'm gearing up to move eight hundred miles away, so I won't be involved when the discernment process resumes. (We suspended it when the COVID-19 pandemic began because continuing such intense conversations on Zoom seemed like a terrible idea.) I don't know how it will proceed or conclude, but I do know these different means of seeking truth will complicate the pursuit of consensus. Even if a theological agreement is reached, how to explain and justify it will remain a difficult question because we have members reaching the same conclusion via wholly different paths.

Before this discernment process began, I would have recommended robust commitment to Christian community as the primary counterweight to our knowledge crisis. It's a recommendation I've read from many writers and pastors wiser than I, and I'm not saying they're wrong. I still think thick community is incredibly important; I will talk about it repeatedly in this book. Yet I no longer think it's enough.

My church is *good* at community life. We're not a Sunday social club. We take our covenant with God and one another seriously. The congregation started as young people living in community houses together, pooling resources and sharing meals. That evolved as most got married and left their early twenties behind, but we kept our commitment to three adjacent neighborhoods in which almost all our members live. We bought houses near one another. We share tools and shovel one another's sidewalks and hang out multiple times a week. When we started this discernment process, a process we knew had rent other churches in two, we reminded ourselves of how much we value our community. We promised we would hold to our covenant and keep sight of our calling to "love each other deeply, because love covers over a multitude of sins" (1 Pet. 4:8).

It still all but broke us. Between people with different assumptions, conversations about how to discern truth were nerve-wracking and disheartening. Dear friends suddenly seemed to be unintelligible strangers. Some members left. I suspect all of us thought about it at least once. I rode home from a particularly painful meeting searching "church" on Google Maps, tapping through all the results nearby though I already knew what every single one was, fighting tears and panicking that my whole community seemed to be coming undone. *How could this happen to* us? I wondered. *We* promised *each other it wouldn't.*

Those promises weren't nothing. I don't think I'm naive to believe the community will survive the discernment process mostly intact and without animosity toward or from those who have left because of this.

Still, as a community we should have been better bound by truth as well as love. We should not have been caught by surprise. We should never have tried to discern such a weighty matter without first, together, learning discernment itself. We should have first determined how, *specifically*, our community would "test and approve what God's will is—his good, pleasing and perfect will" (Rom. 12:2). Robust community life did us so much good, but it alone could not keep the knowledge crisis from prowling into our sanctuary.

The Argument Piece

The third experience was the time another friend of mine told me about a weird pattern of conversations she'd been having with her parents. They'd never been stridently political, but that changed when state mandates intended to control the spread of COVID-19 left them frequently stuck at home in a newly empty nest. In that social vacuum, they developed a cable-news habit, and cable news began to change them.

Its fury began creeping into their minds, its complaints and cadences into their speech. In the middle of mundane text chats with their adult children, they'd suddenly break off on a political tangent, ranting about this outrage or that injustice, all of it irrelevant to the moment at hand. At first, my friend and her siblings didn't know how to respond. By turns they tried ignoring the political tirades or pushing back with arguments of their own, often ending up equally frustrated or angry.

Finally my friend hit on a new strategy. "Why are you angry?" she would respond when a parent lurched into cable mode. "You're about to have a grandchild," she'd say, reminding them of her pregnancy. "You're okay! We're okay." Her parents would pause, reset, and refocus on the topic at hand. It was as if a spell had been broken, and by the time their granddaughter arrived their cable-news fixation was no more.

My friend's success with her parents stood in marked contrast to my failure to persuade Jim it was safe to buy a house near his family. She'd invited them to look away from their screen and out into the world, to remember the goodness in their lives, the ordinary hopes and joys never written into the cable news narrative. I'd argued about politics, foolishly thinking I could overcome Jim's fear if I simply showed him a few more facts.

The Catholic novelist and theologian G. K. Chesterton arrived at this realization a century before I did. If you argue with someone convinced of conspiracy theories (or similarly enveloping falsehoods), he wrote in *Orthodoxy*, "it is extremely probable that you will get the worst of it; for in many ways his mind moves all the quicker for not being delayed by the things that go with good judgment." If this person believes "men have a conspiracy against him, you cannot dispute it," Chesterton continued, "except by saying that all the men deny that they are conspirators; which is exactly what conspirators would do. His explanation covers the facts as much as yours."[2]

When we encounter a mind thus confused, Chesterton advised that "we should be chiefly concerned not so much to give it arguments as to give it air, to convince it that there was something cleaner and cooler outside the suffocation of a single argument."[3] Instead of fact-checking, maybe throw a party. Play a game. Take a walk. Go to church. Remember you're about to have a granddaughter. Remember "neither death nor life, neither angels nor demons, neither the present nor the future, nor any powers, neither height nor depth, nor anything else in all creation, will be able to separate us from the love of God that is in Christ Jesus our Lord" (Rom. 8:38–39).

My friend gave her parents air, and when they'd taken a breath, the suffocating frenzy of cable news no longer satisfied. I argued politics, and Jim bought a camper.

Putting Pieces Together

If something in these stories feels familiar, if you've seen this suffocation in your family or church, if a certain disquiet has begun to engulf you when you read the news or browse social media or otherwise attempt to engage our ever more complex information environment, I am writing for you. And I'm writing for myself, because engaging that environment is a necessary hazard of my work in journalism—which is to say, there is always a risk the confused mind may be my own.

For my own benefit as much as that of anyone else, I need to be able to name the crisis, identify its rotten fruits, and find the air they have not befouled. It is to that threefold project we'll now turn.

Naming the Crisis

Defenceless under the night
Our world in stupor lies;
Yet, dotted everywhere,
Ironic points of light
Flash out wherever the Just
Exchange their messages:
May I, composed like them
Of Eros and of dust,
Beleaguered by the same
Negation and despair,
Show an affirming flame.

—W. H. Auden,
"September 1, 1939"

Soon after our twins were born, usually late at night—
when the prospect of waking up again just a few hours
hence made it hard to fall back to sleep—I often found myself
reading discussions among new mothers on the forum site
Reddit. I never participated myself, for the main attraction

was seeing other people describe what I was already experiencing. Their worries, questions, and gripes gave form and vocabulary to my own. It felt a bit like finally grasping the word stuck on the tip of the tongue or scratching an out-of-reach itch.

This is true beyond those exhaustion-addled days of early parenting: discovering the name of a problem—and the very fact that it has a name, that it is a thing that exists outside your own head—can be crucial to comprehending (and tackling) it.

To that end, the precise name for what I've been calling our "knowledge crisis" is "epistemic crisis." The first word derives from "epistemology," the branch of philosophy that seeks to understand understanding itself.[1] Epistemology asks questions like these: What do we know? How do we know it? What's the difference between knowledge, opinion, and conjecture? Is the world really as we perceive it? Can we trust our senses, our reasoning, our memory, one another? If truth exists, as Christians affirm it does, can humans access it rightly?

Doing epistemology feels a bit like looking at a mirror instead of the reflection in it. It doesn't feel terribly natural, and it may seem like a needlessly academic place to begin this book. I get that—but I'm beginning here because I think ignorance of epistemology is *exactly* what made this crisis possible. In the span of a few decades we massively increased the quantity of information the average person encounters daily, much of which makes or assumes major truth claims. But we didn't equip ourselves for those multiplying encounters. I suppose we assumed we could handle it. We could not.

I'll delve into that equipment and how we can acquire it in the final three chapters of this book. But first, we need to understand our vulnerabilities in its absence. We need to understand what ignorance of epistemology does.

Introduction to Epistemology

Most of us, most of the time, don't think about epistemology—and really, how could we? Whatever we believe, we have to live as if knowledge is attainable and we, individually and as a species, are fairly competent in attaining it. I could never learn a new skill if I spent every moment questioning whether learning is possible. I wouldn't write for a living if I wondered whether real communication could take place. We have to live as if true knowledge can be gained and shared, because it isn't possible to function otherwise in ordinary life.[2]

It *is* possible to function otherwise in the public square, however, and that's increasingly what we're doing. We can't agree about what we know or how we know it. The border between knowledge and opinion is disputed territory. Whether truth exists and can be shared between us is up for debate.

We try to do theology without agreeing on how truth about God can be found. We try to do politics at the usual level of analysis for established knowledge ("What should we do about this?") without realizing we haven't agreed on the knowledge itself ("What *is* this?"). But noticing the need to settle that lower-level question is no guarantee against frustration either when every potential source of knowledge is subject to doubt. Our epistemology is a mess—and we don't even know we have an epistemology.

Signs of the resultant epistemic crisis are everywhere. It's a big part of the decades-long decline of trust in the traditional news media. Mainstream news outlets are rejected for being flawed or biased (an oft-deserved critique!), but the pseudonymous digital rumormongers rising to replace them are worse. The epistemic crisis is implicated in the gullibility and quarrelsomeness that has us spreading fabrications and fallacies on social media, the proliferation of so-called satire intended to fool rather than enlighten and bemuse, and the popularity of political and religious memes that consist of apocryphal quotations, cheap manipulations, and bad math.

The crisis is not a single-party phenomenon, but it presents a little differently along the political spectrum. Since 2015, the most quotable indicators of our epistemology problem have come from the right. Former president Donald Trump didn't invent the term "fake news," but he certainly popularized it—and helped broaden it. The phrase originally meant made-up stories with salacious, clickable headlines designed to attract web traffic and the ad revenue that comes with it.[3] After Trump began to dominate national politics, however, "fake news" was used to refer to everything from honest errors in reporting to malicious deception. It became an insult too, deployed to dismiss even accurate journalism deemed embarrassing or antagonistic.

From the right we also got "alternative facts," a phrase of then-White House counselor Kellyanne Conway,[4] as well as former New York City mayor Rudy Giuliani's announcement on a Sunday news show that "truth isn't truth."[5] All three phrases cast an epistemic fog, directing their hearers to slippery, expedient doubt: Doubt your own memory. Doubt the media if it reports anything you dislike. Doubt anything and anyone that could make your side look bad or give the other side a win.

These phrases say that political victory matters more than truth and that success or convenience in the moment is more important than the long-term effects of epistemic carelessness or outright deception. The epistemology these words represent has obvious advantages if power is your priority, and it will endure after the specific phrases fall from our lexicon.

Some on the left, meanwhile, will have us doubt our own senses and reasoning. This is an overgrowth of postmodern attention to identity, context, and perspective—the notion that what you can know is dependent on who you are, where you are, and what you can see from that vantage. There's a vital insight here, but adopted as a *complete* epistemic framework, it can preclude communication rather than adding nuance to it. It says you can't see what I see, so you can't know what I know or challenge what I believe.

"Over the past decade," writes Columbia University political scientist Mark Lilla of this phenomenon, "a new, and very revealing, locution has drifted from our universities into the mainstream media: *Speaking as an X.*" Lilla continues, drawing on his work as a professor:

> This is not an anodyne phrase. It tells the listener that I am speaking from a privileged position on this matter. . . . So classroom discussions that might once have begun, *I think A, and here is my argument,* now take the form, *Speaking as an X, I am offended that you claim B.* This makes perfect sense if you believe that identity determines everything. It means there is no impartial space for dialogue. White men have one "epistemology," black women have another. So what remains to be said?[6]

Few of us are creatures exclusively of right or left. We encounter (and may participate in) all these epistemic patterns. With enough time, with a reliable internet connection and a hectic schedule, with snatches of news read but not really analyzed, with poignant videos raising our emotions and calculated memes stirring our fury, with good intentions but insufficient prudence, these confused patterns can easily muddle our thinking.

We can become certain about things that don't warrant certainty and doubtful of documented facts. In the throes of epistemic crisis, we look like nothing so much as the fool critiqued throughout the book of Proverbs: always seeking out information that pleases us (17:24), dismissive of wisdom (12:15), lacking common sense (10:21), quick to quarrel (20:2), and too happy to hear ourselves talk (18:2).

The next six chapters will explore the nature of our knowledge crisis in greater depth. We'll tackle "fake news" and "cancel culture," wild populist conspiracism and dubious elite expertise, and the place of emotion and experience in understanding. Then we'll turn to strategies for overcoming this crisis in ourselves and our communities—ways to develop a practical epistemology, good habits, and the conviction to help others do likewise. But first, I'll sketch the effects of epistemic crisis in our politics, social lives, and faith.

Political Implications of Our Crisis

The political implications seem particularly vivid as I'm writing this in the first half of 2021, but our knowledge problem isn't new, only newly visible. Recent political turmoil didn't create it, nor did any single incident, party, movement, or politician. Our epistemic crisis is bigger than discrete factors like these; it will persist as they fade from memory. Its political effects are characterized by distrust, animosity, and escalation.

The distrust is visible in, well, our distrust of each other and nearly every public institution. In the half-century Gallup pollsters have been tracking Americans' trust in major institutions, it has declined almost across the board. Confidence in the church dropped from 65 to 42 percent from 1973 to 2020. Confidence in Congress went from 42 to 13 percent over the same time. Newspapers went from 39 to 25 percent, television news from 46 to 18, the presidency from 52 to 39. Among the institutions that didn't see a precipitous drop over this period— the Supreme Court and the broader criminal-justice system, for example—many had little public trust to lose when polling began.[7]

Lack of confidence in an institution isn't necessarily a bad thing. Sometimes it's well deserved! It can be a precursor to needful reform. But the distrust I have in mind here isn't a constructive skepticism of concentrated power, which might be the healthiest habit of the American political mind. It's darker, more destructive, scornful and suspicious yet also quite credulous; it's always eager to believe the worst. It's more interested in trolling and complaining than in the slow, mundane work of making things better.

The philosopher Hannah Arendt describes this "mixture of gullibility and cynicism" in *The Origins of Totalitarianism*, her seminal 1951 book on anti-Semitism, imperialism, and totalitarianism itself. Arendt argues that in "an ever-changing, incomprehensible world the masses [have] reached the point where they [will], at the same time, believe everything and nothing, think that everything was possible and that nothing was true."[8]

Arendt argues that this combination is a propagandist's dream because a public in this state may not object to being deceived by leaders they like. "One could make people believe the most fantastic statements one day, and trust that if the next day they were given irrefutable proof of their falsehood, they would take refuge in cynicism." Then, "instead of deserting the leaders who had lied to them, [the public] would protest that they had known all along the statement was a lie and would admire the leaders for their superior tactical cleverness."[9]

For all our incessant *reductio ad Hitlerum*, ours is not a totalitarian society like Nazi Germany and Stalinist Russia, of which Arendt wrote. But she evokes a state uncomfortably familiar. There's a caginess in our political discourse, a frustrating tic of insinuation, dodges, and bad faith. Truth and falsehood have become irrelevant in the pursuit of power to use for oneself and against one's enemies.

Too often, fact and context matter less than a desired narrative, and both our major political tribes are guilty here. Trump's most ardent supporters were known to insist he was "playing three-dimensional chess," by which they meant his glaring mistakes and failures were secretly brilliant, careful strategy no one else could understand.[10] Thus, a series of polls by YouGov and *The Economist* revealed about one in four Americans implausibly believed the freewheeling then-president "consider[ed] carefully what he [said] before commenting."[11]

Recall the media mishandling of the Covington Catholic case, the 2019 story with the viral video of a teenage boy (who attended a Catholic high school called Covington and wore a Trump hat) smiling at an elderly Native American man amid a raucous protest crowd in Washington.[12] The context was far more complicated than initial coverage made out, but there was a distinct unwillingness to surrender first interpretations as more details emerged—a seeming determination, as C. S. Lewis put it in *Mere Christianity*, to "cling to the first story for the sheer pleasure of thinking your enemies are as bad as possible."[13]

"I failed the Covington Catholic test," wrote journalist Julie Irwin Zimmerman in *The Atlantic*. "I was all-in on the outrage," she reflected, furious over a story she later realized was a "Rorschach test" administered by "an online mob for whom Saturday-morning indignation is just another form of entertainment."[14] Zimmerman's mea culpa was perceptive and wise. It was also, unfortunately, the exception rather than the rule.

Animosity Out Front

Trust is a liability in politics this cunning. I'm reminded of Paul's famous warning about people who would "gather around them a great number of teachers to say what their itching ears want to hear," who "will turn their ears away from the truth and turn aside to myths" (2 Tim. 4:3–4). They will turn aside from trust too and put animosity in its place.

Political scientists call this animosity "negative partisanship."[15] Americans are increasingly bound together politically not by positive shared goals or convictions so much as by hatred for the other team. Out with mutual pursuit of the common good, in with "owning the libs" (or the cons, as the case may be). Our knowledge crisis isn't the only reason for negative partisanship's decades-long rise, but it's undoubtedly a contributing factor. Epistemic confusion makes us easy prey for demagogues and garden-variety politicians alike, and antagonism is their most reliable bait.

In my neighborhood, as in many around the country, this antagonism has taken a curiously visible form: yard signs. They proliferated gradually, but by mid-2020 you could hardly go a block without seeing one, or ten. What I found interesting—so much so that I wrote about the phenomenon for *The Week*—was that although it was an election year the signs weren't primarily about the election. "In this house," the most popular option declared, "we believe: Black lives matter; women's rights are human rights; no human is illegal; science is real; love is love; kindness is everything."

Signs like this made clear how their owners would vote, yes. But the sign owners I interviewed consistently described them as something more significant to their self-conception. The signs were long-term signals of political rectitude to neighbors and strangers alike.

One woman described her sign as a way to "identify ourselves as friendly and safe." She happily recounted a time she overheard a passerby point to her sign as proof that "this neighborhood is nice people." The sign was also a warning to "people who may not be sympathetic that this neighborhood will stand up for people who need it," she told me. In fact, she said, she won't welcome into her home anyone who doesn't agree with the "In this house . . ." creed.[16]

As I wrote then, I'm not sure if some of my discomfort with the yard-sign discourse is merely temperamental. (I can't imagine displaying *any* political yard sign, election season or not.) But the root of what troubles me about the choice to use one's front yard to announce political proclivities—whatever they may be—is that it feels like an escalatory move. It's a way to take the political sorting, signaling, and sneering we've learned from our favorite social and traditional media and introduce it, like an invasive species, into our real lives and relationships. It makes our neighborhoods more like politics on the internet, which is exactly what I *don't* want to do. My neighborhood is good; adding Twitter won't improve it.

Faster Goes the Treadmill

And it's not just yard signs. I find I'm writing about escalation more and more these days. I used to discuss it mainly in the context of foreign policy, but of late the word has plenty of domestic uses.

In 2004, then-candidate Howard Dean dropped out of the Democratic presidential primaries in part because he yelled "Yeah!" during a campaign rally. His "scream" was endlessly discussed: the recording, which misleadingly excluded the sounds of the noisy crowd to whom Dean was speaking, was played nearly a thousand times on cable news in the following week.[17] Would it be played even once today? The Dean scream was a major gaffe nearly two decades ago, but now? Who would care?

There's a concept in psychology called the "hedonic treadmill" that is useful for understanding this escalation. The idea is that our sense of what's normal dictates what we feel is necessary for contentment and happiness. The more comfort you're used to having, the higher your baseline for feeling okay.

If you've ever moved from a small living space like a dorm room or studio apartment to something much bigger—your own house, perhaps—you know what it's like when the treadmill speeds up. Within a few weeks of moving, going back to the smaller space is unthinkable. "I don't know how we did it," you'll say. "Could I have cooked this dinner in that tiny kitchen?" It's not impossible to slow the hedonic treadmill and adjust your baseline down, but it is difficult. This is why the season of Lent and the spiritual practice of fasting are so challenging. Our brains and bodies rebel as the treadmill slows.

In politics, the treadmill isn't about comfort but thrill, and our political treadmill in the United States is running very quickly now. Everything is incredibly dramatic. We're always drawing lines in the sand, standing against evil, manning the resistance, taking our country back. It's no longer enough for our political opponents to be misinformed; they're lying. They're not wrong; they're evil. They're not Democrats but "Demon-rats," not Republicans but "MAGAts."

Keeping the hedonic treadmill running requires epistemic crisis because reality isn't this exciting. Scandals happen, sure. Politicians certainly lie. Incompetence and laziness can be found in any bureaucracy. Some corruption is predictable too, at a certain scale. And yes, some voters do hold extreme, even abhorrent, beliefs—but they're the exception, not the rule.

A 2019 study called "The Perception Gap" found Americans imagine each other in caricature, with Democrats substantially overestimating extremism in Republicans and vice versa. "Americans have a deeply distorted understanding of each other," the researchers concluded. Crucially, they observed that political media consumption and making political posts on social media are both correlated with *greater* misunderstanding: "People who said they read the news 'most of the time' were nearly three times more distorted in their perceptions than those who said they read the news 'only now and then,'" the report says. Moreover, the researchers found that the "political content we see on social media is . . . disproportionately from people with a more distorted understanding of the other side."[18]

Consumption of political content made people *more* likely to unfairly vilify those with whom they disagree, and almost every type of media the study examined was a negative influence. Someone with more information was, paradoxically, more likely to be misinformed. That's a symptom of a knowledge crisis if there ever was one.

Social Implications of Our Crisis

Our scrambled epistemology isn't confined to political matters. It shapes our social lives too, because so much of our communication and entertainment has migrated to screens during the past thirty years.

I never feel older than when I write about screen time. I know it's tempting to dismiss this stuff as the cranky ranting of a technophobe, and I know that because I'm often tempted to dismiss it myself. I love the internet at least as much as I hate it. After all, I owe my whole career to it. A few generations ago, there was no scenario in which a no-name writer in the flyover states—a young woman with a theology degree, no less—could have accumulated the steady work I have with coastal media outlets week in and week out. The internet enabled me to make those professional connections, and it's vital to the work itself. The research I can complete in an afternoon would have been a week's work for far greater writers in eras past.

So it's not that I'm anti-internet. Far from it! But do a thought experiment with me: suppose it's 1995 and you're sharing exactly as many news articles and opinion pieces and videos with friends and family as you do now. There's no Facebook, of course, and most people don't have email yet. You painstakingly clip the content you want to share out of the local newspaper and *Newsweek* and, hey, maybe *Christianity Today*. (Thanks for subscribing.) Then you go to a print shop or Staples, some place with copy machines, and you make hundreds of copies of each article. Perhaps there's a news segment you want to share, so you record it on your VCR and get it copied on hundreds of VHS cassettes. Then you package up all your "shares" and head to the post office, mailing your copies and tapes to the people presently on your Facebook friends list. "Please read!" you write in a note for each package, clipping it to a recent Polaroid photo of yourself. "This is *so* important to understanding what's going on in our country right now." The next day, a new newspaper arrives, another news segment airs, and you do it all over again.

What would your friends think of you? What would *you* think of you?

The medium for all this sharing makes a difference. But let me suggest that it makes less of a difference than we might want to think, and the proportion of time and attention most of us spend on content consumption and sharing is disordered.

It's epistemically disordered in that we too often fail to scrutinize the quality and meaning of what we read and spread. But it's also relationally disordered. We use our devices to the exclusion of better things. We let them speed up our hedonic treadmills. We let them foster what in German is called *streitsüchtig*, a word usually translated "quarrelsomeness" but which literally means something like "dispute-addicted"—possessed of a hunger for rancor and a need for an enemy.[19] We let our screens take mental, emotional, and spiritual attention and energy we owe to God and each other. We let them make us lonely—and yet we don't recognize it as loneliness, because the content constantly blasting in our faces is a temporary simulacrum of relationship.

Arendt names loneliness as a contributing factor to the epistemic muddle she describes as a "mixture of gullibility and cynicism." Loneliness was "once a borderline experience usually suffered in certain marginal social conditions like old age," she wrote, but "has become an everyday experience of the ever-growing masses."[20]

The breakdown of thick community bonds Arendt saw seventy years ago has continued in the time since. Ours is an atomized society of individuals with only a dim sense of need for the people outside our historically tiny households.[21] We don't rely on our neighbors to survive a hard winter. We don't work or worship with them. At the height of the COVID-19 pandemic in early 2021, three in ten Americans, including six in ten young adults and half of mothers of young children, reported feeling "serious loneliness."[22] Yet talk of a "loneliness epidemic" was widespread well before lockdowns and other social-distancing measures. A poll in 2019 found one in five young adults in America reported they had no friends.[23]

When we're this lonely, Arendt argues, we begin to lose touch with reality. We need "the trusting and trustworthy company of [our] equals" in order to gain knowledge and grasp truth, she wrote. It is in loneliness that "man loses trust in himself as the partner of his thoughts and that elementary confidence in the world which is necessary to make experiences at all."[24] Being lonely makes us vulnerable to epistemic crisis, and epistemic crisis makes us lonelier. Superficially, we're more engaged and social than ever. But if we could look at ourselves from a bird's-eye view, we'd see isolation and *streitsüchtig* flowing through channels we dug for friendship.

Faith Implications of Our Crisis

These political and relational effects of our knowledge crisis are felt throughout society, but for Christians there's a third and more important concern: how it distorts our faith.

For a few weeks after the storming of the US Capitol and the subsequent inauguration of President Joe Biden, my editors wanted articles about what had happened in Washington and what it meant for our politics going forward. I'd been on the QAnon conspiracy movement beat at *The Week* for a while, so I was looking for column ideas by poking around videos of the Capitol riot and archives of conversations among QAnon adherents who had participated.

One widely shared video showed rioters chanting their demand to "hang Mike Pence." But the strangest thing I found in those archived conversations is that some of the people who entered the Capitol building likely thought Pence was *already* dead. There was a rumor going around that he had been executed by a Trump-run military tribunal sometime in 2020—as were the Obamas, the Clintons, Chief Justice John Roberts, and Biden himself. News reports showing them apparently reacting to current events, the story went, were simply computer-generated. Or maybe holograms. Or actors? Or clones![25]

At first, I was bemused by how outlandish the theory was. I mean, *clones*. (How did Trump even grow them that fast? C'mon!) But then I started clicking through to the social media profiles of the people spreading this nonsense, and soon I had the same pit in my stomach I felt when my former coworker, Jim, refused to buy a house. Many of their bios were festooned with phrases like "conservative Christian," "Bible-believing Christian," "fighting for faith," "John 3:16," "God-fearing," "Christian, wife, and mother." They were sharing Bible verses, sometimes in the same post as their conspiracy theories. They expressed faith that God would accomplish the coup they expected. They thought Jesus—the God who loved his enemies and willingly died for them in a brutal state execution (Rom. 5:10)—was leading a political revolution that began with mass executions. They were professing Christians, just like me, but their vision of Christ was unrecognizable.

Speaking the Truth in Love

Christians are supposed to be people of truth, known for our love. To grow in Christian maturity, Paul wrote to the Ephesians, is to cease being "blown here and there by every wind of teaching and by the cunning and craftiness of people in their deceitful scheming" and instead to learn to "[speak] the truth in love" (4:14–15). But perhaps no part of Scripture expresses this with more depth and beauty than the Johannine literature, particularly the Gospel of John and the Epistle of 1 John.

John's Gospel begins this theme with its opening ode to Jesus as "the Word," who "was with God" and "was God," through whom "all things were made" and without whom "nothing was made that has been made" (1:1–3). The Greek word *logos*—which we translate as "Word"—has a fuller meaning, as its similarity to "logic" suggests. When John calls Jesus "the Word," he identifies him as the reason and order of the universe. Justin Martyr, one of the earliest Christian theologians, wrote that the *logos* "who is with God and is begotten before the creation" is "the intuition planted in human nature of an inexpressible reality."[26] Jesus as *logos* is the truth by which the whole world hangs together, Justin taught, and Christ "is the *logos* of whom every race of men and women were partakers."[27]

Jesus himself makes this claim while talking with his critics (in John 8) and his disciples (in John 14). In both passages he links truth and love, and he describes them as foundational to Christian faithfulness. "I am the way and the truth and the life" (14:6), he tells his disciples, and his followers "will know the truth" (8:32). Jesus calls his people to love, promising we will be guided in this by the Holy Spirit (14:5–17), the "Spirit of truth" (14:17).

As for his opponents, Jesus charges that they're unable to love him because they don't know God and therefore can't recognize God's truth. "If God were your Father, you would love me, for I have come here from God," he says in John 8. "Why is my language not clear to you? Because you are unable to hear what I say. You belong to your father, the devil, . . . [and] there is no truth in him. When he lies, he speaks his native language, for he is a liar and the father of lies" (vv. 42–44). It is precisely *because* he tells the truth, Jesus says, that these critics can't understand him. They can't recognize *logos* itself.

The First Epistle of John explores this truth-love-faith connection further in a long pastoral meditation on the nature and expression of love. "This is how we know what love is," the letter explains. "Jesus Christ laid down his life for us. And we ought to lay down our lives for our brothers and sisters . . . not love with words or speech but with actions and in truth" (3:16–18). As Christians, our faithfulness to the truth should be evidenced in our love, and our love, with God's help, should be expressed in truth.

A Failure of Discipleship

So what are we to make of professing Christians who believe absurdities—and cruel ones at that? Most American Christians don't believe anything quite so outlandish as the clones and executions theory, yet belief in that theory is not the aberration we might hope. "In my experience and in my conversations among pastors, we are growing more and more alarmed by the prevalence of belief in conspiracy theories and far-fetched political ideas" in the American church, Daniel Darling told me in an interview for a column I wrote at *Christianity Today*.[28]

Darling is a pastor and author whose books include *A Way with Words: Using Our Online Conversations for Good*. His assessment of the growing knowledge crisis in American churches is backed by national survey data published in an early 2021 Lifeway poll: fully half of Protestant pastors in America said they "frequently hear members of their congregation[s] repeating conspiracy theories they have heard about why something is happening in our country."[29]

"With most pastors I talk to, it's a fraction of their congregations, perhaps among the most politically engaged or the most plugged in online," Darling told me. "And yet it is enough of an element that it has many pastors worried," especially about "how captive many [Christians] are to their preferred media outlets, which are growing more and more extreme, and how seemingly resistant many are to hearing reasonable rebuttals."[30] That resistance, if it grows unchecked, could easily become the stuff of church splits. At the very least, it is a serious challenge of discipleship, an impediment to our progress toward Christian maturity in truth and love.

Faithful life together doesn't require ideological uniformity. We don't need to have the same views on current events or public policy or even every theological question. (My first book, *A Flexible Faith*, is about the value of diverse perspectives within the body of Christ.) But Christian faithfulness does require sincere pursuit of truth in love. Falling into a knowledge crisis risks grave damage to our church communities, our public witness, and our individual faith.

Epistemic confusion does not make us more loving. It does not bear good fruit. It does not help us "live a life worthy of the calling [we] have received" (Eph. 4:1).

It is not of Christ.

"Our World in Stupor Lies"

I've never been much for reading poetry, but in 2020, as the COVID-19 pandemic made so much of life unrecognizable, I found myself revisiting the poets of World War I and the interwar years. The Great War unmade the world that was, and its poets captured well the sense of unmooring, uncertainty, and unsourced dread that pervades our public life once more.

At the tail end of the interwar period came W. H. Auden's "September 1, 1939," a poem named for the day Germany invaded Poland and World War II's hostilities formally began. Auden wrote of a time of "anger and fear" that circulates throughout the land and "obsess[es] our private lives." The poem's best-known lines speak of love and evil, but in the final stanza the poet turns to truth:

Defenceless under the night
Our world in stupor lies;
Yet, dotted everywhere,
Ironic points of light
Flash out wherever the Just
Exchange their messages:
May I, composed like them
Of Eros and of dust,
Beleaguered by the same
Negation and despair,
Show an affirming flame.[31]

Almost a century later, we are again in stupor, and we again need points of light. We have an epistemic crisis breaking our brains, polluting our politics, and corrupting Christian community. This book is my attempt to offer an "affirming flame."

Media

Folly and error, avarice and vice,
Employ our souls and waste our bodies' force.
As mangey beggars incubate their lice,
We nourish our innocuous remorse.
. . . .
The Devil pulls the strings by which we're worked:
By all revolting objects lured, we slink
Hellwards; each day down one more step we're
 jerked
Feeling no horror, through the shades that stink.

> —Charles Baudelaire, "To the Reader"
> (trans. Roy Campbell)

Every journalist makes mistakes. I certainly have, and that means I've had to issue corrections.

If a mistake is small and insignificant—like a typo, and especially one that's easily identifiable as such—it's okay to simply correct it. At *Christianity Today*, I'll shoot a quick email to my editor asking her to make the switch. At *The Week*, I do it myself but always alert at least one other editor to what I'm doing. It's good to leave a record of what you've changed and why, in case anyone has questions later.

Greater mistakes—say, a factual error or misquotation—require greater transparency. The standard procedure is to make an in-text correction and then add an editorial note at the end of the article (or, in print, in the next issue) documenting what was wrong, explaining what was changed, and expressing regret. *The Week*'s format for this note is designed for visibility. It starts in bold, italicized text in capitalized letters: ***CORRECTION***. If an error is egregious, we might move the editorial note to the top of the page or, in an extreme case, issue a complete retraction and apology. (To my knowledge, nothing so dramatic has happened in my time with the magazine.)

A few times I've found mistakes in my own columns after they were published, but occasionally a reader or subject of my work has contacted me or my editor requesting a fix. That latter way is how I learned of the single worst error I've ever made, one that still makes me a little nauseous to remember.

It was early 2020, and I'd written an opinion piece for *The Week* about Liberty University's initial response to COVID-19. The Virginia school stood out from most institutions of higher education, including other evangelical Christian colleges, in its decision to keep its dorms, which housed about sixteen thousand students, open through the end of the semester. Liberty's then-president Jerry Falwell Jr., who at the time was well known for his vocal support of Donald Trump, said he expected "most" of the students to come back to campus after spring break and resume dorm life. Falwell made that prediction in the context of a radio interview in which he called COVID-19 "this flu," said he was "not worried about it," and declared the media response to be "just politics"—an effort to "destroy the American economy just to hurt Trump."[1] He repeatedly tweeted and made other public comments to similar effect.

The thrust of my article was a criticism of this rationale for his decision. Mostly I focused on his statements and on push-back from within the Liberty community. But in a short parenthetical aside, citing a local news outlet in Virginia, I wrote that in "an unfortunate slip of the tongue, Falwell initially resisted moving to online instruction because, he said, the school's extant online classes, which instruct about 85 percent of Liberty's student body under normal conditions, are 'really not the same quality of education' as residential courses."

The words were correct, but my interpretation was dead wrong. Here's the quote in full, which I encountered for the first time in an email from Scott Lamb, who was then Liberty's senior vice president of communications and public engagement: "I don't see us doing the same the other schools have done. When they say they're going online, they don't really mean online, they mean some hybrid of online and normal education—it's really more Skype lectures and emails between the professor and the student—and so it's really not the same quality of education that we provide online and that they receive here on campus."

Lamb shared a link to a YouTube video of Falwell's entire talk, which I hadn't realized was available online. "You are not the first to take him out of context," Lamb wrote, "and the other journalists amended their pieces when they examined the context of the original quote."

I read Falwell's whole quote five times, watched the relevant segment of the video at least thrice, seriously considered the possibility I was going to puke—and then pulled myself together and forwarded the email to all my editors. "He's right about this," I wrote to them. I had "read an excerpted quote and did not realize how misleading it was. We should definitely correct." We fixed it within a few minutes, deleting my parenthetical material entirely and adding the requisite **CORRECTION**. "We regret the error," it concluded.

I did regret it, enormously. And when I wrote back to Lamb, telling him what we were doing to rectify my mistake didn't seem adequate. Making a factual mistake—say, writing "Oregon" when it should have been "Washington"—is bad. Misquoting someone, particularly in a way that falsely suggests malfeasance, is awful. I hadn't changed my mind about Falwell's rationale for Liberty's pandemic policy, but I was mortified I'd written about him so unfairly, not least because his criticism of the hybrid options some schools cobbled together was perfectly apt.

And so, after I'd explained our correction process in my reply to Lamb, I added, "I also want to apologize for this mistake—it was absolutely not my intent to mislead, and I would *never* have included that quote had I realized how inaccurate was the framing I relayed." Lamb's reply was prompt and gracious, a welcome reminder that whatever our differences, we were both Christians and committed to truth.

What's Wrong with the News?

It can be a strange thing to be a Christian—an evangelical one at that[2]—and a member of the media. The strangeness is not that I'm unique; there are plenty of Christian journalists, including at secular outlets. Rather, it's that many of my fellow Christians (and especially evangelicals) are reflexively suspicious of my industry.

Trust in the media is on a long downward trend across American society.[3] Even graded on that curve, white evangelicals are unusually distrustful of the press.[4] "You tease about the mainstream media being 'Satan's newspaper,'" *Washington Post* reporter Sarah Pulliam Bailey wrote in a column framed as a letter to evangelicals soon after the 2016 presidential election. "When I tell you I'm a journalist, I hear your cynicism. Listen, I was raised in an evangelical home. I know the media is supposed to be the butt of many jokes and the source of many of our problems. . . . [But] the jokes aren't funny anymore."[5]

Bailey used to be an editor at *Christianity Today*, where I am now a columnist, and the cynicism she describes is something I've encountered as well. It's most striking in conversations with my mom. She's proud of me and my work, and always eager to support outlets that publish my stuff, but if we discuss the media more generally, her attitude toward the press turns sharply negative.

She's far from alone in that view, and some of this negativity has good cause. The press isn't innocent of contributing to our epistemic crisis, but neither are we—as the press's audience and as social media users. There are serious problems with how our news media works; how we as readers, listeners, and viewers consume its products; and how we interact with content and one another on social-networking sites. Traditional and social media are where many of us have most tangibly encountered our epistemic crisis. It's where our knowledge problem is easiest to spot in this age of "fake news." Even casual consumers of news can easily realize something is wrong here. In this chapter, we explore the nature of the problem and begin to examine how Christians should respond.

"Uniformly Left, Left, Left"?

The primary objection Americans typically raise to the news media is a charge of deliberate, ideological bias. This is what many people mean when they express concern about "fake news." "Eight in 10 Americans say that when they suspect an inaccuracy in a [news] story, they worry it was intentional," a 2020 Gallup/Knight Foundation poll of twenty thousand Americans found, "because the reporter was misrepresenting the facts (52 percent) or making them up (28 percent). Only 18 percent say they think the inaccuracies were innocent mistakes."[6]

Sometimes this accusation comes from the left, which charges the press with being too deferential to corporate, government, and military establishments and too prone to "both-sides-ism," which legitimizes fascism and other unsavory political factions. More often, however, charges that the press is ideologically biased come from the right,[7] and somewhat fairly so: polling finds fewer than one in ten full-time journalists identify as Republicans.[8] Though a slight majority consider themselves politically independent, journalists' campaign donation patterns consistently show a strong preference for Democrats, at around 90 percent.[9] Radio host and *Washington Post* columnist Hugh Hewitt's phrasing of the allegation—that "Manhattan-Beltway media elites are uniformly left, left, left, and they are now extensions of the Democratic Party"—goes too far; yet insofar as there is political bias in the US media, it undeniably leans center-left.[10]

It would be naive to think this has *no* effect on coverage. But as journalist Matt Taibbi argues in *Hate Inc.: Why Today's Media Makes Us Despise One Another*, the effect at reasonably reputable outlets isn't the straightforward, willful deception Americans tend to imagine. "The public largely misunderstands the 'fake news' issue," Taibbi writes. Outlets like TV news stations and newspapers "rarely fib outright. Most 'lies' are errors of omission or emphasis. . . . Most of what's 'fake' is in the caricature: of our own audiences, and especially of despised groups."[11]

Fox News will decline to report embarrassing stories about Republicans, for instance, and MSNBC will do the same for Democrats.[12] A politically biased reporter won't lie to you; she'll merely tell you to look at *this* instead of *that*. And perhaps she's right about where you should look—perhaps *this* really will give you a better understanding of reality than *that*. Or perhaps she's wrong. It's a judgment call, and journalists' political views inevitably influence their judgment about political topics.

Many entire outlets choose a political viewpoint as well, meaning judgment is rendered at an organizational level.

Those judgments influence what news we receive as well as its framing and commentary. Yet focusing on political bias (which 66 percent of respondents to a 2020 poll said is their top criticism of the media) as a *primary* criticism misses multiple other, better indicators of what feels amiss with the news.[13] There is something off here, but it's generally not *intentional, ideologically motivated* inaccuracy, as so many Americans fear. The problem with the press is not malice but ordinary human foibles, disagreements, and practical constraints—plus some of the same epistemic confusion affecting everyone else.

To understand why our news environment is askew, we need to look beyond political bias to other kinds of bias: profit, entertainment, and speed. We also need to recognize that journalists have true blind spots, as we all do, and that the media is presently entangled in an intense internal debate over industry norms of objectivity and activism.

Profit and Entertainment

Profit bias is exactly what it sounds like. The press is a business with two sets of customers: the audience and the advertisers.[14] (This is typically true even of nonprofit outlets, which sometimes run ads in addition to soliciting donations and always want to gain and retain readers or viewers.) News outlets need an audience to sell ads, and communication to large groups of people is the very point of the press. Ideally that audience will be stable or growing. Accomplishing this requires giving customers what they want or are perceived to want, and though that product varies widely by outlet and format, it too often means sensationalism designed to inflame and excite.[15] Profit bias and entertainment bias are thus closed tied.

However sophisticated we may think we are, we like to be entertained. We like to be thrilled. We like to learn that the other guys are exactly as bad as we suspected they are. "If it bleeds, it leads," as the saying goes. More accurately, if it's interesting enough to make you watch or click or buy the magazine, it's more likely to get published. That's not the only consideration in the calculation of what's newsworthy, nor is entertainment bias equally distributed among different types of news media. A cable news show is quite different in this regard from a longform print report; an outlet like *Christianity Today* has controlling principles that override base ploys to attract as many eyeballs as possible. (As a rule of thumb, the more loud noises, bright colors, and moving parts an outlet or story features, the more it's intended to entertain.)

The digital era has allowed the media to fragment and diversify; we no longer have three television networks and one local paper competing for a broad swath of viewers. Consequently, the entertainment-profit dynamic is becoming ever more customized to audience preference. The media can tell you exactly what you want to hear. Again, that doesn't mean deliberate lies, but it can mean a misleading curation of the truth.

The fine-grained audience data now available makes it possible to microtarget advertising on social media, delivering stories only to audiences who will like them. It's also possible to track *by the second* which topics and headlines bring in new readers and subscribers and to steer coverage accordingly. Journalist Jesse Singal, who writes a column about media for *Spectator World* and also runs an independent email newsletter, has observed that whenever he writes about issues of gender and sexuality, he sees an uptick in paying newsletter subscribers that no other topic produces. "One of my concerns about the silo-ization of everything is how the very blunt [and] visible financial incentives could drive people to just hit the same notes over and over and over," Singal has said.[16]

At *The Week* in the first few months after the Trump presidency ended, we noticed that any Trump-related stories brought in unusually high traffic, which meant unusually high ad revenue. Trump was out of office, but people were still eager to read about him. Becoming aware that Trump was a driver of online traffic had a strong knowledge-of-good-and-evil feel (Gen. 2:15–17). It introduced a temptation to lower our standards of newsworthiness and churn out Trump stories for the money.

To their credit—and this is part of why I've been at *The Week* for nearly a decade, which is a lifetime by industry standards— our editors did not do that. They said it was okay to make small tweaks to our coverage with this data in mind (like illustrating a story that already included Trump with a photo of him instead of someone else involved), but they nixed the idea of dramatically bending our coverage for profit.

The move to digital platforms has also exacerbated the profit and entertainment biases by giving outlets far more competition for advertising. "As Jim Moroney of the *Dallas Morning News* explained to me, newspapers in the pre-internet days were cash machines," Taibbi writes in *Hate Inc.*:

> If you wanted to find a worker for hire or sell a car, the local paper was the only game in town. "These were scarcity businesses," is how [Moroney] put it. It was the same with local radio and TV stations, limited in number because each needed FCC licenses. There were only so many 30-second spots on the air. If you had a radio show or a daily newspaper, you didn't have to wind up the local Junior Anti-Sex League to torchbearing action every week to sell copies. You made enough on classified and local ads that you could safely not indulge in fearmongering, if you so chose.[17]

Now advertisers have nigh unlimited options of where to place their ads, almost all of them charging less and offering more reach than that local paper. If they can't rely on other revenue sources, some outlets sensationalize to survive.

Speeding Past Blind Spots

Even well-funded outlets, however, aren't immune to speed bias. Journalists are almost always on a deadline, and that haste often produces a predilection for familiarity and the status quo.[18] This is less about ideology than efficiency, but it can have an ideological effect. When a reporter needs to finish a story quickly, turning to known sources helps—and status quo sources (elected officials, career bureaucrats, think-tank experts, corporate public relations staff) are by nature likelier to be accessible than more heterodox voices.

Should reporters deliberately seek out a wider range of views and topics to include in their work? Yes—and that's one reason why we, as news consumers, must express a preference for a more measured news cycle, serious topical selection, and in-depth reporting. What we pay for (and click on and tweet) is what we'll get.

In the meantime, however, the narrower range of views that speed produces is not deliberate suppression of other views. As an opinion writer, I have longer deadlines and more leeway with my source choices than straight news reporters do, yet I regularly find myself returning to the same sources for expert comment. When my toddlers are screaming in the other room and my to-do list is a mile long, it's quicker to contact people and think tanks I've worked with before. I know how to reach them; I know they'll be well informed; and I know they know me and trust my article will treat them respectfully. That can save precious hours of time in our endlessly roiling news cycle. I diversify as much as I can, but I can't do it with every story.

The only way to lessen speed bias is to give journalists more time to do their work. That would mean slower delivery of news and less output overall. Unfortunately, the message that news consumers have sent for decades is not "slower, less, and better" but "faster and more, even if it's worse." In the aftermath of the 2016 election, Taibbi notes, polling showed confidence in the press dropped—but ratings rose: "People believed us less, but watched us more."[19] This is an incredibly perverse market signal, telling media companies to double down on the very choices that erode public trust.

Like speed bias, blind spots can be found at outlets of every scale and income and among journalists of every political persuasion. I can't list them all, of course, but I can say that ignorance of religion may be the blind spot at the nexus of "most important" and "fastest growing" in America. As religiosity declines in the United States, and Christian religiosity specifically (by which I mean not only faith but also cultural exposure to Christian stories, holidays, rituals, and the like), ways of thinking and turns of phrase that were once normative in America are becoming newly strange in public conversation.[20] Journalists, like all our compatriots, are becoming less familiar with information Christians could once assume was common knowledge.

I regularly think about a 2019 Associated Press headline that, after the famous cathedral burned, announced: "Tourist mecca Notre Dame also revered as place of worship." This headline made it to print even though "mecca" is a metaphor from Islam and Notre Dame was a Christian house of worship for centuries before the concept of tourism emerged.[21] The headline was a laughingstock among religion reporters, but to date it remains unchanged.

This inappropriately casual treatment of a beloved cathedral in a moment of tragedy is the sort of thing conservatives might cite as evidence of "liberal media bias" against Christians. I don't think so. My guess is that the headline wasn't written by the article's coauthors, one of whom has been on the Catholicism beat for years. A final headline is usually an editor's doing, and I suspect this one was the work of a well-intentioned, possibly early-career editor working on a tight deadline and unaware of their own blind spots. It's probably not that they're "left, left, left." It's that they didn't know what they didn't know.

The Objectivity Debate

The final factor Americans tend to ignore in our rush to allege political bias in the media is the current internecine conflict over objectivity and activism. All the other biases and sources of error I've described are longstanding issues; the internet or cultural shifts may have exacerbated them, but in broad strokes they've been unchanged for the past few decades. The debate over objectivity and activism is something new.

Until the early years of the twentieth century, the American press made little pretense of objectivity. Partisans regularly printed false and inflammatory pamphlets about their political opponents that would never pass muster today.[22] Even more moderate newspapers of that era tended to be open about their political preferences. Objectivity as we think of it was not expected or desired. (You can still see evidence of this history in the names of some older newspapers; my husband grew up in a Southern town with a paper called the *Times-Democrat*.)

In the mid-twentieth century, however, objectivity became the norm. To some extent this was required by the federal government's Fairness Doctrine, which from 1949 to 1987 issued broadcast licenses contingent on an outlet's willingness to "devote a reasonable portion of broadcast time to the discussion and consideration of controversial issues of public importance" and to do so fairly by "affirmatively endeavor[ing] to make . . . facilities available for the expression of contrasting viewpoints held by responsible elements with respect to the controversial issues presented."[23] In other words, a licensed TV news station had to discuss serious issues and interview—as it often worked in practice—Democrats and Republicans in pairs.

Beyond the Fairness Doctrine, some of the mid-century objectivity norm was simply a different version of the profit bias: media outlets wanted the biggest, broadest audience they could muster, and the strategy of choice was a neutral, inoffensive style that purported to offer the bare facts. The goal was a product palatable to most of the country, and objectivity was the sales pitch.

Lest I sound too cynical, however, let me hasten to add that the objectivity norm was not only about legislation and profit. It was also a strong principle for many American journalists. The mythos of the dogged reporter following the truth no matter where it led and no matter who it angered was a sincere aspiration, and it still is for many journalists today. Objectivity might not always be perfectly achieved, the thinking goes, but surely we should try.

My horror over my misquoting of Falwell comes in part from this professional lineage. In fact, how a news outlet handles its errors has long been (and remains) a useful gauge of credibility. Willingness to issue corrections and retractions (preferably before they find themselves at the tip of the libel lawsuit's sword) marks a bright line between outlets that, however partisan their editorial perspectives, retain regard for truth and those that do not.

This is why, philosophy professors Cailin O'Connor and James Owen Weatherall explain, even cable news channels—as much as we might object to their editorial slant and sensationalism (and I vehemently do)—are "in a very different category" from "fake news" sites intended to deceive and fringier outlets like *Infowars*. In *The Misinformation Age: How False Beliefs Spread*, they write: "What *makes* them different is that Fox, CNN, and MSNBC generally retract false stories in light of new evidence. A self-correcting editorial process is at work. One can quibble about how long it takes to make the retractions, and whether whatever damage was going to be done had

43

already happened. But in cases where the facts are simply and demonstrably wrong, these media sources have corrected the errors—and in many cases, they have done so because other news sources have policed them."[24]

Sketchy online outlets do not do this. They don't have this editorial process because they don't care about factual accuracy and because sharing news is only a means to some nefarious end. (If an outlet you frequent has *no* corrections, it would be prudent to consider carefully whether its writers have a pre-ternatural ability to avoid human error or whether they simply have another agenda unconcerned with truth.)

Correction of demonstrable error is a persistent and valuable legacy of objectivity journalism. Across the media industry, however, objectivity is under furious debate. Is it a path to fairness or to injustice? A commitment to accuracy or to keeping the average American in happy ignorance? Should journalists aim to convey facts or, in the much-disputed phrase of CBS correspondent Wesley Lowery in a 2020 *New York Times* op-ed, "moral clarity"?[25] Should we tell our audience what *is*, or what *ought to be*?[26]

Defenders of the older model say reporters (as opposed to opinion writers like me) should imitate the detective, not the judge. "The truth has traditionally been very important to journalism," wrote Singal in 2021, "but a larger and larger chunk of the overall media pie is dominated by partisan and hyperpartisan actors for whom it is a secondary concern. In my view, the right is much further down this road than the left," he said, offering examples from the 2016 and 2020 elections. But at a growing number of prominent, center-left outlets, Singal added, "there is what feels like a heightened sense among many mainstream journalists (particularly younger ones) that they are not only observers but active participants in vital social-justice battles . . . and this attitude leads directly to unjournalistic editorial decisions which degrade public trust in our institution."[27]

I share Singal's worries. Straight reporting isn't activism. It's tasked with collecting information, not rendering judgment, and it should attempt to relate the world as it is, not a vision of the world as it ought to be.[28] While both information and judgment have their place in journalism, the former must precede the latter. We need reporters to establish facts—doing the vital work of interviewing eyewitnesses, obtaining secret government records, interrogating powerful officials, and so on—before that second project of judgment can begin. When I write opinion columns, I rely on the groundwork of reporters at newswires like Reuters, the Associated Press, and Religion News Service, along with those at outlets like NBC News, the *Washington Post*, and *Politico*. They tell us what happened; then people like me present a case for what it means and what we should do about it.

The preservation of straight news reporting is also necessary because it isn't always wise to render instant judgment. Early media coverage of the horrific mass shooting in Atlanta in 2021 offers a case study of what happens when reporters rush to judge when they should still be collecting information. The attack was quickly and widely framed by major media outlets as an anti-Asian hate crime, a narrative that made sense given other recent violence against Asians and Asian-Americans.[29] But that's not what the murderer confessed. He "told detectives he carried out the attack as a way of getting rid of [sexual] temptation."[30] Nor is it what people who knew him thought likely,[31] or what prosecutors and investigators[32]—including the FBI[33]—concluded. The available evidence suggests misogyny, sexual sin, and grossly distorted theology are more accurately to blame.[34]

Moreover, even when facts are established, one man's moral clarity is another's "mountains of highly politicized, vituperative content."[35] The proper place to apply one label or the other is the opinion section (and, depending on the outlet, a particular journalist may sometimes work as a reporter and sometimes give her opinion—the line between reporting and opinion divides work, not people).

That said, I don't believe the media should (or can) return to the mid-century model of objectivity. The concept of journalistic objectivity as it's widely understood suggests reporters are like machines, free of their own opinions and capable of sharing pure, unfiltered truth. That's false, and journalists' use of social media, where we publicly broadcast our views, has made the fiction impossible to maintain. Moreover, claiming objectivity can create a dangerous confusion if opinion content is mistaken for straight reporting or misinterpreted as an illicit attempt to package bias as fact. I've seen both misunderstandings time and time again.

Yet even without such confusion, the expectation that journalists will be totally objective is damaging to our discourse, because it feeds an impossible expectation.[36] The most careful, candid reporter cannot produce a perfect representation of reality. Even the choice of what stories to cover is the product of a sort of bias, because in choosing one story we inevitably neglect another. This often is not about an intent to deceive, or ideology (at least not consciously—though that is changing among some journalists, as Singal describes). It's just that journalists, including reporters, are humans with opinions and a finite number of hours in the day.

So why try to hew to an impossible standard? The *Washington Examiner*'s Tim Carney defines a columnist as "a reporter who clearly lays out his own judgments and analysis of what he's reporting" or, with a bit more snark, "a reporter who doesn't pretend to have no opinions."[37] Shouldn't all reporters reject that pretense?

That doesn't mean jettisoning straight news, turning all reporting into opinion and activism. Rather, it means pairing a commitment to truthful reporting—striving for accuracy, not "moral clarity," which is the province of the opinion section—with transparency about journalists' biases. (I discovered Carney has a practice, one I may replicate, of keeping at the top of his Twitter profile a link to a regularly updated statement of all his major views and financial affiliations as context for his writing.) We shouldn't hide our views, and, as Lowery wrote in the *Times*, we should pledge to "diligently seek out the perspectives of those with whom we personally may be inclined to disagree and [to] be just as sure to ask hard questions of those with whom we're inclined to agree."[38] Telling our audience what we think makes it easier for readers to sort fact from opinion, should opinion creep into what ought to be straight news.

"Fake News"

This review of traditional media's contribution to our epistemic crisis has inevitably touched on social media throughout. It's nearly impossible today to speak of one without the other. But I do want to explore social media more directly, and as we make that shift, it's a good time to ask: What do we mean when we say "fake news"?

I've used quotation marks around "fake news" each time I've mentioned it so far, and that's because the term has several contradictory usages all jostling around together in common parlance. The phrase originally meant fabricated online articles formatted to look plausibly real. Their publishers' goal is to fool people into sharing the fake stories and to collect the ad revenue that site traffic brings.[39] Fake sites in this sense are often designed to look like a local newspaper, an easy style to imitate. Some include a disclaimer—usually located on an obscure "About" page the average visitor never sees—labeling the site as "satire." This might provide legal cover, but it's as much a lie as the reports themselves. Satire reveals; fake news deceives.

This fake news works as a business model because without real journalism's constraints, its writers can say whatever they want to get as much traffic as they can. They can write rage- and shock-inducing headlines that create not mere curiosity but a biological urge to click: our adrenaline gets pumping when these stories appear in our newsfeeds, and we *just have to know*. The freedom to deceive is profitable, and fake-news articles often spread more rapidly than the truth.

Shortly before the 2016 election, for example, an article titled "Pope Francis shocks world, endorses Donald Trump for president, releases statement" was shared or liked 960,000 times on Facebook. The story had the pope explaining his plans to vote for Trump because of his dissatisfaction with the Justice Department's handling of an investigation into Hillary Clinton, who at that time was the Democratic presidential nominee.

Of course, the pope is not an American citizen, cannot vote in our elections, and did not endorse any candidate for US president. The story was made up. The website that published it had the standard disclaimer on its "About" page, which described the site as a "fantasy news website" disseminating "satire or pure fantasy."[40] Nevertheless, that article became "the single most-shared election-related news item on Facebook in the three months leading up to the [2016] election," per a calculation in *The Misinformation Age*. "By contrast, the most-shared article from a reputable source in the same period was a *Washington Post* opinion piece . . . shared 849,000 times."[41]

A 2018 study by three scholars at the Massachusetts Institute of Technology (MIT) documented a similar discrepancy on Twitter. "We found that falsehood diffuses significantly farther, faster, deeper, and more broadly than the truth, in all categories of information, and in many cases by an order of magnitude," said Sinan Aral, one of the report's coauthors and an MIT professor. Fake reports were found to be "70 percent more likely to be retweeted than true stories," and they reached fifteen hundred people in one-sixth of the time it took a true story to spread that far. Crucially, this disparity was not attributable to activity by bots (automated accounts). Humans were reading and sharing the lies.[42] Though some of those shares were likely done for the purpose of debunking, many were not.

This means there's no quick technological fix. The dissemination of fake news is an epistemic problem at least as much as a technological one.

"Fake news" is used in at least two other senses, both of which feed misunderstanding. Sometimes we use the phrase to describe unfair or misleading stories that are still technically true, and sometimes we use it for fair and true stories we dislike and want to discount. The latter is a blatant contributor to epistemic crisis and such a response is always wrong. It sows unjustified doubt and precludes good-faith debate.

The former is a trickier case. We *do* need to talk about the kind of journalism that misinforms without outright lying. For example, suppose my town's violent crime rate has been on a downward trend for thirty years. A particular year may not have had fewer crimes than the year before it, but the overall trend line has a steadily declining slope. Say in 1990 there were fifty murders, and that gradually dropped to two murders in 2020. Then, the police department reveals we had four murders in 2021.

As a local reporter, I have a choice. Do I write this story?

Police Announce Spiking Crime:
Murder Rate Doubles in One Year

Or do I write this one?

Three-Decade Decline in Violent Crime Holds
Despite Annual Fluctuation

Both are completely factual, but the second headline communicates far more truth. (Incidentally, this hypothetical isn't a stretch. Crime statistics are often reported in the style of the first headline, which contributes to Americans' frequent insistence that crime rates are rising when they are falling.[43]) Still, I don't think calling the first headline "fake news" accomplishes anything good. It's not fake in the way the pope story is fake. Imprecise language catering to sensationalism or ideological bias is the proper charge here, and equally dubbing these two articles "fake news" makes it more difficult to tell fact from fiction.

What's Wrong with Social Media?

For consumers of social media, telling fact from fiction has become constantly necessary. Gone is the optimism of the early 2000s, when I earnestly told my mom that Facebook was, in fact, a *good* thing that would make the world *better* by facilitating real-world friendships. Now I'm more inclined to echo *New Yorker* columnist Susan B. Glasser in her condemnation of social media as "the most efficient distribution network for conspiracy theories, hatred, and outright falsehoods ever invented."[44]

Social media is the filter through which so much of our consumption of traditional media now happens. Even if you don't get news through social media, the news you consume elsewhere is probably shaped by it, because the journalists who produce that news almost certainly use those networks. Twitter has emerged as the poison of choice in journalism, a choice cemented in 2016 when Trump's Twitter use took advantage of the longstanding journalistic assumption that anything the American president utters is inherently newsworthy. By the time Trump was banned from Twitter five years later, the habit was firmly set, and now whole news cycles are regularly molded by Twitter controversies.

Journalists are far from alone, however, in our overuse and misuse of social media, which didn't create misinformation but, Glasser says, is uniquely powerful as a distribution mechanism.[45] We were all sinners before Facebook, but Facebook gave us unprecedented means of amplifying our sin and calling it virtue.

Social media is deliberately structured to be habit-forming, manipulative, and emotionally escalatory. It invites us to "flit from headline to headline, skimming in search of some new outrage or drama," writes professor and editor Jeffrey Bilbro in *Reading the Times: A Literary and Theological Inquiry into the News*:

> For all our hunger for the next bit of breaking news, we quickly forget it once we've extracted the emotional charge it can give us. We are soon hungry for the next outrage, the next unbelievable headline, the next political scandal. We have an intense desire to know *something*, but the object of that desire remains indeterminate and vague. So we hurriedly scroll through our newsfeed looking for something to latch onto. . . . This restless curiosity, this craving for some new bit of entertainment, makes us incredibly vulnerable to the wiles of advertisers and politicians and ideologues. We become susceptible to the latest groupthink because our thoughts are dictated by trending jargon and viral hashtags.[46]

Our thought patterns and knowledge are not the only things social media affects for the worse. Our physical brains change too. To say that they "break," I think, is not too strong a metaphor.[47]

Author Nicholas Carr was a Pulitzer finalist in 2011 for his exploration of the subject in *The Shallows: What the Internet*

Is Doing to Our Brains, which remains a landmark work on this phenomenon. "Over the past few years I've had an uncomfortable sense that someone, or something, has been tinkering with my brain, remapping the neural circuitry, reprogramming the memory," Carr begins his book. "My mind isn't going—so far as I can tell—but it's changing. I'm not thinking the way I used to think." The internet, he says, with piles of research to back up the instinct, "is chipping away my capacity for concentration and contemplation."[48]

Carr's starting point for his development of the book was an essay he'd published three years earlier in *The Atlantic*.[49] When that essay came out in 2008, Twitter was just two years old and was a silly place where you pointlessly announced your breakfast. Instagram didn't exist. Facebook seemed innocuous; Carr didn't even mention it in his article, an unthinkable choice today. The risks our brains faced then, real though they were, look laughably meager now. The degradation of attention spans that Carr described has massively accelerated in the years since, time in which social media and smartphone use have become ubiquitous. Our habitual distraction is debilitating; "addiction" is not entirely metaphorical.

But it's not only that. The brokenness I'm describing is more than distraction. Carr focuses on the medium over the message. "In the long run, a medium's content matters less than the medium itself in influencing how we think and act," he asserts.[50] I agree, but what we're seeing now is that the content itself cannot be discounted as a potent force of epistemic disorder and relational discord.

Borrowing from the epigraph at the beginning of this chapter, the way social media's "folly and error, avarice and vice / Employ our souls and waste our bodies' force" will be a recurring theme throughout this book. For now, however, I'll confine myself to four ways it fosters epistemic confusion.

First, it encourages distraction and uncritical content consumption, presenting a trivializing mix of serious content with memes, ads, and personal posts from our family and friends.[51] It also wraps most content in a friend's personal endorsement. When I see an article or graphic shared by a loved one whose good character I value, my inclination is to approach that content very differently than I would if I encountered it in the wilds of the internet.

We are social beings, powerfully influenced by our communities, and the familiar faces peppered through our social media feeds wrongly communicate that it is safe to drop our epistemic guard.[52] The same effect can happen with public figures with whom we have no personal relationship but have an artificial sense of "knowing" from their daily appearance in our newsfeeds among our real friends.[53]

Second, we fail to realize or remember the extent to which the content we encounter on social media is tailored by algorithms to set our lizard brains on fire. A 2018 Reuters poll of Americans and Europeans found just three in ten respondents correctly understood that "the individual decisions about what news stories to show people on Facebook" are made by "computer analysis of what stories might interest you." Four in ten said they didn't know; the remaining 30 percent were split almost equally between believing it was random and believing those decisions were made by journalists and editors employed by either Facebook or outside news organizations.[54]

This ignorance encourages us to drift with the algorithm, to share misinformation and fail to identify content designed to take our money or rile our anger and fear. Social media runs on human emotion, and its most efficient fuel is not the friendly connections it ostensibly exists to foster; it is political rage, the one sort of spleen for which American society consistently sanctions public venting.[55]

Ad-funded social networks like Facebook make money not by the mere fact of user accounts existing but by steady user engagement. They are engineered to produce frequent, active use—not passive browsing but clicks and comments and shares.

The experience is gamified. It trains our brains. We sincerely enjoy those accumulating likes. We enjoy even more the rush that inflammatory political content brings, and because a lot of politics, even now, is quite boring, lies and half-truths are best equipped to provide the excitement we crave. Facebook wants clicks, and lies get clicks. Bad faith gets clicks. Folly, error, avarice, and vice get clicks, and thus "we slink / Hellwards; each day down one more step we're jerked / Feeling no horror, through the shades that stink."[56]

Third, social media "radical[ly] modif[ies] existing types of [real-life] social-network interactions," as Nicholas A. Christakis and James H. Fowler write in *Connected: How Your Friends' Friends' Friends Affect Everything You Feel, Think, and Do*. Among those modifications are a "vast increase in the scale of our networks and the numbers of people who might be reached to join them" and a "broadening of the scale by which we can share information and contribute to collective efforts."[57]

Remember our thought experiment in chapter 1. I asked you to imagine yourself in 1995, using analog technology to share exactly as many news articles and opinion pieces and videos as you do now. Christakis and Fowler are making the same point. In past eras, it was difficult to take in and pass along the volume of information (especially political news and commentary) ordinary people (with no real political activity beyond voting) now routinely absorb and spread online. The physical distance inherent in social media also removes the protective constraint of regular, face-to-face interaction with the audience of our sharing.[58]

Finally, our use of social media solidifies our own views and makes us partly responsible for the views others adopt. In neither case is this necessarily a good thing. Research and personal experience have shown that when we make statements in public, we don't like to reverse them. Psychologists have found people will doggedly cling to wrong beliefs (like which of two lines is longer), even in the face of strong evidence to the contrary (like seeing each line measured by the same rule), if they have *publicly* committed themselves to the incorrect view.[59] We do the same thing with news and politics as we do with beliefs of no consequence, like the length of the line. That means each time we post something on social media, we become just a little less open to new evidence on that issue. We become a little less reachable by persuasion. We become a little more epistemically isolated and unreasonable.

We also exert a little bit of influence on our friends. This is the flip side of receiving content from loved ones, and it's a graver responsibility than we tend to realize. "Not many of you should become teachers, my fellow believers, because you know that we who teach will be judged more strictly," advises James 3:1, resonating with a warning from Jesus that proud and unloving teachers will be "punished most severely" (Luke 20:45–47).[60] The "teachers" in these passages are religious leaders teaching in the context of church and synagogue communities, respectively, but we should all heed these cautions if we act as teachers of our communities online. We would often do better to stay silent than to summon the divine scrutiny that teaching entails.

"We all stumble in many ways," James continues. "With the tongue we praise our Lord and Father, and with it we curse human beings, who have been made in God's likeness. Out of the same mouth come praise and cursing." Social media incessantly invites exactly that unholy pair. "My brothers and sisters, this should not be" (James 3:2, 9–10).

Faithful, Factual, Fair

So what do we do with a media environment like this? How do we navigate it faithfully, factually, and fairly? As followers of Jesus we "are advised to imitate his life and habits, if we wish to be truly enlightened and free from all blindness of heart," wrote Thomas à Kempis at the start of his devotional classic *The Imitation of Christ*. "Let our chief effort; therefore, be to study the life of Jesus Christ," Thomas goes on, for "all is vanity, except to love God and serve Him alone."[61] Is it possible to create and consume traditional and social media content with any resemblance of Christ?

I think the answer *can* be "yes" but that the question is too narrowly conceived. Our concern here isn't merely how to be a responsible news consumer or how to be a disciplined social media user. It's about a society-wide epistemic crisis that is evident in the press and online networks but by no means confined to them. There's much more to describe about the nature of our knowledge problem—the way we use shame and exclusion to narrow the bounds of conversation, the attraction of conspiracism and the decline of trust in expertise, the place of emotion and experience in knowledge—before we turn in the final three chapters to ways we can curtail the problem in our lives and communities. The problem is of a whole, and the remedies must be too.

For now, then, I'll end this chapter with wisdom from well before the internet as we know it. Writing in 1942, when "the common sense of Europe had been undermined and battered down by Nazi propaganda," author and theologian Dorothy L. Sayers metaphorically described words as "fields of force." Then she pressed the analogy between language and perilous scientific ventures a little further:

> It is as dangerous for people unaccustomed to handling words and unacquainted with their technique to tinker about with

these heavily-charged nuclei of emotional power as it would be for me to burst into a laboratory and play about with a powerful electro-magnet or other machine highly charged with electrical force. . . . At the present time, we have a population that is literate, in the sense that everybody is able to read and write; but owing to the emphasis placed on scientific and technical training at the expense of the humanities, very few of our people have been taught to understand and handle language as an instrument of power. This means that, in [England] alone, 40 million innocents or thereabouts are wandering inquisitively around the laboratory, enthusiastically pulling handles and pushing buttons, thereby releasing uncontrollable currents of electric speech, with results that astonish themselves and the world.[62]

This innocent ignorance is dangerous enough to our life together, Sayers warns—but not all are so innocent. Also using language among us are "the demagogue who can sway crowds, the journalist who can push up the sales of his paper to the 2-million mark, the playwright who can plunge an audience into an orgy of facile emotion, the parliamentary candidate who is carried to the top of the poll on a flood of meaningless rhetoric, the ranting preacher, the advertising salesman of material or spiritual commodities."[63]

To that list today we might add the cable-news pundit who browbeats his guests and calls it honest debate, the Instagram influencer who serves pretty half-truths to her following of millions, the podcaster whose voice inside your head begins each morning and ends each night, and the public pseudo-intellectual who passes off glib quips and insults as reasoned thought. Unlike their unsuspecting marks, these unscrupulous figures know well the potential of language, which they deploy for power, fame, agenda, and profit against "people who were not armed to resist it and had never really understood that it was a weapon at all."[64]

In Sayers's time, the verbally unscrupulous, however powerful, were relatively few in number and limited in technological means. Today, we—the entire public—are invited by social media to become orators ourselves. We can no longer anticipate assault from a limited category of people. At any moment, anyone in our acquaintance may play the demagogue or playwright or pseudo-intellectual on our newsfeed.[65] We can all wield language as a weapon against one another with too little understanding and too much speed—without, in Sayers's phrase, a "wary determination to understand the potentialities of language and to use it with resolution and skill."

Responsible and humane use of language in public is a skill that requires cultivation. It is not something we are born knowing, nor is it something we are all taught, though it is certainly something anyone willing to develop epistemic virtue can learn. Before we come to that, however, we'll examine the public inhumanity of the online mob.

Mob

You will be walking some night
in the comfortable dark of your yard
and suddenly a great light will shine
round about you, and behind you
will be a wall you never saw before.
It will be clear to you suddenly
that you were about to escape,
and that you are guilty: you misread
the complex instructions, you are not
a member, you lost your card
or never had one. And you will know
that they have been there all along,
their eyes on your letters and books,
their hands in your pockets,
their ears wired to your bed.
—Wendell Berry, "Do Not Be Ashamed"

In the mid-1990s, I spent about a year in China, in a regional
capital city with a population of several million. My mother
was studying with a professor there while teaching English at
a local university, and the language job came with housing in

the form of a hotel-style room with its own bathroom but no kitchen. For most meals, the cheapest and easiest option was to walk to a nearby street of restaurants built of tarps. In the morning we'd head over for congee or delicious fresh-cut noodles at one of a variety of stalls; for dinner we nearly always went to the shop right at the start of the block, and over time we became the communication-impaired friends of the family who owned it.

We lingered long enough over a meal there one day for the scene of our brief walk home to transform. A small crowd clustered at a street corner, and in its center we caught sight of a young woman wearing a sandwich board. Cheeks red, she stared fixedly at the ground while apparently contentious conversations flurried around her.

From what we could gather from bystanders (our Mandarin was limited), she was being punished for petty theft. I have a vague idea that there were some old vegetables strewn about, as if they had been thrown at her, though this may be my own addition to the story, my brain's attempt to fit an unprecedented experience into a more familiar framework of historical American punishments like the stocks. My mother hurried us home.

I remember feeling unsettled as we walked away, disturbed in a way I couldn't then articulate. Now I'd explain it as the single strongest culture shock of that year: my first experience of a public-shaming ritual. Looking back nearly three decades later, however, the shaming no longer strikes me as strange. I see public shaming as a means of punishment regularly here in the United States—not imposed by the government on street corners with sandwich boards but online, where you needn't find a rotten tomato to join the rebuke.

Cancel Culture

The first case of online shaming I recall seeing in the wild became the prototypical story of the genre: the tweet, flight, and firing of Justine Sacco. A publicist with fewer than two hundred Twitter followers on her personal account, Sacco was traveling from the United States to South Africa in 2013 to visit extended family. She'd sent out a handful of snarky tweets along the way, and shortly before boarding her final flight, she tweeted again, "Going to Africa. Hope I don't get AIDS. Just kidding. I'm white!"

Sacco was trying to make a dark joke about inequality, racism, and unfair allocation of resources. Suffice it to say, the joke did *not* land. It was shared derisively by a few larger accounts and soon became the biggest topic on Twitter worldwide. While Sacco slept on her flight, #HasJustineLandedYet began trending globally. Twitter users figured out what plane she was on and used flight trackers to answer the hashtag's question in real time.

By the time Sacco landed in Cape Town and turned on her phone, she'd gone from anonymity to infamy. A man who followed the controversy—not a paparazzo, just a random man—waited for her in the airport and photographed her arrival. He posted her picture on Twitter, observing under cover of his own pseudonymity that she'd chosen to wear sunglasses in a futile bid to hide her face. "I don't think Justine's 'a horrible person that needs to be punished,'" the man would later tweet. "Let's not pretend like we all haven't joked or said something in private that we regretted after. Let's wait for her apology instead of following the herd [and] being nasty."[1] Perhaps it was self-admonition come too late.

Sacco was fired. Twitter cheered—the desired denouement had arrived, and fast. In the weeks that followed, Sacco's reputation was trampled further, with clickbait sites combing through her digital record for reasons to relive the thrill of #HasJustine LandedYet. As time went on, however, she was largely able to reclaim her reputation. It was a multiyear process, but she was ultimately rehired by the same company that fired her, a neatly symmetrical redemption that isn't available to all those who, like Sacco, find themselves at the center of what we now would call "being canceled."

The nature of "cancel culture"—the term for the broader phenomenon of which Sacco's experience was an early example—is widely debated. It is increasingly an issue of partisan politics, hyped on the right as a critical threat to civilization and dismissed on the left as either an imagined "boogeyman" or bigots' fear of well-deserved consequences. But even many critics of the phrase acknowledge there's *something* there.[2] There's something new about how our society applies public shame, and that newness is entwined with mobbish group behavior online.

Though this *something* has been developing for several decades (Brookings Institution scholar Jonathan Rauch sounded a prescient warning two decades before Sacco's ordeal in 1993's *Kindly Inquisitors: The New Attacks on Free Thought*), it has accelerated in the social media era, and "cancel culture" has become the favored label. Google Trends, which tracks public interest in topics by measuring search-engine traffic over time, shows a flat line for "online shaming" and "cancel culture" from 2004 to late 2018. Then the spikes start, first small, then rising so quickly the upward trend line goes nearly vertical.[3] I say "line" in the singular because trends for the two phrases move in nearly perfect parallel, which suggests that whether or not "cancel culture" is a useful or durable term, we understand it means public shame administered by a digital crowd.

What we may not understand is how this use of shame contributes to epistemic crisis, to our uncertainty around truth and the public discussion and debate about it. I think online shaming is powerfully shaping our information environment— and not for the better. It's also part of a bigger cultural shift on matters of shame, guilt, punishment, repentance, forgiveness, redemption, reconciliation, and restoration, all of which should be of particular interest to Christians because we have been re-deemed and tasked with reconciliation (2 Cor. 5:18). Before we come to all of that, however, I think it's wise to specify exactly the meaning of "cancel culture" I have in mind.

Defining Cancellation

The single most useful taxonomy of cancel culture I've en-countered is a 2020 article by *New York Times* columnist Ross Douthat that postulates ten theses on the subject. His first thesis is a definition: "Cancellation, properly understood, refers to an attack on someone's employment and reputation by a de-termined collective of critics, based on an opinion or an action that is alleged to be disgraceful and disqualifying."[4]

There are several pieces of this definition that are worth our notice. One is that the opinion or action, though deemed "disgraceful and disqualifying"—perhaps vulgar, cruel, and/ or unethical—is not a criminal act. Cancel culture has been much linked to the #MeToo movement, in which prominent people (mostly men) were publicly accused of various sexual assaults or coercions against people (mostly women) who were professionally or personally under their authority. The link is understandable, chronologically and topically. But #MeToo is often about criminal behavior. Groping is a crime. Posting a bad tweet, like Sacco's ill-considered joke, is not. Its punishment, if punishment arrives, must be social and economic, not official, and that's the sort of punishment cancel culture delivers.

The other pieces to notice in Douthat's definition are the specifications of reputation and employment. Elsewhere in the column, he explains:

> You are not being canceled if you are merely being heckled or insulted—if somebody describes you as a moron or a fascist or some profane alternative to "Douthat" on the internet—no matter how vivid and threatening the heckling becomes. You

are decidedly at risk of cancellation, however, if your critics are calling for you to be de-platformed or fired or put out of business, and especially if the call is coming from inside the house—from within your professional community, from co-workers or employees or potential customers or colleagues, on a professional message board or Slack or some interest-specific slice of social media.[5]

Sacco's case is again a good example here, as she was not only labeled a horrible racist but also fired and, for a while, was un-employable in her field.

Douthat's other nine theses narrow and qualify his definition in several useful ways, one of which I'll mention here: cancel culture is not a new phenomenon, he concedes, because "all cul-tures cancel; the question is for what, how widely, and through what means." There has never been a human society without social censure. That's a given. But cancel culture feels like—and is—a new thing because "the internet has changed the way we cancel, and extended cancellation's reach."[6]

Cancel culture is often compared to the anti-communist Mc-Carthyism of the 1950s, which is an okay analogy. A better one, I think, is medieval outlawry.[7] "Outlawry required forfeiture of goods to the king and liability to be killed with impunity," says historian Melissa Sartore in *Outlawry, Governance, and Law in Medieval England*. "An outlaw was stripped of any property and was essentially a 'friendless' and 'lawless' man. He had no more rights than a hunted animal."[8] He could not go home or resume his normal means of livelihood. What he could do, however, was go to a distant village or a burgeoning city, where no one knew his face or name, and begin a new life.

That isn't possible now. "Under the rule of the internet there's no leaving the village," Douthat observes. "Everywhere is the same place, and so is every time."[9] It doesn't matter if you move to a different city or delete your Twitter account or issue a public apology. Unless, like Sacco, you find a way to rehabilitate your reputation, your cancellation can last as long as Google exists.[10]

Critique and Accountability

To Douthat's insights, I'll add two more points. The first, from *The Atlantic*'s Graeme Wood, is a "distinction that saves the term *cancellation* from uselessness and hypocrisy." As he goes on to explain, "Cancellation is not criticism; cancellation is the absence of criticism. It is the replacement of criticism with a summary punishment. The punishment ranges in seriousness and could include withdrawal of a job or just an invitation, but the salient point is that it is meted out instantly and without deliberation, often as the result of a mob action. When this switcheroo becomes a habit, the normal way of doing things, we can call that 'cancel culture,' and it is indeed a sign of intellectual and institutional rot."[11]

When Sacco posted her tweet, the collective response was not "Hmm, I think I get the joke you're trying to make here, but your glib tone isn't appropriate for this topic." The response was "You're a racist, and you should be deprived of income, banished from polite society, and subjected to creepshots at the airport." The first response would have been criticism— criticism many would agree the tweet warranted. The second was "the replacement of criticism with a summary punishment" by a Twitter mob.

Second, those who discount worries over cancel culture sometimes say it is simply a method of accountability—and who would be against accountability? Surely only those who deserve it most. But accountability and punishment aren't the same thing.[12] The former is a process, the latter a conclusion. If we're really proposing to hold someone accountable, that means engaging critically with what they said or did. Perhaps that engagement will end in a negative judgment, but perhaps the accountable person will persuade us she was in the right (cf. 2 Cor. 7:8–13). That result is preemptively eliminated when we dispense summary punishment and call it accountability.

The Pitfalls of Public Shaming

Cancel culture exacerbates our epistemic crisis in two ways. One stems from the fact that it has no due process. We have no legal or metaphorical social contract that allows thousands of strangers on the internet to decide we should be punished for our views or comments, what the punishment should be, and when it should end.[13] As flawed as our legal system is, it at least attempts to give fixed answers to those questions. Likewise, when Christian congregations or denominations perform church discipline, everyone involved has agreed (or should have agreed) to be there and to abide by the rules alleged to be broken.[14] But no one signs up to be at the center of a social media scandal—I haven't assented to the discipline of Twitter user @dickjokez420 and his fifteen thousand followers—and there are no stable rules for what's considered scandalous. Cancel culture ostracizes people with the "wrong" ideas, but the category of "right" ideas is too rapidly evolving.

Public theologian Russell Moore has related a story of a young man he met who was terrified of being canceled. "I found that this adolescent isn't someone saying, or even thinking, offensive or controversial things," Moore said. He was worried he might say something offensive or controversial without realizing its meaning.[15] He felt the uncertain dread evoked in Wendell Berry's poem "Do Not Be Ashamed," which is excerpted at the start of this chapter (and is a favorite of Moore's). I'll repeat some of that excerpt here:

> You will be walking some night
> in the comfortable dark of your yard

and suddenly a great light will shine
round about you, and behind you
will be a wall you never saw before.
It will be clear to you suddenly
that you were about to escape,
and that you are guilty: you misread
the complex instructions, you are not
a member, you lost your card
or never had one. . . .[16]

This surprise shamefulness that comes from violating a previously unknown moral code is what has that young man worried—and I have friends with the same amorphous fear that they will somehow find themselves in that light, against that wall, despite their best intentions, because the boundary of acceptable opinion moved when they weren't looking.

Their fear is not unique.[17] I don't share it, but there's a certain ironic protection in my job: if you air your controversial opinions for a living, there's not much of a "gotcha!" in the discovery that you hold a controversial opinion. Yet outside this line of work, some who witness cancellations will react with fear. A 2020 survey found two in three Americans self-censor their political views and one in three "are worried about missing out on career opportunities or losing their job if their political opinions became known." In the same poll, 31 percent said they'd support the firing of a business executive for making a personal donation to the Trump campaign, and 22 percent said the same about the Biden campaign.[18] Others will respond with reflexive suspicion of mainstream ideas and information sources, with embrace and development of conspiracy theories (which we'll get into in the next chapter), and with an impulse to transgress. If something is banned, some people will find it *more* appealing. Verboten ideas have a certain allure, and if you're already canceled, why not sample more of the forbidden fruit?[19] Why not entice others to try to it too? At least then you'll have some company.

Either of these reactions are more likely, I suspect, among those who live, work, go to school, or consume news in a space where they're in the ideological minority—where it may well feel "they" are watching you, "their hands in your pockets, their ears wired to your bed," their eyes on your tweets. This is part of why moral panic over cancel culture has emerged on the right rather than the left, inverting older stereotypes of right-wing censoriousness and left-wing liberality. Because mainstream media (as I discussed in the previous chapter) has a center-left tilt—and because we're all constantly exposed to media via our phones—many right-leaning Americans *always* feel they're in the scrutinized minority.

The Overton Window

Now, no one of good conscience objects to true accountability or would deny that sometimes people *should* lose their jobs over an offensive belief or action. (An extreme and therefore simple example: If you learned your kid's kindergarten teacher was the Grand Dragon of the Ku Klux Klan, would you be cool with that?) There's nothing wrong with drawing a boundary of acceptable opinion. As Douthat says, every society does this— and should. Some opinions *are* immoral.[20] The problem comes when people draw the boundary too narrowly, redraw it too frequently, and build upon it a high wall that, once crossed, leaves the offender forever tainted.

There's a useful concept in political science called the "Overton window." It says societies always have a limited range of ideas generally deemed legitimate (not *right*, necessarily, but *reasonable*). When you look out a window, there's a whole world out there, but you can see only part of it. The window's edges limit your view. In the same way, public consensus limits what ideas—especially political ideas and policy proposals—are considered worthy of debate among reasonable people.[21]

We're never without an Overton window, but the window can grow, shrink, and move. In a society where nearly everyone has the same religion or a country governed by a totalitarian state that bans dissenting opinion, the window will be small. In a pluralist society like ours that has constitutional free-speech protections, it'll be larger.

Sometimes people can deliberately move the edges of the window. For instance, the temperance movement in the nineteenth and twentieth centuries so successfully shifted American views of alcohol that our nation amended the Constitution to ban it. Today, Prohibition is far outside our Overton window in most of the country.

What makes cancel culture distinct, then, is not that it enforces the edges of an Overton window or even that those edges shift. It's that the edges are moving at an unreasonable pace and are mostly moving closer together. You never noticed that wall in your yard, the wall you're now backed up against, because *it wasn't there before*. Our "social-media environment . . . issues new commandments every fortnight or so," as Baylor University humanities professor Alan Jacobs has noted with only some exaggeration.[22]

"The dangerous forms of 'cancel culture,'" Moore argues, "happen when standards are contradictory and inconsistent."[23] We cannot talk to each other constructively—we cannot seek truth together or even establish facts around contentious subjects—if we incessantly erect ever-closer boundaries of conversation and threaten to destroy the careers and reputations of those who want to know what's on the other side.[24] Our Overton window will move over time, but it must not move so rapidly and mercilessly that it stifles debate and research, making some people scared to say what they believe is true and leaving others, of a more contrarian ilk, fixated on proscribed ideas and content.[25]

No Way Home

The other way this cultural tic becomes a problem, Moore says, is when "immoral or dangerous ideas are censured but with no means for someone holding them to change his or her mind."[26] This brings me to cancel culture's second contribution to epistemic crisis: permanent rejection. It is why cancel culture is about public *shame*, not public *guilt*, and it is shame without an avenue to repentance, forgiveness, reconciliation, and restoration.[27]

We often speak of shame and guilt interchangeably, but they're different. Guilt is about action, while shame is about identity. Guilt says, "You did a bad thing." Shame says, "You are a bad person." Guilt is usually individual, and its opposite is innocence. Shame is communal, and its opposite is honor accorded to you by others. To be shamed is to be subjected to the judgment and exclusion of the crowd.[28]

Some cultures use shame to enforce ethical norms, while others favor guilt. (We find both in the Bible.) An honor-shame culture is not worse than an innocence-guilt culture—*if* it has communal rituals to remove shame once applied. "In a traditional culture, when someone experiences shame, a web of people will try to restore lost 'face,'" explained Andy Crouch of *Christianity Today* in a 2015 examination of social media's role in modern shaming. "Indeed, many honor-shame cultures strive to prevent the loss of face in the first place," he wrote. "Conflict that would be tolerated in a guilt-innocence culture is suppressed or redirected in order to prevent ruptured relationships—one reason that many honor-shame cultures prize politeness and indirectness in situations in which disagreement could erupt."[29]

Western culture used to have a strong honor-shame element; outlawry is a very shame-based punishment, for example, as is any sort of ostracism. But we shifted to a guilt model in no small part because of the Enlightenment's focus on the rights and responsibilities of the individual and the legal systems that thinking tended to create. Now we've brought back shame, but our hyperindividualistic culture has no communal rituals of redemption.[30]

We take honor but can't seem to return it. We don't know how to restore one another's "face" once it's lost. We demand apologies but have no means of communal reconciliation. When we shame someone, as cancel culture does, we declare them a bad person, tear apart their life, require public prostration—and then turn our backs and walk away.[31]

This is harmful to our public conversations and epistemology because it stifles conversation and fosters a wary distrust. Who might be lurking among your followers to amplify your bad tweet and launch a global hue and cry for your ouster? *Better to keep quiet, just to be safe*—or even to join the next mob that runs through your feed, just to make clear you're on the right side of the boundary line.

Christ's Command of Forgiveness

Graceless shaming also diminishes the work of Christ. If we believe God delivers us from evil (Rom. 7:24–25) and removes our sin "as far as the east is from the west" (Ps. 103:12), if we believe we are made into new creations in Christ (2 Cor. 5:16–19), we will not speak of anything as a permanent stain on ourselves or other people. No bad opinion or action is more powerful than the blood of Christ. There is no wrong Jesus did not conquer, no bad tweet or offensive comment or mistaken idea that gets an exception clause to God's redemption. And if that is true—if no evil exists unvanquished by Christ (1 Cor. 15:54–57)—then our behavior should reflect that truth.[32]

What would that reflection look like in practice? If we're speaking only about Christians, that question is easy enough to answer—though the answer is anything but easy to obey. "Christianity has a lot to say about sin, repentance, and forgiveness," Jacobs writes. "It tells us that we all sin. It tells us that when we sin against a sister or brother, in thought, word, or deed, we must seek to make it right, and to ask that person's forgiveness. And if we feel that someone has sinned against us, we are to tell that person so, to give them the opportunity to repent" and to offer forgiveness and reconciliation after genuine contrition and repentance.[33]

For Christians, there's no way around this. Commands of forgiveness, repentance, and reconciliation are unambiguous throughout the New Testament. "If your brother or sister sins against you, rebuke them," Jesus told his disciples, "and if they repent, forgive them. Even if they sin against you seven times in a day and seven times come back to you saying 'I repent,' you must forgive them" (Luke 17:3–4). Matthew records the command as "not seven times, but seventy-seven times" (Matt. 18:22), and in Mark's Gospel we're told to forgive before praying, "so that your Father in heaven may forgive you your sins" (Mark 11:25). In Luke's account of the Lord's Prayer, Jesus teaches us to say, "Forgive us our sins, for we also forgive *everyone* who sins against us" (Luke 11:4, emphasis added).

If we profess to follow Jesus, we cannot be content with our sin, nor can we withhold forgiveness and ceaselessly hurl shame. Our inclination must always be toward mercy. This isn't because Christians are apathetic about justice or opposed to accountability or any nonsense like that. It's because we have also been forgiven, and, in Christ, our shame has been removed.

"As God does not abandon the godless to their"—more aptly, our—"evil but gives the divine self for them in order to receive them into divine communion through atonement, so also should we—whoever our enemies and whoever we may be," urges theologian Miroslav Volf in his exceptional work on forgiveness, *Exclusion and Embrace*.[34] "Therefore, as God's chosen people, holy and dearly loved," we must "clothe [our]selves with compassion, kindness, humility, gentleness, and patience," as Paul wrote to the Colossians: "Bear with each other and forgive one another if any of you has a grievance against someone. *Forgive as the Lord forgave you.* And over all these virtues put on love, which binds them all together in perfect unity" (Col. 3:12–14, emphasis added).

There's room for debate over how this applies in our massive, digital public square, where we find ourselves following—and, to an extent, involved in—controversies that do not directly concern us. When Justine Sacco tweeted her comment about AIDS, I worked in social media management (maybe my worst job ever, and I was once a busy restaurant's combined expediter, busser, and dishwasher), so I saw the hashtag about her pass through my Twitter feed in real time. But if my Wi-Fi connection had been spotty for a few hours, I might have gone to my grave without ever hearing Sacco's name. Whether she kept or lost her job had no bearing on me. It's difficult to see how she could owe *me* repentance, or how *I* could owe her accountability or forgiveness. She may have been a perpetrator, but I was hardly her victim, nor were we in any sort of relationship (friends or colleagues or fellow congregants or official and constituent) that might have given me a right to rebuke her. How could we reconcile if we'd never conciliated in the first place? How could we repair what we never had?

The same is true of just about every case of public shaming. If I have some relationship with the person being shamed, I can speak to her in private or in the right communal setting. Real confession, contrition, and restoration can take place. But if I don't know her, if we haven't even the barest relationship and she has done me no direct harm, how can I imagine I'm right to join the mob?

I'm not sure exactly how to name the sin of mass online shaming, but it is somewhere around the intersection of gossip and "bitterness, rage and anger, brawling and slander, along with every form of malice" (Eph. 4:31). Or perhaps it has to do with what the great medieval theologian Thomas Aquinas called "presumption," the sin of attempting things "above our ability," typically under the delusion that we are more capable, knowledgeable, or virtuous than we truly are.[35] At any rate, I cannot picture Jesus mobbing someone online, and even if he had the right to do so, I do not. "What business is it of mine to judge those outside the church? . . . God will judge those outside" (1 Cor. 5:12–13).

Unanswered Questions

Ah, and what of those outside the church? "When a society rejects the Christian account of who we are, it doesn't become less moralistic but far more so, because it retains an inchoate sense of justice but has no means of offering and receiving forgiveness," Jacobs writes. "The great moral crisis of our time is not, as many of my fellow Christians believe, sexual licentiousness, but rather *vindictiveness*."[36]

As a culture writ large, Catholic writer Leah Libresco Sargeant has argued, we "need a way to find an answer to the following questions: What do we do with people who have committed a wrong that they themselves cannot put right? And is it possible for me to make full amends for the wrongs that I've done, whatever their size?"[37]

I'm not sure we *want* to find a way, though. We love to consume stories of forgiveness and redemption, but we don't so much like to participate in them. We have no means of restoring honor after public shaming; I suspect that's the case, in part, because our vindictiveness doesn't want it restored. Instead of the costly way of repentance and forgiveness, Volf posits, we've set our hopes on "the twin strategies of *social control* and *rational thought*."[38] Why seek the truth together in love when you can shame someone into (at least publicly) confining themselves to your Overton window of choice? The resultant enduring shame is very much like Christians' ideas around original sin, except there's no savior coming to make us clean.[39]

Sargeant identifies three different tactics, all inadequate, for coping with this "untenable situation."[40] Some respond with indefinite ostracism (and not only online: more than one in four adult Americans report estrangement from a close family member).[41] Once canceled, always canceled—or, at least, until your cancellation is superseded by someone else's more fascinating offense.[42]

Others "deny the seriousness of sin," dissembling in the face of immorality and minimizing real wrongs so relationships can be preserved without repentance or acceptance of correction.[43] They're like the townspeople G. K. Chesterton chides through his character Father Brown, a Catholic priest and detective: "It seems to me that you only pardon the sins that you don't really think sinful. You only forgive criminals when they commit what you don't regard as crimes, but rather as conventions. . . . You forgive because there isn't anything to be forgiven."[44]

Still others perform what Christians might dub a sort of works righteousness, constantly pledging to "do better" and "be better" and "educate themselves" out of offense. They assiduously track those fortnightly new commandments and update their vocabularies and Instagram stories accordingly, all with a fervor the dissemblers will deride as virtue signaling—and so it is, I suppose, though it often is part of a perfectly sincere pursuit of virtue.[45]

These tactics might seem workable, for a while, at the individual scale. Collectively, however, they don't get us to the forgiveness we need. They don't take away the shame. They don't solve our problem of the missing communal ritual of redemption and the damage that absence contributes to our epistemic crisis.

I'm not sure what could solve the problem. We don't agree on whether or how to remove shame once applied, or even on why it should be applied in the first place. Christians have an answer to the problem—Christ—but try tweeting *that* suggestion at the next mob and let me know how far you get. Perhaps our society will find a way to redeem the canceled, or perhaps we'll repent of our unmerciful public shaming, though I can't say I'm terribly optimistic.

Whatever happens, however, I do know the task for Christians is to refuse to find ourselves, in Volf's words, "accomplices in war, rather than agents of peace. We find it difficult to distance ourselves from our selves and our own culture, and so we echo its reigning opinions and mimic its practices. As we keep the vision of God's future alive, we need to reach out across the firing lines and join hands with our brothers and sisters on the other side."[46] And to that end, we'll now turn to a subject where I myself find it particularly hard to take Volf's gospel advice: conspiracism.

Schemes

The blood-dimmed tide is loosed, and everywhere
The ceremony of innocence is drowned;
The best lack all conviction, while the worst
Are full of passionate intensity.
Surely some revelation is at hand;
Surely the Second Coming is at hand.

—W. B. Yeats, "The Second Coming"

The conspiracist movement known as QAnon began on October 28, 2017, with a cryptic post on a foul online message board called 4chan. In two days, it prophesied, former presidential candidate Hillary Clinton would be arrested. "Expect massive riots organized in defiance" of the fate coming to Clinton and her fellow schemers, the post warned, promising the National Guard would suppress the violence. The post ended by urging readers to conduct a "Proof check: Locate a [Guard] member and ask if activated for duty 10/30 across most major cities." Two hours later, a second post said Clinton had already been detained.[1]

She hadn't, of course, and the "proof check," if attempted, would have failed. That didn't matter. The movement grew.

Polling on QAnon tends to be somewhat messy, as researchers are still figuring out what questions get the most accurate answers.[2] Still, surveys can give us some sense of the phenomenon's scale. Research in 2020 and 2021, when the movement first came to national attention, showed few Americans knew precisely what QAnon was and few were willing to link themselves to it. Self-described Q believers typically came in around 3 to 5 percent of American adults.[3]

But when polls asked about the *content* of QAnon instead of its name, those numbers spiked. A mid-2021 survey by the Public Religion Research Institute (PRRI) found 15 percent of American adults endorsed all the major QAnon beliefs pollsters mentioned, and some individual tenets got even higher support. That 15 percent is "more than 30 million people," PRRI founder Robby Jones told the Associated Press. "Thinking about QAnon, if it were a religion," he added, it's comparable in scale to "all white mainline Protestants" in the United States.[4] White mainline churches have met in this land for four centuries, and QAnon matched them in less than four years.

Trust the Plan . . .

The basic QAnon story has two parts.[5] The first is that there's a hidden cabal in government, the media, and other powerful institutions that is guilty of child sex trafficking, cannibalism of a sort, Satan-worshipping human sacrifice, and world domination.

This nightmare has been revealed to the public—an exposé believers call "the Great Awakening," borrowing from Christian revivals past—by the pseudonymous author of those message board posts. He's known as Q, and he's ostensibly a high-ranking military intelligence official compelled by conscience to enlighten patriotic Americans. When Q's prophecies (or "drops," as they're called) don't pan out, adherents either conclude the cabal interfered or that Q was distracting his enemies with misinformation.[6]

The second element of the QAnon story is hope. As the story was originally told, then-president Donald Trump was the movement's messiah figure, its Jesus to Q's role as John the Baptist, working at great personal cost to defeat the cabal. At Trump's direction, cabal members like Clinton would be executed in an imminent event called "the Storm." Q believers had only to "trust the plan" and "enjoy the show," as Q often urged. Then, in late 2020, Q drops stopped. The pseudonymous prophet went silent and, at least as of this writing, hasn't posted again. Trump lost his reelection campaign, and the Storm didn't break on Inauguration Day 2021.[7]

In the time since, Q belief has fractured. Some adherents have left the movement, concluding Q was discredited. Some cling to the original hope of Trump's triumphal return. Others insist he is secretly in power *now*, adopting something like the Biden-is-a-clone story I shared in chapter 1. Still others are transforming QAnon into a political movement that expects practical action from its members instead of a rescue from on high (or from Florida, as the case may be). Run for school board, Q influencers advise. Or city council, or leadership positions in your state's Republican Party.[8] Work your way up to take down the cabal.

. . . or Some Other Plan

As I write this in mid-2021, QAnon remains very much a part of our national conversation. In a year or five or twenty it may fall into obscurity.

But for our purposes here—exploring why people engage in conspiracism, how that contributes to our epistemic crisis,

and how Christians should approach conspiracist thinking—
the lifespan of QAnon is irrelevant. The "paranoid style of
American politics," to borrow a phrase from a 1964 essay by
historian Richard Hofstadter, will persist long after QAnon
fades.[9] Habits of "heated exaggeration, suspiciousness, and
conspiratorial fantasy," in Hofstadter's summary, are nothing
new, and there's no reason to think they'll ever cease to appeal.
For now, however, QAnon is a useful case study for thinking
about conspiracism because it's both extremely unoriginal and
unusually comprehensive.

Many Q ideas are longstanding tropes of conspiracist thinking, all mashed together and repackaged for our moment. The
child-trafficking claims, for example, sound a lot like fears of a
"white slave trade" from the early 1900s.[10] Q-linked allegations
about COVID-19 being a Chinese bioweapon resemble allegations against German pharmaceutical company Bayer during
the 1918 Spanish Flu epidemic—and anti-COVID-19 vaccine
theories are almost identical to 1990s rumors about childhood
shots.[11] The idea that Biden has been cloned recycles claims
about then-president Jimmy Carter from the late 1970s.[12] Cannibalism is a rip-off of the centuries-old blood libel, a spuri-
ous anti-Semitic charge that Jews kidnap Christian children
to steal their blood.[13] And all the rest—global totalitarianism,
evil masterminds, satanism, and the like—is a pretty standard
sampler of American conspiracist fears.

QAnon is also broad in form. In *The United States of Paranoia*, a study of four hundred years of American conspiracism,
journalist Jesse Walker posits "five primal myths" that under-
gird our theories. "By using the word *myths*, I don't mean to
suggest that these stories are never true," he explains:

> I mean that they're culturally resonant ideas that appear again
> and again when Americans communicate with one another:
> archetypes that can absorb all kinds of allegations, true or not,

and arrange them into a familiar form. One is the Enemy Out-side, who plots outside the community's gates, and one is the Enemy Within, comprising villainous neighbors who can't be easily distinguished from friends. There is the Enemy Above, hiding at the top of the social pyramid, and there is the enemy below, lurking at the bottom. And then there is the Benevolent Conspiracy, which isn't an enemy at all: a secret force working behind the scenes to improve people's lives.[14]

QAnon works together *all five* myths. Its candidates for the Enemy Outside include China, wealthy figures with foreign and/or Jewish roots, and child traffickers. Enemies Within include nearly all elected Democrats, many ordinary Democratic voters, and even more child traffickers. The Enemy Above, of course, is the cabal, and the Enemy Below includes antifa (violent, far-left activists) and immigrants alleged to be voting illegally to steal elections for Democrats. The Benevolent Conspiracy is the Storm.

This sprawl and malleability give QAnon a very slippery feel and, for my money, a degree of durability.[15] But even if it's soon subsumed or superseded by new suspicions of secret schemes, the Q movement will remain a handy illustration as we examine the place of conspiracism in epistemic crisis.

Conspiracies, Conspiracy Theories, and Conspiracism

One reason people believe tales of conspiracy is that conspiracies *do* happen. Many of the real conspiracies that are well known today first came to light in the 1970s, often in the Enemy Above format and via mainstream sources, like prominent newspapers and official probes.[16]

The 1970s were when Americans learned about COINTEL-PRO, an FBI program of infiltrating disfavored political groups to spread internal discord, foment paranoia, and even break up participants' marriages to discourage them from political activism. It's also the decade when news broke of the CIA's Operation CHAOS, a domestic surveillance project that targeted Vietnam War protesters and other leftist groups. It's the decade of the Watergate scandal and a congressional investigation known as the Church Committee. The committee reported "a host of executive-branch abuses," as Walker sums it up, including "politically motivated IRS audits, CIA assassination plots, an effort to intercept and read Americans' mail, and a particularly creepy program called MKULTRA," which entailed "the 'surreptitious administration' of LSD 'to unwitting nonvolunteer subjects in normal life settings.' More bluntly, the CIA had dosed people with acid without their consent."[17]

Look beyond the 1970s to any other decade in American history and you'll find other cases of verified conspiracy, often—though not exclusively—in the same Enemy Above pattern. Sometimes conspiracies happen, which means sometimes conspiracy theories are true.

That reality raises an important distinction I'll make before we move on to other reasons people believe. My concern here is not so much conspiracies themselves or specific conspiracy theories; it's the *conspiracist mindset*. Nancy L. Rosenblum and Russell Muirhead, who are politics professors at Harvard and Dartmouth Universities, respectively, explain the difference this way:

[Conspiracy theorizing] engages in a sort of detective work. Once all the facts—especially facts ominously withheld by reliable sources and omitted from official reports—are scrupulously amassed, a pattern of secret machinations emerges. The dots are woven into a comprehensive narrative of events. Warranted or not, classic conspiracism is conspiracy with a theory.

The new conspiracism is something different. There is no punctilious demand for proofs, no exhaustive amassing of evidence, no dots revealed to form a pattern, no close examination of the operators plotting in the shadows. The new conspiracism dispenses with the burden of explanation. Instead, we have innuendo and verbal gesture: 'A lot of people are saying . . .' Or we have bare assertion: 'Rigged!'—a one-word exclamation that evokes fantastic schemes, sinister motives, and the awesome capacity to mobilize 3 million illegal voters to support Hillary Clinton for president. This is conspiracy without the theory.[18]

Conspiracism is what animates QAnon, and that's why I favor calling it a "movement," not a "theory." "Do your own research" is a favorite slogan, but QAnon doesn't run on research. It runs on fandom and memes. There's no demand for the stereotypical conspiracy theorist's wall of photos and newspaper clippings meticulously linked by a spiderweb of red string. "Trust the plan" is an expression of faith even though you *don't* know the details and can marshal only thin, digital rumors of hard evidence. "Enjoy the show" is what you say to an audience, not to a detective.

Though Rosenblum and Muirhead draw a sharp distinction between conspiracy theorizing and conspiracism, I think there can be overlap between the two. It's possible to embrace a conspiracy theory in a conspiracist way: neither doing nor requiring meaningful research, choosing to "trust the plan" not because you've obtained classified documents or interviewed officials involved but because, in one way or another, the theory "says something true about [your] anxieties and experiences . . . even if it says nothing true about the objects of the theory itself."[19]

Conspiracies happen, and conspiracy theories may be true or (far more often, I think) false. But conspiracism is always epistemic poison. This accusatory, credulous mindset, more than any individual theory, is what contributes to our epistemic crisis. It treats confirmation bias as confirmation, rumor as research, and innuendo as proof. It isolates its victims and builds their community on a foundation of sand. It falsely labels ideas and behaviors unconnected to reality as a heroic search for truth. And all those downsides, ironically, are part of conspiracism's appeal. They're part of why people believe.

It Just All Makes So Much Sense

If conspiracism were a drug, users would describe the high by saying, "It just all makes so much sense." They would mean this in two ways. First, our brains like intelligible patterns and explanations. "We find human faces in the moon, armies in the clouds," observed the Scottish philosopher David Hume in 1755, "and by a natural propensity, if not corrected by experience and reflection, ascribe malice and good will to everything that hurts or pleases us."[20] This tendency is called "apophenia": the human predilection to detect pattern and significance in random, meaningless information.[21]

Conspiracism pathologizes this normal human habit. It has us not only perceiving patterns where they don't exist but actively searching for and fabricating them. It meets feelings of fear and confusion with a grand, complicated narrative of moral conflict and invites us to stuff every day's headlines into the story. Under sway of conspiracism, our interpretation of the news becomes "distinctly personal," Hofstadter wrote, as "decisive events are not taken as part of the stream of history, but as the consequences of someone's will."[22] Everything is deliberate, never accidental. It's always malice, never human fallibility. Always evil, never merely stupid.

The other reason conspiracism "just makes sense" is that people like to be right. Conspiracist thinking offers powerful confirmation of the rightness of our desires, beliefs, and subconscious assumptions about what the world is and what it should be. In QAnon, most of the story's villains are Democrats and/or secular elite figures. Not coincidentally, most Q believers are Republicans or further to the political right, and many would describe themselves as conservative and/or evangelical Christians.

Remember the 15 percent of Americans who signed on to major Q beliefs? Among Republicans and self-identified white evangelicals, that number roughly doubles in most polls.[23] Some studies have put white evangelical assent as high as 50 percent.[24] Likewise, half of American Protestant pastors in 2021 reported "frequently" hearing conspiracy theories from their congregants.[25]

These Q adherents *already* worried about godlessness and spiritual warfare in American government when Q told them the cabal isn't merely godless but downright satanic. They *already* disliked Clinton's politics when they came to believe her guilty of child trafficking. That dislike is part of why they believed it. It just all makes so much sense.

People Like Community

The six months on either side of the 2020 election were a boom time for long magazine profiles of QAnon supporters. I read a lot of these articles, and themes of loneliness and community were common. In some cases, Q believers were already feeling isolated when they came upon QAnon. For others, the embrace of Q itself led to broken relationships. Either way, Q believers reported finding a new, Q-centric community, mostly online but in person as well. This is a social conspiracism.

That communal element strengthens conspiracist movements, particularly when social media is involved. It feels good, and it insulates participants from pushback and motivates them to stay convinced. "When we encounter opposing views in the age and context of social media, it's not like reading them in a newspaper while sitting alone," Turkish sociologist Zeynep Tufekci argues in the *MIT Technology Review*. "It's like hearing them from the opposing team while sitting with our fellow fans in a football stadium."[26]

That combative, tribal environment encourages loyalty to your own team and animosity toward outsiders—and toward whatever the outsiders try to tell you about your team's beliefs. "This is why the various projects for fact-checking claims in the news, while valuable, don't convince people," Tufekci says. "Belonging is stronger than facts."[27] Are you going to listen to some dweeb journalist who's probably part of the cabal anyway, or are you going to listen to your good friends on Facebook?

Our cultural stereotype of a conspiracy theorist conjures an unwashed loner locked away in his basement, piecing together evidence—the cobweb of string and all that. But conspiracism is increasingly a group project, and the group itself is crucial to the mindset's attraction. It's the conspiracist version of what C. S. Lewis called the "inner ring," a digital update to "the sacred little attic or studio, the heads bent together, the fog of tobacco smoke, and the delicious knowledge that we—we four or five all huddled beside this stove—are the people who *know*."[28]

Once admitted, no one wants to leave the people who *know*. It would mean losing friends, perhaps the only friends you have left. And it would feel like betraying those in the trenches with you, those happy few standing against a glaring evil most of society refuses to see.

People Like to Help

That invocation of heroism brings me to the third element of conspiracism's appeal: people like to help, and there is so much that needs helping. There are "wars and rumors of wars," nation rising against nation, "famines and earthquakes in various places," creation itself in "bondage to decay" (see Matt. 24:6–7; Rom. 8:21). Surely it can't go on like this? "Surely some revelation is at hand; / Surely the Second Coming is at hand"?[29]

Conspiracism pops up to answer the longing in W. B. Yeats's poetic words with a confident "yes." A revelation *is* at hand, and *you* can know it *first*.[30] You can get a glimpse of the second coming before it comes. You can see the patterns, prepare for the Storm, be privy to the plan. And maybe you can help defeat this lurking evil and speed the triumph of the good. "The best all lack conviction"—but not you. Maybe you'll only play a small part, but you can be one of the good guys.[31] You can help bring to justice evildoers who are guilty of blasphemy, murder, and rape. You can participate in the salvation of the world.

Conspiracism in the Church

Christians are already participating in the salvation of the world, already serving a just God who will right every wrong, already looking for the second coming. Shouldn't that make us immune to conspiracism?

It should, but it doesn't. Sometimes it seems to make us *more* vulnerable. "People of faith believe there is a divine plan—that there are forces of good and forces of evil at work in the world," evangelical pastor and scholar Ed Stetzer explained in a 2021 interview with *FiveThirtyEight*. "QAnon is a train that runs on the tracks that religion has already put in place."[32]

In case it seems like Stetzer and I are nut-picking here—selecting a few outliers and holding them up as representative of the whole—remember those survey results. Polling around QAnon *is* messy, but 30 to 50 percent white evangelical endorsement of QAnon beliefs isn't statistical noise (and white evangelicals weren't the only Christian group with above-average Q support). Not all conspiracists are Christians, and not all Christians have fallen into conspiracism, but the two are linked in America today.

Q deliberately cultivated Christian conspiracism by quoting Scripture passages and using Christian vocabulary in his drops. Sometimes it was awkward, and sometimes it verged into heresy, but it successfully implied the movement was at least Christian-adjacent.[33] Yet we'd be deceiving ourselves to imagine that sales pitch is the sole reason large swaths of the American church have fallen down the rabbit hole. I reached out to three pastors who are dealing with conspiracism in their congregations and/or denominations for insight into why this is happening and what Christians should do about it. Their thinking and mine coalesced around three themes: theology, politics, and authority.

Theology

The evangelical churches and schools of my childhood were, I see in retrospect, a culture under the sway of apocalyptic fascination and sometimes a paranoid political style. The adults teaching my generation largely came of age amid all those conspiracy revelations of the 1970s, which perhaps not coincidentally was when Hal Lindsey's *The Late Great Planet Earth* was the national bestseller of the decade.[34] Lindsey opened his book with questions strikingly like those being considered here: "How do we know in what direction we should go? How can we separate truth from opinion? In whom can we trust?"[35]

These "basic and visceral questions of man" can ultimately be answered only by God, Lindsey said, and he presented his book as a pure conveyance of the divine plan for the very near future. "Let's give God a chance to present his views," he wrote in the introduction. *Late Great* connected contemporary events to scriptural passages, with special attention to the book of Revelation. Though Lindsey didn't explicitly commit to a timeline for Christ's return, many of his readers concluded the 1980s were looking like a solid time for the end of the world.

The 1980s had come and gone without apocalypse by the time I was able to absorb any of this. Russia, a key figure in Lindsey's interpretation, had ceased to be part of the Soviet

Union and had never invaded Israel as he'd foretold. The antichrist hadn't appeared. There was no rapture. But even if the specifics didn't work out, the mindset Lindsey's work fostered—the belief that Christians could and *should* scan the headlines for hidden evidence of scriptural "events soon to come and events already unfolding"—stuck around.[36]

This stance toward history and Christians' place within it treats the Bible (and especially the apocalyptic literature, like Daniel and Revelation) "as something of a secret decoder ring" for current events, explains pastor and theologian Joel Lawrence. But that's not the purpose of Scripture, and this thinking "can easily mutate into a vulnerability" to conspiracism, Lawrence warns. It "provides people of faith with a confidence that the vicissitudes of history can be easily understood," he says, "and that we have access to the knowledge necessary to make sense of the seeming chaos and contingency of historical movement."[37]

But our confidence should be in Christ, not our own understanding (Prov. 3:5), and we usually *don't* have that access; even Jesus didn't know the day and hour of his own return (Matt. 24:36). We shouldn't spend our time playing casting director for the apocalypse; our place is to live hopefully and faithfully in love.

Though most often seen in evangelical and charismatic circles of American Christianity, this misguided view of history isn't confined there.[38] And I think that explains, in part, why pastors and other Christians are so vehemently rebuffed when they push back on conspiracism in their churches and relationships. Conspiracism is mistaken for a biblical directive. It can start to feel like part of Christianity itself.

That commitment to conspiracism has made some Christian leaders wary of speaking against it, Derek Kubilus, vicar of Uniontown United Methodist Church in Ohio, told me in an email interview.[39] Kubilus said he is disappointed that "more 'high profile' Christians have not started talking about [conspiracism in the American church] in any kind of public manner." Yet "I understand their hesitancy," he continued. "No one wants to lose a third of their congregation or readership," and that's a real possibility for pastors who challenge conspiracism in their flocks, as Kubilus knows from experience.

But that silence is worrisome, the vicar wrote to me, because he believes conspiracism is "the most profound cultural crisis we've experienced [in the US church] in my lifetime, and there has never been more at stake. Pastors, priests, and Christian influencers need to start speaking up." *Late Great* theology makes that difficult to do.

Politics

Christians' political loyalties, inevitably, are a factor too, and one all three of the pastors I interviewed for this chapter highlighted. Ben Marsh, pastor of First Alliance Church Winston-Salem in North Carolina, said conspiracism isn't a big problem in his own congregation, but he's seen it elsewhere in his denomination, in which he said there are "pastors who directly shared Q information (both knowingly and unknowingly)," "churches currently divided over Q," and "heartbroken pastors whose elders are fighting over Q."[40]

Like Derek Kubilus, Marsh has become an informal consultant on the subject for other pastors and Christians since he appeared in a CNN story on QAnon. He reaches out to fellow pastors to warn them conspiracism is likely coming to their church—if it's not there already. Even among clergy, Marsh said, sometimes politics is a consuming concern, and conspiracism is tolerated or embraced as a tool for political victory for the right. "Sadly, many pastors are too passively accepting of Q," he said, "because 'the enemy of my enemy is my friend' and many evangelical pastors view the left as being the only enemy worth fighting."

Clear across the country in California, Dr. James Kendall of Grace Community Church described the same disordering of Christian priorities. The underlying problem, he wrote in our email interview, is that "politics has become a religion for many in America (on both the left and the right) including those who attend church." He went on:

> The culture wars and elections have become their religion. They form their tribes based on politics and political ideology more so than because of religious affiliation. . . . All of this grieves me deeply. It saddens me to see so many who have lost their focus, who are more concerned with the affairs of this earth than they are with the Kingdom of God. It grieves me to see Christians attacking each other rather than standing as brothers and sisters. It saddens me to see people believing the craziest of [conspiracist claims] because it justifies their hatred for their political enemies.[41]

Marsh's critique of misplaced allegiance is needful, but so too is his reminder that conspiracism born of overattention to political ideology and power is not solely a right of center problem. I've looked rightward in this chapter because that's where QAnon mostly lives, and QAnon happens to loom large in American politics at present. Yet we should look left as well.[42]

Kubilus said he's begun to encounter left-wing conspiracism too. "Some of the ways those on the left talk about the hastening of the day when Donald Trump goes to prison alongside his children," he mused, "the way I've heard them spread rumors about those in the Trump orbit . . . all of it is very reminiscent of QAnon, and part of me worries that it is a nascent version of what we've already been experiencing on the right." Maybe it won't be a full-blown movement complete with a message-board prophet, but a left-wing conspiracism used to justify hatred for political enemies is hardly a stretch.

Authority

Since I began writing about epistemic crisis a few years ago, I've frequently encountered the same complaint from American pastors. Most recently it popped up in my interview with Kendall, the senior pastor in California. "The main issue I face is only having one hour a week to try to influence people," he said, "when they can get five hours a week from a TV host, fifteen hours a week from a talk radio host, or many hours beyond that from a blog, YouTube channel, or online group."

This is a complaint about attention, habit, and influence, but it's also about authority—or rather, its lack. Pastors have lost much of their authority as "arbiters of truth," Kendall told me, recounting a quip he's heard that "many pastors are only trusted insomuch as they agree with [Fox News host] Tucker Carlson." One reason the American church is so deep into conspiracism and the epistemic confusion it brings is because we pay too little or no heed to pastors and other spiritual leaders who try to pull us back out.

Questioning authority is very American and very Protestant, and sometimes such questioning is vital. Sometimes authority is wrongly claimed, or rightly claimed but wrongly used. Still, for Christians, committing to a church community means accepting spiritual authority. "Have confidence in your leaders and submit to their authority," the author of Hebrews advises, "because they keep watch over you as those who must give an account" (Heb. 13:17). Likewise, in his second letter to the Corinthian church, Paul speaks of "the authority the Lord gave me for building you up rather than tearing you down" (10:8) and repeats the point in nearly the same words later (13:10; see also 1 Thess. 2:6–7).

Any church is in trouble if its leaders exercise authority in a manner unworthy of respect, but it's equally in trouble if worthy authority is ignored or rejected. The latter is the error into which much of the American church is now lurching, Kubilus contends. Many pastors encounter "an unspoken assumption that we will always be affirming and affable in every encounter, and that we will never presume to tell our congregants that they are wrong," he said, and if a pastor violates that assumption, a "quick Google search will help you find a congregation where your liberal/conservative/conspiratorial/woke/anti-woke/nationalist needs will be met." When pastoral guidance and political allegiance conflict, the pastor will probably lose.

Three Steps against Conspiracism

So how do we retake mental territory conspiracism has invaded? The best course is to forestall that occupation in the first place, and that will be among the concerns of the final section of this book. My conversations with the three pastors suggested sweeping projects of Christian education and discipleship in which we learn to read Scripture as Scripture, not as a decoder ring; learn to keep politics in its proper place among our priorities; and learn to submit to good spiritual authority. All of that is important, but how to achieve it is beyond the scope of this volume.

Here, then, I'll conclude with three smaller proposals for grappling with conspiracism when we find it in our loved ones or ourselves: (1) don't argue; (2) look at the fruit the mindset is bearing; and (3) don't seek a false sense of security that doesn't come from God.

Don't Argue

This is a lesson I've learned through hard experience, as I recounted in the introduction. When conspiracist thinking derailed my former colleague's plans, I argued—and I accomplished exactly nothing. That's how arguing with conspiracism typically goes. Challenging the conspiracist's sources and claims, if there are sources cited and fixed claims levied at all, feels like emptying a spring-fed lake with a slotted spoon.[43] There's no victory to be had.

G. K. Chesterton understood that well. The conspiracist perspective, he wrote, tends to be sweeping, complete, "unanswerable." The conspiracist is wrong, but "if we attempt to trace his error in exact terms, we shall not find it quite so easy as we had supposed. Perhaps the nearest we can get to expressing it is to say this: that his mind moves in a perfect but narrow circle."[44]

Chesterton recommended abandoning attempts to breach the circle by argumentative force. Instead, he advised, invite the conspiracist into the far bigger circle of reality, and especially into the joys of ordinary life. Offer him air—"something cleaner and cooler outside the suffocation" of the conspiracist mindset—but also know he must be willing to draw a breath. "In these cases it is not enough that the unhappy man should desire truth," Chesterton said; "he must desire health."[45] He must recognize that the air he has been breathing is stifling and polluted; argument can make that recognition more difficult.

Kubilus has come to the same conclusion from his pastoral work. "Argument gets you nowhere," he wrote to me. "In fact, in my experience, it only drives it deeper. Debates, reviewing evidence, snark, sarcasm, ostracizing, anger . . . all of it is a dead end." Conspiracism can't be defeated by direct attack, nor can you ever offer air to a stranger. "I tell folks to think about helping [conspiracist] friends and neighbors as a long-term treatment plan," Kubilus said, using the same apt medical metaphor Chesterton employed one hundred years before. "It's not something you can clear up with a single 'come-to-Jesus meeting' or 'tell-it-like-it-is' session. It takes time and trust and vulnerability."

That means listening—not to refute but to understand. Find out what anxieties the conspiracism assuages or feeds, what experiences it explains, what real emotional, social, and/

or spiritual needs it meets. Giving air means addressing those anxieties, experiences, and needs. You'll never be able to prove Biden isn't a clone or Clinton doesn't drain children of their blood, but you can prove yourself a trustworthy friend, and compared to a good friendship, an absurd story about a faraway politician may lose its pull.

Look at the Fruit

This next suggestion is a medicine more easily self-administered than the last—in fact, it's something worth asking ourselves from time to time about *any* significant mindset or habit we adopt. It's also a question that, once trust has been established, we can ask loved ones who have fallen into conspiracist thinking: What kind of fruit is this bearing?

In the Sermon on the Mount, Jesus tells his listeners to examine prophets according to the fruit they produce. A false prophet's appearance may be deceiving, he says, but "by their fruit you will recognize them. Do people pick grapes from thornbushes, or figs from thistles? Likewise, every good tree bears good fruit, but a bad tree bears bad fruit. A good tree cannot bear bad fruit, and a bad tree cannot bear good fruit" (Matt. 7:15–18). No matter how much sense a prophet makes—no matter how large a community his followers build or how strongly they feel they're helping the world—he's still a bad tree if he bears bad fruit.

"The question that seems to hit home the best is to ask, 'Has QAnon given you more peace, made you more patient or kind or forgiving?'" Kubilus said. "If someone is in the right place to process that question, it becomes immediately obvious that no, QAnon has only made them more angry and paranoid and resentful. That can be a turning point for some."

Not every conspiracist movement has a single prophet figure like Q, but with or without that central source, conspiracism imitates prophecy—purporting to reveal unrecognized truth about the world. The standard Jesus gave us can be applied beyond QAnon, and conspiracism will always be revealed for the poisonous plant it is. This mindset does not foster the fruits of the Spirit in us, that list of "love, joy, peace, forbearance, kindness, goodness, faithfulness, gentleness and self-control" Paul sent to the Galatian church (Gal. 5:22–23). It is far more recognizable in several of the vices Paul says will grow without the Spirit: "hatred, discord, fits of rage, dissensions, factions" (5:20).

I said earlier that a theme of loneliness often pops up in profiles of QAnon adherents, but it's worse than that. To research conspiracism is to read story after story of relationships riven and decency disintegrating.[46] "I have fielded dozens of emails from broken families from across the US since I appeared on CNN," said Marsh, the North Carolina pastor. I didn't need him to share those stories with me because I've read so many already.

In Canada, a QAnon influencer named Romana Didulo hyped the mass executions Q adherents believe are coming for their powerful enemies. "YASSS!!!" wrote one of her fans in reply, adding a praying-hands emoji. "I'm so happy we have you," said another, posting a heart emoji. Didulo, who claims to be the rightful ruler of Canada, "is the only one that is saying anything hopeful or anything that makes sense," said a third supporter. A fourth expressed a touch more nuance: "As much as I hate to see people being put to death, it has become necessary because the jerks just won't stop what they are doing."[47] This is bad fruit.

On Reddit, there's a forum called QAnon Casualties that people whose family and friends are caught up in Q conspiracism use as a makeshift support group. It hosts thousands of accounts of marriages ended, friendships severed, and parents estranged. "[My grandma] only ever calls anymore about updates to" her conspiracism, says one post. "If I ask her how she is doing, she launches right into 'news,' warnings, and predictions. If I try to tell her something about my life that I'm planning or excited for, she cuts me off to tell me more about conspiracies."[48] This is bad fruit.

In Michigan, Reformed pastor Vern Swieringa parted ways with his church over conspiracism. First, congregants began sharing QAnon videos. Then, many of them came to believe the COVID-19 pandemic was a hoax. Swieringa pleaded for precautionary measures, citing his wife's lung damage from a previous illness that made her unusually vulnerable to the disease. Congregation and pastor could not find common ground. "We agreed to separate at that point, and so it felt pretty cordial at the time," he told Business Insider Australia. "But I found out later that there were really hard feelings amongst the congregation, and many of them felt like I abandoned them. It was heartbreaking."[49] This is bad fruit indeed.

Don't Seek Fake Security

I wrote at the end of the previous chapter that I find it particularly difficult to "reach out across the firing lines" where conspiracism is concerned. I argued with my former coworker Jim because it is my strong instinct to argue when I hear this stuff. Every bit of me hates sincerely listening when a loved one explains their conspiracist ideas, though I know that's what's needed. I find it physically difficult to sit still and give a hearing to what I strongly believe to be utter nonsense.

The funny thing is, I could easily be a conspiracist myself. I grew up around *Late Great Planet Earth* theology, and as you'll learn if you look up my political commentary, I'm a libertarian. The Enemy Above myth makes sense to libertarians. We're nothing if not suspicious of state power and the stories it tells. The idea that a government agency is dysfunctional or inhuman—or that people possessed of too much power may have abused it—is not a difficult sell to a libertarian crowd.

Despite all that, conspiracy theories are never my default explanation for the "chaos and contingency" I see in the world, to borrow Joel Lawrence's phrase. For me, an inescapable conclusion of working in journalism—especially covering foreign policy and criminal justice issues, which is a euphemistic way of saying I spend a lot of time thinking about war, death, torture, crime, prison, and associated horrors—is that though true conspiracies happen, evil frequently makes no effort to hide.[50]

Evil happens in plain sight, and if it seems obscure, that is often because we have ignored, downplayed, or tried to justify it. Bad things are often exactly what they appear to be. War crimes happen out in the open and go without consequence. Political scandals happen because public figures are just that selfish, shortsighted, lazy, wasteful, lascivious, stupid, and cruel. Sometimes we look at a single incident and think, "There's no way that could be unplanned. There's no way that whole bureaucracy could be so incompetent or that law could be so badly written or that official could be so unfeeling." I assure you: they can.

In this complex, fallen world, rife with glaring and often systemic evil, longing for the second coming, conspiracism boils everything down into a simple message of false security. It says things are bad because of secretive, bad people's deliberately bad choices. If you can catch and punish the bad people, you can stop the bad things.

There is a satisfying explanatory power here. I understand the appeal. But it is false, and worse, it pretends to provide security that should come only from God.[51] It promises the thin justice of retribution, not the full justice God has promised, a justice attended by the great mercy of the cross. It cultivates a false fear, a false feeling of control, a false conception of where history is going, and a false notion of how we should spend our time.[52] Conspiracism is a con artist and usurper.

God says as much through the prophet Isaiah. "Do not call conspiracy everything this people calls a conspiracy; do not fear what they fear, and do not dread it," Isaiah records God telling him (Isa. 8:12). "The Lord Almighty is the one you are to regard as holy" (8:13), the one to whom we owe our attention and respect, the one who will shepherd his people's future, the one in whom we should place our trust (see 8:11–17). Those who put their trust elsewhere, Isaiah warns, will receive in return "distress and darkness and fearful gloom" (8:22).

That corrupt harvest is precisely what conspiracism delivers. It points us to a false second coming, which means we look away from the real one. It takes a trust undeserved, a faith wrongly placed, a belief too easily given. And from here we'll turn to its odd but often close companion of belief too much withheld: the death of expertise.

Skepticism

Sometimes it seems as though some puppet-player,
    A clenched claw cupping a craggy chin
Sits just beyond the border of our seeing,
    Twitching the strings with slow, sardonic grin.
    —Angelina Weld Grimké, "The Puppet-Player"

In early June 2020, New York City was in the final days of a three-month stay-at-home order of the COVID-19 pandemic. It was also in the early days of mass protests following the death of George Floyd in Minneapolis, demonstrations city officials had permitted despite public-health bans on large gatherings.

In conversation with then-mayor Bill de Blasio, a reporter for the Orthodox Jewish outlet *Hamodia* asked about this double standard: Why was city government enforcing the pandemic rule on religious services with more than ten attendees while allowing tens of thousands of people to gather for demonstrations? The query was particularly pressing for *Hamodia*'s readers, because some Jewish services have a mandatory minimum attendance of eleven, meaning the ten-person limit was effectively a total ban.[1]

The mayor dismissed the inquiry. "When you see a nation, an entire nation, simultaneously grappling with an extraordinary crisis seeded in 400 years of American racism, I'm sorry, that is not the same question," de Blasio said, "as the . . . devout religious person who wants to go back to services."[2]

Sure, it's not the *same* question. But it's certainly a reasonable and relevant question. In fact, de Blasio's framing of the protests as concerning long history and severe sin—not simply policing policy and procedure—only makes the relation more apparent. Both protest and worship are unnecessary for immediate physical survival, so why permit one but not the other? Or conversely, both involve a sense of moral obligation flowing from deeply held convictions about humanity, so why enforce the gathering ban against just one?

The answer, unspoken but blaring, is that de Blasio thought the protests were important and the religious services, at least by comparison, were not. He wasn't "following the science," to use a phrase that was so often sounded in those months that it devolved into parody. He was making a judgment call—maybe a good call, maybe a bad call, but undeniably an ideological call.

At least de Blasio had the decency to (almost) admit it. Too many other officials and experts tasked with crafting public-health guidance that summer did not, and that duplicity was harmful to more than physical health. It was harmful to epistemic health, sabotaging the public reputation of expertise itself.

The Death of Expertise

The death of expertise, as former Naval War College professor Tom Nichols argues in a book by that name, "is not just a rejection of existing knowledge."[3] It is "more than a natural skepticism toward experts," whom he defines as those possessed of "an intangible but recognizable combination of education, talent, experience, and peer recognition."[4] Rather, Nichols argues, what "we are witnessing [is] the *death of the ideal of expertise* itself, a Google-fueled, Wikipedia-based, blog-sodden collapse of any division between professionals and lay-people, students and teachers, knowers and wonderers—in other words, between those of any achievement in an area and those with none at all."[5]

That this is happening seems fairly easy to demonstrate. Nichols reports hearing stories from experts of all sorts—not only academic types like doctors, teachers, and lawyers, but also plumbers, electricians, mechanics, and more—who regularly find themselves arguing with uninformed or misinformed laypeople convinced they know just as much or more than the expert. It happens to pastors too. "One of my best friends is a pediatrician," said Derek Kubilus, the Methodist minister I quoted in the previous chapter, "and we often lament together that we are both experts in fields where we are expected to help people who already consider themselves to be experts!"

Or consider the ubiquity of online ads promising to reveal "one weird trick" to lose weight or cure acne or get better sleep that medical experts have allegedly been hiding from you. "Doctors hate him!" is often the headline, and the ads usually have an amateur, hand-drawn look intended to evoke an underdog uprising against establishment knowledge.[6] The remarkable longevity and omnipresence of this ad format means it works. It means there's a large audience for whom the ideal of expertise is already dead.

The question, then, is who killed it and whether it can be revived. Nichols devotes most of his attention to laypeople's role in destroying the public-expert relationship, and his accusation of public hubris—unwarranted self-confidence and defiance against those who know better—is both important and fair. We'll come to that in a moment. But the other half of this, the half that has become starkly apparent in 2020 and 2021, the immediate backdrop to my writing here, is expert failure. I'll examine both parts before turning to how interactions between the public and experts can be better with the cultivation of Christian virtues of respect and humility in habits of good faith and gracious apology.

The Necessity of Trust

The death of expertise would be less of a problem in a different time and place.[7] Before the Enlightenment and Scientific and Industrial Revolutions, there was far less specialized knowledge to be had. Ignorance could lead to catastrophe, but more limited technology tended to contain the fallout. We don't live in that age anymore. Now "we live in a society that works because of division of labor, a system designed to relieve each of us of having to know about everything," Nichols observes. "The fact of the matter is we cannot function without admitting the limits of our knowledge and trusting in the expertise of others."[8]

The most suspicious among us lives by means of enormous trust in strangers every day. Have you ever traveled across a bridge? You trusted the expertise of its engineers, builders, maintenance workers—experts whose name you'll never know. Have you eaten a piece of cheese in a restaurant? You trusted the expertise of the farmer and cheesemaker to produce an uncontaminated product, of the refrigerator manufacturers and truck drivers to get it safely to the kitchen, of the chef to select it, and of the dishwasher to ensure you receive it on a clean plate. Every time you fly on a plane or take your dog to the vet or walk over a manhole or let your kid swing at the park or hire a plumber, you rely on expertise, often the expertise of total strangers that you can't meaningfully evaluate.

Modern life requires this. What separates our daily experience from that of a premodern peasant is, significantly, trust placed in experts we will never meet. A democratic and "complex society" like ours "can't dispense with elites," as media scholar and former CIA analyst Martin Gurri argues in *Revolt of the Public and the Crisis of Authority in the New Millennium*. "That is the hard reality of the situation."[9]

Democratized Knowledge, Public Hubris

The other hard reality is that expertise has never been so difficult to trust as it is now. Part of this has to do with the media through which many experts speak. Experts aren't immune to all the biases, pressures, and incentives of traditional and social media we examined in chapter 2. They're asked to explain an ever more complex world in fewer and fewer words.[10] That's a remarkably difficult job, and people with dual expertise in their own field *and* public communications are rare. Perfectly competent and well-intended experts may come off as naive, unfeeling, or downright incapable on Twitter or cable news.

Another aspect, though, is that as access to knowledge has expanded, we in the public have tended to confuse our ability to easily look something up online with possession of true expertise. We've taken democratic principles about the moral equality of humanity—"All men are created equal"—and applied it to expert knowledge, an arena of life in which humans are incredibly *un*equal.[11] A structural engineer and a nurse have equal worth and both equally reflect the image of God. But that doesn't mean I'll let the nurse inspect my home or the engineer treat my infection.

Nichols recounts a story of a student at his university arguing with a renowned astrophysicist on the faculty. After some banter back and forth, the student retreated, saying, "Well, your guess is as good as mine." "No, no, no," the expert answered, "*My* guesses are much, *much* better than yours."[12] Democratization of knowledge has made it possible for the whole public to respond to expert pronouncements as that student did, wrongly imagining our guess is as good as that of someone who's made the issue at hand their life's work.

And while it's true that sometimes the layperson is right and the expert is wrong, *on average*, the uneducated—or Google-educated—guess is worse, and it is hubris to think otherwise. If "doctors hate him," as those ads scream, it's not because the disparaged individual is revealing some secret truth the medical establishment hid. It's because he's spewing uninformed nonsense and demanding undeserved respect. *Any* expert working in good faith to advance knowledge in their field would hate that, and so they should. They have a responsibility to preserve, expand, and pass on their expert knowledge, and pretending "your guess is as good as mine" does not serve that duty well.

The combination of expert use of social media and the democratization of knowledge has another effect too: expert failure is far easier to spot and endlessly tout as "proof" of expert illegitimacy. Experts were never infallible, nor can they be. There are always limits to what humans know, and building new knowledge and revising old errors is a vital part of developing expertise. Mistakes are made in the short term, but in the long run this process of expert correction moves us toward truth.[13]

What's new is that nonexperts can watch this process in real time. We can watch both true failure and unsettled, intra-industry debate of new (and maybe not so great) ideas, a conversation that has significantly moved into performative, public spaces like Twitter.[14] In "the industrial age, the pratfalls of authority had been managed discreetly, camouflaged by the mystique of the expert at the top of his game," Gurri explains. "Today failure happens out in the open, where everyone can see. With the arrival of the global information sphere, each failure is captured, reproduced, multiplied, amplified, and made to stand for authority as a whole."[15] A bad tweet or a botched CNN segment can serve as justification for believing we know better than a given expert or the practitioners of an entire field.

That illusion is possible to maintain because of the infinite trove of information we can access online. Experts and elite institutions have lost what Gurri calls "the monopoly on information."[16] Because of that loss, every expert claim is subject to dispute and under suspicion of illegitimate (especially political) motivation. If you don't like what an expert is saying and believe you know better, someone—maybe many someones—on the internet will agree. They'll tally every expert failure and offer gratifying alternative advice or explanations. Modern media makes it easier than ever to "gather around [us] a great number of teachers to say what [our] itching ears want to hear" (2 Tim. 4:3).

Expert Failure

In fairness, some of that itch is the tickle of expert failure. The expert guess is better, but it's not perfect. Experts get things wrong.

You may recall that in chapter 2 (on traditional and social media) I shared survey data showing that when Americans suspect inaccuracy in the news, many of them worry it's intentional and ideologically motivated. They suspect journalists are deliberately lying to promote a political agenda. The reality, I argue in that chapter, is that for all the problems in journalism, willful deception like this is quite rare (and when it does happen—as with famous cases like those of Stephen Glass, whose deception at *The New Republic* was dramatized in the 2003 film *Shattered Glass*, or Janet Cooke's "Jimmy's World" story—we typically learn about it through the exposé work of other journalists).

The same is true of expert failure. Deliberate falsehood is unusual, and when it does occur, it's often exposed by other experts who care about the integrity of their field.[17] This is particularly true of more academic areas of expertise, hard sciences most of all, where intensely specialized knowledge makes public scrutiny nearly impossible. Researchers question and build on one another's findings, so willfully falsified (or simply shoddy) research is frequently caught and debunked when fellow scientists attempt to use it in their own work. Many industries and academic fields have professional associations precisely for the purpose of censuring liars and hucksters who endanger the reputation of the whole group.

Still, expert failure needn't be purposeful to contribute to the death of expertise, as the past few years have demonstrated ad nauseam.

Personal Hypocrisy

"Pass the potatoes, not COVID," Denver Mayor Michael B. Hancock tweeted the day before Thanksgiving 2020. "Stay home as much as you can, especially if you're sick. Host virtual gatherings instead of in-person dinners. Avoid travel, if you can."[18]

Less than an hour later, Hancock hopped on a plane to fly from Colorado to Mississippi to spend the holiday with family.[19] He was far from the only politician to violate pandemic restrictions of his own making, and that sort of hypocrisy has predictably bad effects on public confidence in expertise.[20] *Rules for thee but not for me* fuel conspiracism too—and understandably so. They paint experts as self-interested manipulators who control more than they inform. They make it seem, as journalist and poet Angelina Weld Grimké wrote, "as though some puppet-player / A clenched claw cupping a craggy chin / Sits just beyond the border of our seeing, / Twitching the strings with slow, sardonic grin."[21] No one trusts a puppet master.

Noble Lies

If hypocrisy is what selfish expert failure looks like, noble lies are expert failure in an altruistic mode. The concept of a noble lie is as old as Plato, who in the *Republic* proposes maintaining sharp class divisions in his ideal society by "contriv[ing] one of those lies that come into being in case of need . . . some one noble lie to persuade, in the best case, even the rulers, but if not them, the rest of the city." Such deception, the dialogue suggests, can be appropriate if that is what it takes to make the people "care more for the city and one another."[22]

That is not a convincing argument in our society—at least, not for those on the lie's receiving end. When experts are caught in noble lies it discredits their future announcements, perhaps irreparably, or at least until memory fades or a sincere apology is given.[23]

The biggest noble lie of COVID-19 was about masks. At the beginning of the pandemic, when it was becoming apparent this would not be a quick, distant worry like other epidemics of recent memory, prominent federal officials told the public we absolutely should not buy or use masks to slow the viral spread.[24] "Seriously people," tweeted then-surgeon general Jerome Adams, "STOP BUYING MASKS!"[25] Dr. Anthony Fauci, chief of the National Institute of Allergy and Infectious Diseases, took a similar tack. Within a matter of weeks, however, not only had the guidance been reversed but mask mandates became the federal recommendation.[26]

The reason for the lie was pretty noble. As Adams's tweet hinted, it was about conserving medical supplies for health care workers. But it was still a lie, one that may have permanently suppressed how many Americans were willing to wear a mask. And that backlash was evidently insufficient a lesson for experts like Fauci, who would go on to tell other noble lies.[27] "When polls said only about half of all Americans would take a vaccine, I was saying herd immunity would take 70 to 75 percent," he told the *New York Times* in late 2020. "Then, when newer surveys said 60 percent or more would take it, I thought, 'I can nudge this up a bit,' so I went to 80, 85." The real number is "somewhere between 70 to 90 percent," he added. "But, I'm not going to say 90 percent."[28]

That strategy isn't "humility," as Fauci cast it. A noble lie is just a lie.

Politicized Judgment

Now we come to de Blasio's failure in telling the *Hamodia* reporter that mass protests were permissible though far smaller religious gatherings weren't. While the public sometimes rejects expertise on political grounds, experts sometimes subvert their own message because of their politics.

The undeniable double standard for the protests was conspicuous well beyond New York City. Some public-health experts and journalists spoke as if COVID-19 adjusted its contagion along political lines.[29] An apt *New York Times* headline captured the situation well: "Are Protests Dangerous? What Experts Say May Depend on Who's Protesting What."[30] The degrading effect of that double standard was enormous, "proving" every skeptic's suspicion that experts can't be trusted.[31] The puppet strings are exposed!

Reality was a bit more complex. Religious services and right-wing anti-lockdown protests typically took place indoors, while protests related to policing usually assembled outside, where the illness was far less likely to spread. Plenty of individual public-health experts, including Fauci, issued consistent warnings across the board. Still, it was undeniable the *aggregate* public-health messaging shifted depending on who was protesting what. "We allowed thousands of people to die alone," Yale sociologist Nicholas A. Christakis said in that *Times* report. "We buried people by Zoom. Now all of a sudden we are saying, never mind?"[32]

That sense of gross unfairness—that some politically favored groups were allowed to do the thing they felt morally vital while others were denied the same opportunity on ostensibly neutral, scientific grounds—made the assembly-rules fiasco stand out as a case of politicized expert failure. It was not the only such case in COVID's first year. Debates around treatment regimens[33] and viral origins[34] were similarly infected by partisan judgment. And perhaps, given the urgency of the pandemic, we shouldn't be surprised: quick decisions may often be correct, but they are by nature ill examined. Expert decisions are no exception.

Professional Relationships

If we're to peek behind the curtain into experts' conversations in spaces like Twitter, we may as well peek a little more and notice how professional dynamics can be a source of expert failure too. Again, the COVID-19 pandemic offers a wealth of examples. For instance, the knowledge that would form the basis of the mRNA vaccines—the two-shot options from Moderna and Pfizer—languished for years in the research of a University of Pennsylvania scientist, Dr. Katalin Karikó. For *decades*, Karikó was sure this could be a useful medical technique, but it seems she wasn't very popular at her institution and struggled to get professional support.

This all came out after her research became a globally celebrated success. "In published interviews before the public glare grew more intense, she did acknowledge some frustration with the years of rejections from funders, journals, and Penn," reported *Times Higher Education*, an industry magazine for university faculty and staff. "Key points included numerous grant application rejections, her demotion to an adjunct position in 1995 after a few initial years of work on mRNA, and her 2013 departure for BioNTech—now a celebrated maker of a leading Covid vaccine—to what she described as words of sarcastic ridicule from Penn leadership."[35] Another researcher who had worked with Karikó while doing his doctoral research at Penn told the magazine outright that had her ideas "come from someone with an established and influential network," they would have been funded long before the pandemic began.[36]

Positive relationships can contribute to failure too if experts allow their affection or desire for acceptance to cloud their judgment. This happens both online and off, but social media amplifies the effect. "Social media is truly *social* in the sense that it features incredible pressures to form in-groups and out-groups and then to conform to your in-group," argues journalist Matt Yglesias in an analysis of expert failure concerning COVID-19's possible origins. So "if you secure your impression of what 'the scientists' think about something from scanning Twitter, you will perceive a consensus that is not really there. If something is a 70-30 issue but the 30 are keeping their heads down, it can look like a 98-2 issue."[37]

Unrealistic Expectations

All of this contributes to the overarching problem of expert failure: unrealistic expectations. The public often has a sense that experts don't deliver what they promise and that, therefore, their authority isn't legitimate and the respect they want isn't deserved. I contend that for all their failures, experts generally *do* deliver! We can all think of exceptions to that rule—the failures—but our technologically complex and historically comfortable lives are functional, in the day-to-day, because of the many successes.

Yes, that bridge in Minneapolis collapsed in 2007. But hundreds of thousands of bridges in the United States *don't* collapse every day. You *haven't* died of polio or smallpox, diseases eliminated in the United States because of expert work. I can spend my time writing, not scrubbing my family's clothes on a washboard or carrying dirty drinking water from a river or doing any number of similar survival chores, because experts have created wonderful machines and systems to do it for me.

All this settled success, this luxury into which we were born, contributes to our unrealistic expectations, and then we unfairly knock experts for the "failure" of self-revision as they learn and try new things.

While writing this chapter, I happened to see a quote attributed to "That Patriot Mom . . . on Twitter," whoever she may be. "If science was never questioned, you'd still be drinking cocaine, giving kids cough syrup with heroin, spraying people with DDT, and smoking the cigarette brand your doctor recommended," she said.[38] The intended effect—successfully achieved, as far as Facebook commenters were concerned—was to undermine trust in scientific expertise. Of course, what That Patriot Mom neglected to say is that it wasn't social media users like herself who corrected all those failures. It was scientists revising incomplete knowledge with expert research, because questioning science is the basic task of science.

Still, here again the experts deserve a share of the blame insofar as they set us up for too high expectations by claiming greater or different competence than they possess. Experts could get away with reputation inflation in the pre-internet age. No more. No sooner has a failure dropped from expert lips but it becomes the subject of a thousand tweetstorms.[39] Public patience for experts who stray outside their expertise (actors weighing in on politics, politicians critiquing art, scientists commenting on morality, preachers speaking about science) is thinning as well, provided the straying is unpopular.[40]

The sum of all of this is that expertise carries less and less authority, even the authority it deserves. We accept its bounty in the form of running water and babies living past infancy and all the other blessings of modern life, but with ever greater ease we also discount it as bad-faith manipulation. Public hubris and expert failure are a toxic mix. Their product—a sloppy, convenient skepticism of the best (albeit imperfect) knowledge we have—is epistemic poison.

Onward to Virtue

Is there an antidote? The relationship between experts and the public can never go back to what it once was. Public innocence about expertise is gone for good. If the internet disappeared tomorrow, we'd all still remember the failures by the experts it had shown us. (We'd probably add the internet's disappearance itself to their number.)

The impossibility of returning to a naive trust in expertise doesn't leave us hopeless here, but it does mean we have no shortcut around our need for virtue. Experts and nonexperts alike—and we all play each role, to varying degrees and with varying publicity—must learn attitudes of humility and respect, habits of listening and speaking in good faith, and an eagerness to apologize graciously when we are wrong.

The Path for Nonexperts

We are most of us nonexperts on most subjects most of the time, so let's start out on that more modest path toward these virtues and practices. Humility here means recognizing how very much we do not know and will not learn by googling. Respect means acknowledging what experts *do* know, giving due honor (Rom. 13:7) to diligent learning and well-honed technique (1 Tim. 5:17), and acknowledging our constant reliance on expert knowledge. Cultivating humility and respect means not behaving like the proverbial fools who "despise wisdom and instruction" (Prov. 1:7), assume their own intuition is correct (12:15), and scorn prudent advice (23:9).[41]

As a practical matter, that requires adjusting our expectations to make room for expert fallibility. No expert has perfect knowledge or, if they somehow did, could always communicate or apply that knowledge perfectly. Some failure is inevitable. Though egregious, repeated, and demonstrably malicious failure can deservedly discredit an expert, institution, or entire field, "experts being wrong on occasion about certain issues is not the same thing as experts being wrong consistently on everything," as Nichols notes, nor is it the same thing as nonexperts being right.[42] An expert's wrong guess doesn't make my uninformed guess any better.

Also necessary is accepting that revision after learning is a good thing. It's proof of competence, not incompetence. It demonstrates trustworthiness, not unreliability, because updating established knowledge isn't failure. Expert knowledge *should* increase over time, and experts *should* change their advice as that happens. We should welcome those updates, for—as Proverbs bluntly says—"whoever hates correction is stupid" (12:1) and "leads others astray" (10:17).

That balance of honoring expertise while expecting that experts will sometimes fail, and grow, points to the challenge of good-faith interaction on the nonexpert side: to chart a course between anti-intellectualism (in my judgment, the greater temptation of the political right) and scientism (by the same standard, the bigger risk for the left). Expertise isn't only scientific, of course, but the spirit of scientism can corrupt our response to any expert, giving us an inflated notion of what questions expertise can answer and with what degree of certainty. The right blend of circumspection and trust might be something like that advised by the mathematician and public intellectual Bertrand Russell a century ago: "The skepticism that I advocate amounts only to this: (1) that when the experts are agreed, the opposite opinion cannot be held to be certain; (2) that when they are not agreed, no opinion can be regarded as certain by a non-expert; and (3) that when they all hold that no sufficient grounds for a positive opinion exist, the ordinary man would do well to suspend his judgment."[43]

The Path for Experts

In expert mode, a significant facet of our task is to smooth the nonexpert path to these virtues. That is, don't make it difficult to trust true expertise.

Experts are not Plato's philosopher kings. We have no right to tell noble lies—or *any* lies—to nonexperts, nor can we expect to dictate the behavior of other adults. Humility for an expert means realizing it is not their right or responsibility to determine what information the public is capable of handling well—what complex truths nonexperts can be trusted to know.[44]

In a country with leaders chosen by popular vote like the United States, this also means experts can't expect political decisions to be bound to their advice.[45] Especially in the throes of hubris, the public may come to wrong conclusions and may, through their elected representatives, make stupid policies that defy expert knowledge. That's a bad thing and can have awful consequences, but it is a necessary risk we take when we trust a people with self-governance.

Often it seems that when such negative consequences ensue the expert impulse is to shift into condescension and shaming, some dressed-up version of "Well, you dummies should have listened to me and will get what you deserve" or "You should be forced into the correct option you rejected." I understand (and have felt!) that temptation, but experts who want nonexperts to willingly heed their words must treat them with more respect than this response entails.

That goes beyond telling even the complex and difficult truths. It also means demonstrating "*integrity* in life and work," as Gurri exhorts. Experts "must learn to say, out loud for all to hear, 'This is a process of trial and error,' and, 'We are uncertain of the consequences,' and even, 'I was wrong,'" he elaborates. "Honesty means that the relationship to truth [so far as it's known] matters more than ambition or partisan advantage. Humility means that the top of the [hierarchy of expertise and authority] looks to the public as a home it will return to rather than a carnivorous species from which to hide. Truth must be spoken even when it hurts the speaker or the audience."[46]

The book of Proverbs has wisdom for the expert too. It critiques the fool six ways to Sunday, but sometimes finds targets for criticism who make the fool look good by comparison. "Do you see a person wise in their own eyes? There is more hope for a fool than for them" (Prov. 26:12). For experts, being wise in our own eyes may look like conflating our judgment—which could be correct but could also be flawed, incomplete, or simply poorly communicated—with capital-*T* Truth itself.

In a particularly bad cable-news appearance in 2021, for instance, Fauci claimed many of the "attacks on [him], quite frankly, are attacks on science."[47] Experts can have hubris too. Indeed, often with expertise comes the prideful temptation to "love the place of honor at banquets and the most important seats in the synagogues" (Matt. 23:6), a desire Jesus says we should expunge from ourselves, for we "have one Instructor, the Messiah," and "those who exalt themselves will be humbled, and those who humble themselves will be exalted" (23:10, 12).

On the necessity of apology, Proverbs speaks as well: "Fools mock at making amends for sin, but goodwill is found among the upright" (14:9). Though expert failure isn't necessarily sinful, public trust in expertise becomes inconceivable if experts refuse to acknowledge when they are wrong and apologize.[48] One of my colleagues at *The Week*, columnist Damon Linker, has a commendable practice of taking an annual inventory of the opinions he's published in the past twelve months and writing up a year-end column detailing his mistakes—not factual errors that need corrections, which would be fixed much sooner, but expert judgment calls he got wrong. This habit enhances his own expertise and his credibility, because it roots out lingering fallacies in his thinking and shows his readers he's writing in good faith, in pursuit of truth.

Apology doesn't come easily to me. It commonly feels like dramatization, like making a mistake or offense a bigger deal than it really is. In my work I can follow Linker's good example and fess up when I get things wrong, but in private life I find I have to drag the words past my lips. I understand how the requirement of apology is a hard teaching, because it's one with which I struggle to comply. Yet I know that graciously offering an apology must be a Christian distinctive—it's the other side of Jesus's command to generously forgive (as discussed in chap. 3). People of truth cannot cling to error, however comfortable a pose it may be, however safe for our reputations or useful for our politics.

Expertise, wielded aright, is not "an infallible panacea," Christian writer and editor Samuel D. James has mused. "It is the natural consequence of being made in the image of a knowing God, who gives gifts and graces to each, for the good of all. Humility to sit under this kingdom economy is the key to resurrecting a culture of trust—and with it, a flourishing, mutually beneficial age of experts."[49] That is a flourishing we cannot do without, not least amid the emotional manipulation and confusion to which we'll now turn.

Emotion

Feelings come and feelings go,
And feelings are deceiving;
My warrant is the Word of God—
Naught else is worth believing.

Though all my heart should feel condemned
For want of some sweet token,
There is One greater than my heart
Whose Word cannot be broken.

I'll trust in God's unchanging Word
'Til soul and body sever,
For, though all things shall pass away,
His Word shall stand forever!

> —Anonymous, but commonly
> attributed to Martin Luther

The conservative evangelicalism of my youth didn't take a terribly favorable view of emotion. Feelings are mercurial and untrustworthy, I remember hearing. They're often disconnected from reality—something we can't escape, unfortunately, but can work to ignore as an impediment to right thinking.

Faithfulness to God and the truth would be impossible if we succumbed to emotion, I learned, whether through manipulation by other people or the workings of our own deceitful hearts. Jeremiah 17:9—which declares that "the heart is deceitful above all things, and desperately wicked" (KJV)[1]—was a familiar quotation. The Hebrew word rendered as "heart" in this passage (typically transliterated *leb*) is a broad term that encompasses the whole inner being, including what we would call the soul, the rational mind, the will, and the seat of emotion. It's often the word used, for example, when the Old Testament records that someone "said (something) in his heart"—that is, he thought it.[2]

But when I heard that verse, "heart" was interpreted as it is in contemporary American parlance. It was understood to refer to the emotive, nonrational parts of us, which meant our feelings were something bad to be overcome by reason and Scripture through the empowerment of the Holy Spirit. Pop culture might tell you to "follow your heart," but we would follow the Bible instead.

That context is the reason why, for years, I read Paul's famous monologue of the divided self in Romans 7 ("what I want to do I do not do, but what I hate I do," he confesses in v. 15) as a battle between the emotional fallen nature and the rational redeemed mind. I don't think anyone taught me that interpretation in so many words, but linking the troublesome, ungovernable part of the self to feelings made sense given what else I'd been told about emotion. *Of course* the bad part of you produced the feelings, and the good part—the part that reflected the image of God and could be sanctified—was the reasoning mind.

The first stanza of the poem located at the beginning of this chapter was familiar to me too. In pithy, proverbial form, it communicates that our changeable feelings are a path to deception, an enemy of Scripture, and, by extension, a hindrance to our relationship with God. Shove those feelings down, if you are thus plagued, by reading the Bible.

I don't think I knew at the time that these lines are typically credited to Martin Luther, an attribution that's very probably false. I've been unable to find any citation of a specific source in his extensive writings, and anyway, the sixteenth-century German theologian didn't write in rhyming near-modern English. It's possible, however, that this is some anonymous Christian poet's rendering of a comment found in a volume of Luther's "table talks," which are informal remarks that some of his students wrote down when they shared dinner and conversation with Luther and his family.[3]

"The forgiveness of sins is declared only in God's Word, and there we must seek it; for it is grounded on God's promises," Luther said in one such discussion. "God forgives you your sins, not because you feel them and are sorry, for that itself produces sin, and can deserve nothing; but he forgives your sins because he is merciful, and because he has promised to forgive for Christ's sake, his dearly beloved Son, and caused his word to be applied to you: namely, 'Be of good cheer, your sins are forgiven you.'"[4]

If this is the basis of the poem, you can see how seriously Luther's meaning was distorted in the adaptation. Luther was rejecting emotion as stand-alone proof of Christian salvation in two ways. On the one hand, he wanted Christians who struggle to feel themselves redeemed to rest in God's mercy and promise. If you are dealing with depression or persistent doubt or temptation that makes you question whether God truly forgives and wants you, Luther offers reassurance: God has made his good intentions toward you known in unmistakable terms in Scripture. On the other hand, Luther has a caution for those who believe themselves to be in good standing with God solely because of their emotional self-perception. Your emotions about your sins aren't what saves you, Luther warns. Salvation by feelings is not salvation by faith.

The second stanza of the poem does echo Luther's reassurance for worried Christians. But his warning is lost, and when the first stanza is quoted by itself—the only way I'd ever encountered it before I began researching it for this book—*all* of Luther's meaning is gone, and we're left instead with a sweeping condemnation of emotion that the famously emotive reformer's talk never makes.[5]

Hooked on a Feeling

That paradigm of emotion versus Scripture and/or reason was among the earliest explanations I absorbed for people's theological and political differences. We hardheaded conservatives were committed to truth, especially the truth of the Bible, even when it was emotionally difficult. *We* could accept unpleasant realities. *We* could make the tough calls where weaker, more emotional people—those bleeding-heart liberals—would take the easy path. They'd fall sway to peer pressure, follow the whims of secular culture, and bend to their own deceitful hearts. We'd push aside our feelings and stand firm. The slogan of right-wing pundit Ben Shapiro might have become a regular proverb of my younger years too, had we had it back then: "Facts don't care about your feelings."[6]

That idea of the hardheaded conservative is a longstanding trope in US politics, and it's what makes so remarkable the new emotionalism of the American right. It's not that there's no emotionalism elsewhere on our political spectrum; there's plenty.[7] But if the stereotype was ever true (and I think it was always far more complicated than that image allows), it has been fully upended.[8]

While still regularly dismissing feelings as distraction or deception, as in Shapiro's line, the populist right of the 2020s has also embraced emotion in a way that once would have been unacceptable under the "feelings come and feelings go" standard. (A vignette that always sticks with me: at Republican campaign rallies, T-shirts blaring the slogan "F—k your feelings"—not censored, of course—have become a normal sight. Political opponents' feelings are illegitimate, declares a shirt that commits a crude emotional outburst to print.)[9]

This new emotionalism came into focus for me in the weeks after the 2020 election.[10] Some of Donald Trump's supporters, while arguing that he'd won, would rattle off unsubstantiated figures or legal claims that had failed in court. Yet often there was no attempt to present any rationale beyond feelings and desires. Trump's win was an article of faith in the absolute worst sense of the phrase. Anything that supported the idea of the victory was accepted without much scrutiny; anything that opposed it was rejected without pause.

Some prominent Trump supporters made explicit the central role of emotion in their "knowledge" of Trump's triumph. "This is how I feel," said *Fox & Friends* weekend cohost Will Cain on a show in January 2021. "I think Americans—I think Republicans, conservatives—can be forgiven for their skepticism [of then-president-elect Joe Biden's victory], because whether or not an election was rigged, it certainly feels like society is rigged right now."[11]

Speaking at a pro-Trump rally for Christians called the Jericho March, former national security adviser Michael Flynn told supporters to trust only their feelings, not their minds. "It's in our hearts where we truly know what is right. It's in our hearts where we differentiate good and bad," Flynn said. "It's your heart talking to you, not your mind, because your mind is going to say, 'I'm afraid.'"[12]

In an interview with Trumpist youth activist Charlie Kirk, evangelical author and radio host Eric Metaxas—after clarifying that both men "firmly believe[d] that Trump actually won"—argued their conversation should "just stop" examining how, specifically, Trump could be the one taking the oath of office come Inauguration Day. "My attitude is, like, so who cares what I can prove in the courts? This is right. This happened," Metaxas said as Kirk nodded enthusiastic agreement. A few minutes later, Metaxas announced himself "thrilled to be too ignorant of the details" of Trump's election legal battles to analyze them. Kirk grinned.[13]

There's a yawning gap between "The heart is deceitful above all things, and desperately wicked" and "It's in our hearts where we truly know what is right." Even so, I have no doubt there are millions of Americans who might declare "Facts don't care about your feelings" *and* nod along to Cain, Kirk, and Metaxas as they express how they feel. You can see the contradiction.

That dissonance is facilitated by the endless content of the internet, the constant solicitation of emotional outbursts and mob behavior on social media (as we saw in chap. 3), and the ever-narrower audience tailoring of traditional media (as discussed in chap. 2). Should you come across some content too stubborn to be interpreted to your liking, you can simply discard it and—often unconsciously—invite the internet to provide another piece of content you like much more. Feelings don't have to care about facts, because facts can be framed around feelings while still feeling like unfeeling facts.

Feeling and Knowing

There's enormous epistemic confusion in both the extremes I've described, and that confusion raises crucial questions: What's the proper role of emotion in acquiring knowledge? What part, if any, should feelings play as we judge what is right? Do Christians have to suppress our emotions to be able to discern the truth? Or is reason the real obstacle, as Flynn said, feelings being the surer guide?

What I'll argue here is that the expanse between emotion and reason those questions assume is a lot narrower than we tend to think. Feelings aren't uniquely corrupted by the fall, and used rightly, emotion is a powerful tool of persuasion. Our epistemic crisis, which is as much an emotional problem as an intellectual and spiritual one, a matter of fear and grievance as much as mental doubt, makes feeling all the more needful.[14]

The Elephant and the Rider

"Within the Western philosophical tradition, emotions have usually been considered potentially or actually subversive of knowledge," writes philosopher Alison Jaggar in an influential essay on emotion and epistemology.[15] In Plato's dialogue *Timaeus*, for example, the philosopher posits that our reasoning souls were made by the creator god, who then let demigods figure out our physical bodies. They did shoddier work, and we ended up with "terrible and irresistible affections"— emotions—that tempt us to evil. Emotions live in the body, Timaeus says, but don't worry! Your neck is a barrier that helps keep them out of your perfect, rational head. Alas, he adds, men who fail to master their emotions are probably punished by being reincarnated as women.[16]

Thus, "from Plato until the present, with a few notable exceptions, reason rather than emotion has been regarded as the indispensable faculty for acquiring knowledge," Jaggar continues. And while "reason was taken to be objective and universal, . . . emotions [were portrayed] as non-rational and often irrational urges that regularly swept the body, rather as a storm sweeps over the land. The common way of referring to the emotions as the 'passions' emphasized that emotions happened to or were imposed upon an individual, something she suffered rather than something she did."[17] If you want to feel, fine, indulge in emotion—but if you want to *know*, reason is the tool you need.

The trouble with this dichotomy is that it isn't especially real. It's real on paper, of course. We can define the difference between reason and emotion. But it's not real in *us*. We might like to tell ourselves we're ignoring all those pesky emotions in order to issue purely rational judgments based on reason (or the Bible) alone. This is exactly my own inclination: I'm not naturally very emotive, and I enjoy reasoning in its own right. (I've long loved detective fiction, where the hero champions justice by crafting a string of logical inferences, and logic was among my favorite classes in college, one I recommend to every new student willing to hear me out.) But however much I might want to achieve and boast of it, that total bifurcation of emotion and reason is elusive. Very rarely, maybe never, can I—or anyone—actually manage it.

Moral psychologist Jonathan Haidt has made this interplay of emotion and reason—particularly in the process of making moral judgments—his life's work. He's developed a metaphor that makes sense of the integration I'm describing: the rider and the elephant.[18] Mulling on his research and his own experience of the divided self, Haidt writes:

> The image that I came up with for myself, as I marveled at my weakness, was that I was a rider on the back of an elephant. I'm holding the reins in my hands, and by pulling one way or the other I can tell the elephant to turn, to stop, or to go. I can direct things, but only when the elephant doesn't have desires of his own. When the elephant really wants to do something, I'm no match for him. . . .
>
> The rider is . . . conscious, controlled thought. The elephant, in contrast, is everything else. The elephant includes gut feelings, visceral reactions, emotions, and intuitions.[19]

Reading that, you may conclude the reasoning rider is the most important, most real, or most distinctly human part of you, and the emotional, intuitive elephant is a more external and perhaps less human *thing* with which you're forced to contend. Haidt adamantly rejects that split: "Because we can only see one little corner of the mind's vast operations, we are surprised when urges, wishes, and temptations emerge, seemingly from nowhere. We make pronouncements, vows, and resolutions, and then are surprised by our own powerlessness to carry them out. We sometimes fall into the view that we are fighting with our unconscious, our id, or our animal self. But really we are the whole thing. We are the rider, and we are the elephant."[20]

The rider can never dismount and walk away, rejecting the elephant as "terrible and irresistible affections" (or, if you prefer, "deceitful above all things, and desperately wicked"), nor should we try to effect that separation. The elephant isn't stupid, immoral, or a hindrance to careful thinking. Its instincts are a part of cognition and are vital to our ability to choose "the good [we] want to do" (Rom. 7:19).

In fact, neuroscience research has shown that when we suffer physical damage to an elephant part of the brain—the ventromedial prefrontal cortex—we don't become logical and righteous, decisive masters of our sinful passions. Even with their IQ and knowledge of right and wrong intact, patients with that sort of brain damage make poorer decisions or struggle to decide at all, often ending up estranged and unemployable.[21]

Aspiring to that platonic "ideal" is not feasible or wise. And ironically, as Jaggar remarks, "lacking awareness of [one's] own emotional responses frequently results in [one's] being more influenced by emotion rather than less."[22] A rider who doesn't know he's riding an elephant is at the elephant's mercy. He'll use reason or even the Bible to retroactively justify his elephant's path and mistake the result for pure, dispassionate thought. The truth is that when we suppress our emotions, they don't go away. We've merely surrendered the opportunity to regulate them well and submit them to Christ (James 4:7).

Yet, equally, the elephant can't produce reasoned, mature, informed moral conclusions on its own. Rejecting the rider's deliberation, fact-finding, principle, and logic is just as severe a mistake as rejecting the elephant, and it is downright scandalous when Christians indulge in anti-intellectualism.[23] Feelings aren't categorically deceptive, but neither are they always correct. Sometimes our gut instincts are sinful or mistaken. Sometimes our hearts *don't* "truly know what is right." The elephant is necessary for gaining knowledge and assessing truth claims, yet to acknowledge that is no excuse for bucking off the rider. It is no excuse for descending into willful ignorance of facts, disinterest in rigorous reasoning, and, for Christians, failure to diligently study Scripture.

Redeemed Emotion

The divided self of the elephant and the rider, then, is *not* the divided self of Romans 7, as I once assumed. "I do not understand what I do. For what I want to do I do not do, but what I hate I do," Paul writes in verse 15. Why? He's told us, one verse prior, "I am unspiritual, sold as a slave to sin." He continues in this vein through the rest of the chapter:

> Now if I do what I do not want to do, it is no longer I who do it, but it is sin living in me that does it. So I find this law at work: Although I want to do good, evil is right there with me. For in my inner being I delight in God's law; but I see another law at work in me, waging war against the law of my mind and making me a prisoner of the law of sin at work within me. What a wretched man I am! Who will rescue me from this body that is subject to death? Thanks be to God, who delivers me through Jesus Christ our Lord! So then, I myself in my mind am a slave to God's law, but in my sinful nature a slave to the law of sin. (Rom. 7:20–25)

When the apostle laments that he does not do what he wants to do, he isn't expressing dismay over succumbing to his feelings.

He's dismayed over succumbing to sin. And the source of his deliverance isn't his own rationality; it's Christ.

Paul counts his accomplished scholarship as "garbage" compared to "the surpassing worth of knowing Christ Jesus my Lord" (Phil. 3:8). He glories in God's choosing of "the foolish things of the world to shame the wise" (1 Cor. 1:27) and declares himself the "worst" of sinners (1 Tim. 1:15) in need of redemption. He doesn't make an exception to that need for his rational mind or suggest his emotions are the most fallen part of him. If anything, his expression of desire to do God's will ("I want to do good") is evidence of his elephant already turning *against* the temptation to sin. Plato thought that by force of reason a few heroic men could conquer their passions; the gospel message is that the whole of us—any of us, and our elephants included—may be rescued and transformed by Jesus.

"The way I look at it is, Christ is redemptive of our full selves," Christian author and attorney David French, who edits *The Dispatch*, told me in an interview.[24] French noted that he grew up, as I did, in an "environment where emotion in church was viewed as deeply suspicious," and his work as a conservative political commentator has him regularly grappling with the right-wing populist emotionalism typified by figures like Flynn and their fans. I wanted to talk to him about emotion and knowledge because I see in his writing an effort to push back on groundless, emotive claims without veering into naive, self-sabotaging rationalism. "There is a version of your emotions that is fallen, and there's a version that is redeemed," French said. "This is the process of sanctification. I think within the individual Christian, this idea that you might put to death your emotions in favor of your reason is (A) fiction. You're never going to be able to do that. And (B) it doesn't really speak to the way Christ wants you to live your life in full."

Indeed, when the Bible speaks of "put[ting] to death . . . whatever belongs to your earthly nature," the contents of that "whatever" category aren't our emotions and all the other sub-conscious parts of cognition the elephant includes (Col. 3:5; see also Rom. 8:13) but our sins—all the ways we haven't loved God with our whole hearts and our neighbors as ourselves. God made our emotions as surely as he made our logical minds, and both are essential to the outworking of our faith. Neither the *imago Dei* nor the effects of the fall are confined to one or the other. To condemn our feelings as nothing but a capricious source of deception doesn't move us into greater faithfulness. It is to engage in pagan disrespect for creation that God declared good.

Feeling Convinced

If we see that emotions are a useful gift from God that en-hance and complement our reason, then we can also see that, used well, emotion is a valuable tool of persuasion we can't afford to lose when truth is in question and trust on the decline. Ceding emotion to liars, performers, and trolls would be a gross strategic error. Stories that stir our emotions can get through defenses facts can't pass.[25] They can shift the elephant—or at least make the elephant open to shifting in response to new information or argument.

"[Haidt] says, 'If you move the elephant, the rider can't help but come along.' I think that's a really great way of phrasing persuasion," French mused in our conversation. "The open mind flows from the open heart," which means opening hearts is "our fundamental persuasive challenge." In addition,

> If you look at a lot of the great political communicators of the past, you can see how they moved the elephant and how they communicated so powerfully to the heart. One of the down-sides of—and I say this knowing full well that we have a very robust fact-checking operation at *The Dispatch*—but one of the downsides of this sort of fact-check culture of, "You've got a

bad idea. Look. I'm going to tweet or text you this article that's going to change your mind," is we just have ended up aiming all of our fire at the rider.

In chapter 4, I quoted sociologist Zeynep Tufekci, who says "belonging is stronger than facts," to explain why positive experiences of community in conspiracism can make people open to preposterous, baseless ideas.[26] That's true because belonging is a feeling. The rider cares about facts, but deciding whether the rider feels like she belongs is up to the elephant. If the elephant feels embraced, the rider is likely to be persuaded to come along without objection.

Appealing to the elephant is a necessity if we want that part of people to move, and it isn't inherently manipulative. Emotional manipulation is misuse of feelings to distract people from noticing lies, lack of evidence, or invalid logical leaps. But emotional appeal is a legitimate means of persuasion when it is marshaled in support of truth, strong evidence, and valid logic. It helps us come to right beliefs and choices.

The redemption of emotion that can happen in us as individuals can and "should apply to institutions as well, and to populations," French said. "I think that there is a way in which you can stir emotion to do great good. The emotional appeal is a tool like many tools, but it's one that can have great redemptive purpose to make you *want* to do justice, to make you *want* to love mercy, to refer to Micah 6:8."

The dominant emotions in our political lives right now are rage, fear, and resentment. We're often preoccupied with how we have been (or will be) wronged, who has wronged us, and how they may be punished. Experts are among our betrayers; conspiracism purports to predict the coming wrongs; online mobs vent punitive spleen; and in media there's nothing like a sensational revelation of wrongdoing against the audience to draw eyeballs and shares. The rider alone is no match for all this epistemic mayhem. The elephant must be recruited to help.

Feelings Come and Feelings Go

Feelings are an important part of us that God created, united with our reason, made subject to redemption, and wants us to use to his good ends. But feelings are transient. They can be difficult to handle rightly, and dangerous to ourselves and others if disordered or disconnected from reality. They shouldn't be given free rein to rampage through our thinking any more than an elephant should be permitted to wander around the neighborhood. Sometimes feelings don't comport with reality. Sometimes you may want something very badly, like an election victory, and the strength of your emotions may incline you to disregard the facts and disbelieve the truth. Sometimes, as Luther knew, feelings may mislead you about as reliable a reality as the love of God, and your reason may be unable to overcome them.

Luther's advice was to check our feelings against the standard of Scripture. Of course, this is wise. But notice the context in which he gave his table talk: over a meal, among family and fellow scholars, within the community of the church. Joining in the rhythms of communal life and worship help us to know and be known, to come to want as we should, to belong to God and one another.[27] And that belonging is a powerful elephant call able to draw us toward truth, to redirect a wayward elephant or steady it when the rider needs a rest. Instead of a single rider tussling with a single elephant, in church we have a tribe of riders and a herd of elephants who, together, learn where we have been, where we are going, and who we are in Christ.

Who we are and where we've been are central to our next chapter too, in which we'll examine our culture's growing fixation on identity and lived experience.

Experience

There are many social-media-savvy people who are choking on sanctimony. . . . People who depend on obfuscation, who have no compassion for anybody genuinely curious or confused. Ask them a question and you are told that the answer is to repeat a mantra. Ask again for clarity and be accused of violence.

—Chimamanda Ngozi Adichie, "It Is Obscene"

Journalist Katie Herzog used to live in Seattle. That changed after she reported a story for a local paper in 2017 that broached the subject of detransitioners, "people who have transitioned to a different gender and then later transitioned back." As Herzog acknowledged in the second paragraph of the piece, this is "a contentious debate both in and outside the trans community, with various sides accusing each other of bigotry, harassment, censorship, and damaging the fight for trans rights."[1] It's so contentious, in fact, that many of Herzog's sources requested anonymity, and some people she approached for interviews refused to speak on the record at all.

It doesn't seem to have seriously occurred to Herzog, however, that *she* would get blowback for her report, which carefully explained how little research there is on the phenomenon of detransition, centered the voices of detransitioners, included arguments from trans activists who believe detransitioning is a "myth" propagated by "charlatans" and transphobes, and was reviewed by two trans sensitivity readers before publication, both of whom responded positively.[2] One of Herzog's interviewees, author and bioethicist Alice Dreger, told her, "You're going to get slaughtered for this," Dreger recalled to the *New York Times* two years later. "She just laughed," Dreger said, but after the story was published, the warning proved wise.[3]

That report "is, by far, the most-read thing I've ever written," Herzog said in the *Times* story, and it made her "wildly reviled" in Seattle, wary of introducing herself to strangers. Dozens of friends jilted her. Stickers began appearing around the city, slapped onto parking meters: "Katie Herzog (writer at *The Stranger*) is a transphobe," they declared.

Some critics called her a neo-Nazi.[4] Others came after her with anti-Semitic attacks, though she isn't Jewish. Flyers denouncing her went up in local coffee shops, and Herzog "found herself newly unwelcome in queer spaces." Meanwhile, her editors and trans friends stood by the article, which amid the uproar went through another round of fact-checking without requiring any corrections.[5] Eventually, worn down by the harassment, Herzog and her now-wife moved out of Seattle.

Herzog thought she was doing exactly what journalists are supposed to do: tell stories, examine data, explore competing arguments in an important debate so her readers could be better informed. Not only that, but she was doing local journalism, profiling a detransitioned young adult in the Seattle area and including local healthcare providers among her sources. Other journalists had fact-checked and edited her article before it went to print.

But to her detractors, all of that was irrelevant. "When I wrote this piece on detransition," Herzog told me in an interview over the phone, "the main complaint about the piece had nothing to do with the content of the piece. It was that I wasn't trans."[6] As one critic charged, the story "was written by a cis [i.e., not trans] woman without the knowledge and language necessary to responsibly report on the subject in a way that would not feed into the narrative of anti-trans bigots."[7]

The objection wasn't her reporting. It was her identity.

The Identity Assumption

That pushback Herzog encountered—that insistence, in her words, that journalists "should only be reporting on our own communities," which in her case would be "38-year-old lesbians from North Carolina, a pretty boring group"—is but one outworking of a larger assumption about identity and personal experience that's changing the rules of our public conversations, and not for the better. Though this thinking cloaks itself in sympathetic, humanitarian language, it functions to block the pursuit of truth and stifle good-faith conversation. It is adding to our epistemic crisis.

The gist of the assumption is this: if you don't have a given identity or experience (or "lived experience," a phrase intended to communicate that not only did the thing happen to you, but you've since reflected on what it meant), your understanding of related issues is fundamentally limited—maybe totally precluded.

Once you accept that premise, the logical conclusion is twofold. First, people of different identities or experiences are significantly unable to comprehend one another or communicate truth to one another. And second, people who can't claim a given identity or experience must, because of their insurmountable epistemic limitation, defer to those who can. The result, Herzog said, is that your lived experiences or "the color of your skin, or your sex or gender, or whatever, take precedent and are used as a trump card to shut everybody else up."

In this chapter, we'll look at how that assumption works before examining the place of identity and personal history in gaining and sharing knowledge. And we'll consider what to make of the identity assumption as Christians—that is, as part of a people of God that includes "persons from every tribe and language and people and nation" (Rev. 5:9).

Identitarian Deference

Our culture's attention to identity has increased exponentially in recent years, particularly around race and gender. For many of us, this isn't the result of a conscious process of changing our minds. The rider, to repeat chapter 6's metaphor, may not have steered in a new direction, but the elephant has certainly moved. Identity is given a position of honor in our search for truth, sometimes at the expense of free inquiry and good-faith conversation among people with differing experiences, beliefs, and expertise.[8]

In 2013, many of us had not yet noticed this shift. But that was the year Matt Bruenig, a commentator and founder of the democratic socialist think tank People's Policy Project, coined a term for it: "identitarian deference." He defines it as "the idea that privileged individuals should defer to the opinions and views of oppressed individuals, especially on topics relevant to those individuals' oppression."[9]

This isn't as straightforward as it may seem. For example, how do you identify who's oppressed? Identitarian deference (ID) *alone* can't answer that. "On its face, ID would demand that you look to oppressed people to tell you who oppressed people are," Bruenig says. "But to do this, you still have to first know who the oppressed people are." He continues:

To escape this impossible circularity . . . you must have your own independent theory of who is oppressed in order to even practice ID. But where do you get this antecedent theory? You'd have to somehow arrive at it on your own, through reflection, treatises on justice, morality, and so on. Wherever you get it, you necessarily get it in some way that does not involve ID. As such, the only way to get ID off the ground is to have some other understanding of oppression that is totally separate from it.

That then raises the question of what ID adds to the picture. To practice ID, you already must have a detailed theory of what makes someone oppressed. But if you already have a detailed theory of what makes someone oppressed, then what do you need ID for?[10]

The trouble doesn't stop there. After you decide which identities deserve deference, next you have to deal with the fact that people within those groups are rarely monolithic in their thinking. Having the same identity doesn't mean having the same beliefs. Some of the angriest denouncements of Herzog's article came from trans people, but other trans people "were invited to read the piece and give their feedback" before it went live, and they were "entirely supportive."[11] We can't equally defer to both camps.

Perhaps the most common solution to this dilemma is deference to the (real or perceived) majority view among the group in question. This too has problems. What if it's a bare majority of 51 percent? Do you dismiss 49 percent of the group? Or what if there's no majority view because there are more than two sides of the question at hand? Is a plurality good enough? Now you're dismissing the majority. Or what if the majority view changes over time? Is the newest view always the best, or is the oldest and best-established? Or what if the majority view differs from one city, state, or nation to the next? How do we draw epistemic boundaries on a territorial map?

The way most people who practice ID actually choose to whom they'll defer, Bruenig concludes, is "just cherry-picking voices [they] like." They independently decide what they believe, find a person with the relevant identity who agrees, and then retroactively describe their existing beliefs as deference to that person. "This works as a way of resolving disputes," Bruenig notes, "but only by gutting the whole point of ID."[12]

Meanwhile, for those with an identity that can win them deference, the temptation is obvious: to use it to direct, manipulate, or outright end debate. Sometimes this is well intentioned—and maybe conflicted too. Herzog acknowledges she sometimes plays by ID rules, for all her dislike of the game.

"I weaponize [my identity] in my own way, even though I also hate [ID]. I think there are things that I can say as a woman that I almost have an obligation to say," she said, citing as a case in point the debate around due process for those accused of sexual misconduct. When #MeToo stories dominated the headlines, "I felt like I had a superpower—and also an obligation—to say something" about the importance of due process, Herzog explained, "because I'm allowed to comment on this. I'm allowed to talk about sexism and gender and sexual assault and false allegations because I'm a woman. . . . I can always say like, As a lesbian . . . , As a queer woman . . ." and anticipate a reception a straight man making the same argument wouldn't receive.

"ID is so easy to game in this way," Bruenig said in a reflection on his terminology seven years after its introduction. "If what you say receives deference because of what identities you have, then you can use that deference to demand anything that you like no matter how silly or calculated it is."[13] If anyone objects, you can reiterate that they should defer to you because of your identity. If they still object, you can tout it as proof of their unfixable ignorance (if not malevolence).[14] The logic of ID says the reason they aren't deferring is that they don't understand, and they don't understand because they *can't* understand, and they can't understand—not now, not ever—because they don't share your identity. Lack of deference "proves" deference is the only way.

In conversation with someone willing to exploit ID to manipulative or stifling ends, there's no room for "compassion for anybody genuinely curious or confused," as the celebrated Nigerian writer Chimamanda Ngozi Adichie has observed. "Ask them a question and you are told that the answer is to repeat a mantra. Ask again for clarity and be accused of violence."[15] Refusing to defer is itself oppression.

As long as ID is an option, Bruenig reasons, "people will take advantage of it [this way]. And honestly, who can blame them? If we create a button that, when pressed, magically requires everyone else to agree with your ideas and demands, people would be foolish not to press it."[16] The system is self-perpetuating, and, whether sincere or cynical, it's an epistemic mess.

ID in the Wild

None of this has precluded ID's spread. In chapter 1, I shared a brief quote from Columbia University political scientist Mark Lilla, whose description of ID as he encounters it on campus is worth excerpting here at greater length.

> Over the past decade a new, and very revealing, locution has drifted from our universities into the mainstream media: *Speaking as an X* . . . This is not an anodyne phrase. It tells the listener that I am speaking from a privileged position on this matter. (One never says, *Speaking as a gay Asian, I feel incompetent to judge this matter.*) It sets up a wall against questions, which by definition come from a *non-X* perspective. And it turns the encounter into a power relation: The winner of the argument will be whoever has invoked the morally superior identity and expressed the most outrage at being questioned.

So classroom discussions that might once have begun, *I think
A, and here is my argument*, now take the form, *Speaking as an
X, I am offended that you claim B*. This makes perfect sense if
you believe that identity determines everything. It means there
is no impartial space for dialogue. White men have one "epistemology," black women have another. So what remains to be
said? What replaces argument, then, is taboo.[17]

Lilla's book was published in 2017, so (factoring in his publication timeline) the decade he references is 2006 to 2016. I
started college at the beginning of that span, and I can't recall
"Speaking as an X" ever sounding in my classrooms. Granted,
my school was tiny, rural, and politically somewhere between
moderate and apathetic. We weren't anywhere near the cutting
edge of campus culture.

Still, I was a political-science major and never shy about
airing my opinions, many of which put me in debate with professors and fellow students. If we ever cited our identities in
conversation, it was with reference to our chosen ideological
alignments—something like, "If a libertarian like me thinks
this government program is necessary . . ." If we mentioned our
lived experience, it was to give emotional depth and personal
context to more abstract arguments—a way to put flesh to data,
not to deny data's necessity.[18]

When I first noticed demands of ID, often in the university context Lilla depicts, I thought back to my own college
experience—which was still recent, and basically ID-free—and
figured ID was a passing campus fad. Five years beyond Lilla's
decade, however, it's clear I was wrong. Instead of sprouting
and withering on the quad, ID has spread beyond the walls
of academia and into general discourse. Those notions—of
forever-separate epistemologies, impassable communication
boundaries, and arguments won by declaration of identity or

claim of outrage—are now widespread, especially (though not exclusively) on the left.

"I used to read the *New York Times* every week," Herzog said in our interview. "And I would always read the letters [to the editor], and there was this formula for the letters. They would start, like, *As a doctor, here's my expertise to tell you about this story.* And then that has shifted from, *As a doctor . . . , As a teacher . . . , As someone who does something . . .* It has shifted to, *As an X, Y . . . , As a black person . . . , As a white person . . . , As a woman . . . , As a trans person . . . ,* or whatever." Identitarian deference is off campus and proliferating in the wild, supplanting persuasion and the wisdom of expertise with assertions of power.[19]

A Middle Way?

Of course, to demand that we speak as automatons—that we imagine ourselves like brains in vats, uninfluenced by our identities and experiences—is an assertion of power too, and no more defensible than the one made by calculating practitioners of ID.

For Christians, both options are too small. Neither has space for the *whole* of our selves as new creations in Christ: embodied, with a given identity and personal history, but "children of God through faith" as well, no longer separated from one another by race, status, or sex (Gal. 3:26–28). We should be dissatisfied alike, in theologian N. T. Wright's phrase, with "the modern idea that we're all identical [and] the postmodern idea, which collapses into dozens of different competing identities each trying to claim the high ground of the victim."[20] We need a middle way that preserves free debate, makes constructive use of our identities and personal experiences in conversation, and pushes back on epistemic crisis with a "ministry of reconciliation" (2 Cor. 5:18).

Preserving Free Debate

Discovery of knowledge in a free society runs on two rules, argues journalist Jonathan Rauch in his essential 1993 book, *Kindly Inquisitors*:

1. *No one gets the final say:* You may claim that a statement is established as [public] knowledge only if it can be debunked, in principle, and only insofar as it withstands attempts to debunk it.
2. *No one has personal authority:* You may claim that a statement has been established as knowledge only insofar as the method used to check it gives the same result regardless of the identity of the checker, and regardless of the source of the statement.[21]

Identitarian deference runs afoul of both rules. It tries to settle disagreement without doing the hard work of checking and persuasion, and the means by which it seizes the final say is an assertion of personal authority based in a deference-worthy identity or experience. Identitarian deference isn't an argument. It's a cudgel. It makes free debate impossible by walling us off from one another and shutting down even sincere and irenic inquiry when it comes from the "wrong" person. This is counterproductive and unreasonable. It's also shortsighted and naive; if we introduce the magical ID button, what makes us think it will only ever be claimed and used by people we like?

The idea that some people are inherently more capable of knowledge is not new. Underneath ID's progressive mask is "anti-intellectualism at its most rancid," Rauch warns, nothing more than "the age-old tribalist notion that . . . 'we think with our blood,' 'with our national heritage,' or 'with our class.'" Admit that monster to our public square, and it brings along a whole herd of horrors, all denying "that knowledge is available to everyone and comes through public inquiry and criticism, not from the color of your skin or your ethnic heritage or your social class."[22] Identitarian deference proponents might imagine themselves freed from this risk—safeguarded by humanity's forward momentum—but history sometimes swerves. Power often lands in unprogressive hands. Who will hold the button then?

Identitarian deference's strictures can all too easily be used to add oppression instead of undoing it, while the rules of free debate require integrity and protect open inquiry no matter who's in charge. As I am forever warning in my writing on partisan politics, your side may be ascendant now, but you will not always be in control. Make rules for the day you are defeated.

Speaking Humbly as an X

Rauch is careful to distinguish, as Herzog did in her story about the *New York Times* letters, between personal authority and earned authority (which often takes the form of expertise).[23] "Speaking as a veterinarian, here's what you should do about your dog's ringworm" is not in the same category as "Speaking as a woman, here's what I think about cable news." Yet my critique of cable news as a woman might legitimately be different from a critique by a man whose thinking is otherwise quite similar to mine. Watching the same cable segment, we might notice different things or ask different questions because of our different personal histories. My experience as a woman in media could help me spot some sexist detail my co-watcher doesn't notice. Or, as a man, he might have an insight I don't about a male pundit's behavior.

Rejecting ID doesn't mean rejecting those questions and insights. It means using them to open new lines of exploration and communication instead of using them to estrange, isolate, or mute. It means allowing our unique perspectives to extend the conversation, not to end it.[24]

A thinker I've found helpful in making that distinction is Esau McCaulley, a New Testament scholar, pastor, and the author of *Reading While Black: African American Biblical Interpretation as an Exercise in Hope*. McCaulley's book comes in part from his experiences in mostly white academic contexts where, he writes, he "read biblical commentaries that displayed little concern for how biblical texts speak to the experiences of Black believers." He had questions it seemed no one was bothering to ask of Scripture and insights that seemed to have no home in his field of biblical interpretation.[25]

McCaulley doesn't respond to those frustrations with a demand for ID or a claim that he understood things that white Christians could never grasp. On the contrary, his book aims to bring the riches of black Christians' perspective to the rest of the church, adding insight to insight and question to question in a "unified mission in which our varied cultures turn to the text in dialogue with one another to discern the mind of Christ."[26] McCaulley elaborated on this call to mutual learning and humility in a podcast interview about *Reading While Black*:

> I don't think that [black] Christianity is closed off, that the black experience of Christianity is so unique that *only* black people can get it. Insomuch as we have this common object of worship, and we're reading these same [biblical] texts, there are parts where, I think—because black Christians aren't just telling a "black truth"; they're telling *the* truth—that anyone that's on the side of the truth can follow along and say, "Oh, yeah, I find myself agreeing with this." . . . I don't think that anybody can read Scripture alone. I don't think black people can read Scripture alone. I think in God's providence we need one another to properly discern the mind of Christ. . . . Truth emerges from considering things from a variety of angles.[27]

That last line deserves a closer look. McCaulley isn't suggesting that there are different truths for different people or that some people can't access some truth. (Later in the podcast he explicitly cautions against letting our experiences and identities "eclipse the [biblical] text," and he rejects the idea that "it's impossible for someone who hasn't experienced oppression to read the Bible properly.") No, McCaulley is simply saying we need one another to perceive angles on reality we'd miss on our own.

Just as different giftings of the Holy Spirit work together to build up the church, so our different identities and experiences in the body of Christ work together to help us discover knowledge and reveal truth in Scripture and in the world at large (1 Cor. 12:12–31). "The eye cannot say to the hand, 'I don't need you!' And the head cannot say to the feet, 'I don't need you!'" (v. 21). We need people with different perspectives—not only to answer questions we can't but also to ask questions we've never conceived. Recognizing the value in "a variety of angles" isn't capitulation to moral relativism or ID. It's an honest acknowledgment that none of us individually has a God's-eye view.

In practice, the middle way McCaulley charts here may still sometimes find us saying "Speaking as an X"—but the phrase will no longer divide and silence others. Sometimes we might say it to explain the origin of a question we're the first to pose. Sometimes we might say it (as Lilla reports no one in his classroom ever does) to admit our own ignorance or confusion: "Speaking as an X, I feel incompetent to judge this matter. Can you help me?" Sometimes we might say it to introduce a personal story, knowing our experience may be widely resonant—or that it could be a strange exception to what the best available data shows to be the rule.

However we say it—if we say it—"Speaking as an X" should be an exercise in humility and intellectual integrity. It must never be a power play to shutter debate, not on our own behalf or for someone cherry-picking voices to serve their views. Some white Christians are "just saying, 'I'm gonna find a black voice, and I'm gonna amplify it,'" McCaulley says, decrying exactly the habit Bruenig described. "That's paternalistic," McCaulley adds. "Black scholars deserve . . . real analysis. People say they appreciate my voice. I'm like, 'No, appreciate my scholarship. I'm exegeting text here. I'm doing real work, and it deserves to be taken seriously.'"[28] It deserves to persuade not because McCaulley is black but because, with research interests informed by who he is and what he's experienced, he's doing good work to show the church a new angle of God's truth.

A Ministry of Epistemic Reconciliation

A word about that truth is the foundation of my final comment here. God doesn't tell us everything he knows—"now we see only a reflection as in a mirror" (1 Cor. 13:12)—but he is not a God of obfuscation and epistemic muddle.

"This is what the LORD says," the prophet Isaiah records: "'I am the LORD, and there is no other. I have not spoken in secret, from somewhere in a land of darkness; I have not said to Jacob's descendants, "Seek me in vain."'" (Isa. 45:18–19). A God like this would not (and did not!) make a world of people unable to comprehend and communicate truth to one another. Indeed, in the verses that follow, God gives Isaiah a message for the "ignorant" and invites them to "take counsel together" to discuss what they've heard and to then turn to God for salvation (vv. 20–25). This makes sense only if it's at least possible for Isaiah, an Israelite, to communicate God's message to "the nations" (v. 20) and for them to learn and change course as a result.

We're often ignorant of truth, and we often fail to comprehend it when given a glimpse. But God didn't call us to knowledge of reality in an unintelligible world or command us to unity in Christ across impassable identitarian boundaries. If white men have one epistemology and black women another, and the twain can never meet, the whole New Testament vision of humanity redeemed and made one in Jesus is undone.

Our faith does not erase our particulars. When God's kingdom is fully realized, "persons from every tribe and language and people and nation" will still be identifiably themselves (Rev. 5:9). But if our differences of identity and experience are barriers rather than complements, I fail to see how the church can function. How can we disciple, serve, love, and learn from people whose lives and thinking we can never understand?

In three letters to predominantly gentile churches, the apostle Paul, a "Hebrew of Hebrews" (Phil. 3:5), speaks of reconciliation. Without Christ, he says, we were "alienated from God" (Col. 1:19–22) and "without hope and without God in the world" (Eph. 2:12). We were hostile toward one another, divided by a "barrier" of ethnic and religious difference, but with Christ, that barrier is "destroyed" (Eph. 2:14–18). We are reconciled to God and tasked with sharing the "message of reconciliation" in a "ministry of reconciliation" (2 Cor. 5:16–19).

It is a ministry, I submit, that extends to epistemic reconciliation. It includes the proclamation that truth is knowable for all, that our identities do not keep us from conversation, that persuasion is possible. And to begin that work, we'll now turn from diagnoses of epistemic crisis to epistemology proper.

A Practical Epistemology

Creator of all things,
true source of light and wisdom,
lofty origin of all being,
graciously let a ray of your brilliance
penetrate into the darkness of my understanding
and take from me the double darkness
in which I have been born,
an obscurity of both sin and ignorance.
Give me a sharp sense of understanding,
a retentive memory,
and the ability to grasp things correctly and
    fundamentally.
Grant me the talent of being exact in my
    explanations,
and the ability to express myself with thoroughness
    and charm.
Point out the beginning,
direct the progress,
and help in completion;
through Christ our Lord, amen.

      —Thomas Aquinas, "A Prayer for Students"

Each morning while writing this book, I've started my work by saying this prayer. It's a modern translation of a composition by the great Catholic theologian and philosopher Thomas Aquinas, which he prayed before studying, writing, and preaching.[1] I adopted the practice for two reasons.

First, it's so clearly a writer's prayer, and across eight centuries it resonates still as the plea of a master of my craft. Exactitude, thoroughness, charm—these are always the persuasive writer's goal, just as sin, ignorance, forgetfulness, and confusion are ever the enemy.

But second, I hoped the prayer would help to form in me the virtues it models: humility and love of truth. Prayer like this is not "primarily . . . a means of self-expression or an individual conversation with the divine," as author and Anglican priest Tish Harrison Warren explains, but "an inherited way of approaching God, a way to wade into the ongoing stream of the church's communion with him." It is a way to access "a reality . . . larger and more enduring than what [we feel] in the moment," something that "shapes us," that "works back on us to change who we are and what we believe. Patterns of prayer draw us out of ourselves, out of our time-bound moment, into the long story of Christ's work in and through his people over time."[2]

If I'm honest, I must admit there were mornings when my recitation of Aquinas's words had something of the quality of a magical incantation, or payment of a toll to drive the road I wanted, or mechanistic compliance with the instructions of a recipe so the cake would come out right. Do the good thing, get the good results.

But in my better moments—in the moment I chose to build this habit and the moments I determined to continue it though it felt, right then, inconvenient and unnecessary and maybe a bit silly—my intention was not about the flow of any one day or the construction of any one argument. It was about what sort of person I wanted to be. It was an exclamation, aided by the faithfulness of a man who died more than seven hundred years before I was born, that I do believe but need help for my unbelief (Mark 9:24). It was a commitment too, to practice what I'm preaching, in this chapter most of all.

An Epistemology of One's Own

At the start of chapter 1, I argued that our ignorance of epistemology is what got us into our present epistemic mess. We've spent forty years dramatically increasing how much information the average person encounters daily, and we've made no effort to equip ourselves to handle that shift. The previous seven chapters have explored the consequences of that error (and some issue-specific ways for Christians to respond). Now we'll more broadly explore its correction.

In some times and places, you might not need to think consciously about epistemology. Ours is not one of those contexts, nor is there any sign it will become one in our lifetimes. Absent some catastrophic change in our society, our information environment is unlikely to become any calmer or more manageable. The confusion may ebb and flow, improve here, worsen there, but I'm not optimistic that we'll find large-scale fixes for our epistemic crisis. I don't think we'll solve our knowledge woes by tweaking Twitter's content-moderation algorithms or forcing cable news to comply with equal-time regulations or firing experts who get things wrong.

Debates around policy, whether legal or corporate, have their place and value. But they can't and won't get us out of this mess, because the problems that policy might conceivably address are less the cause of the crisis than its symptoms. The real cause is deeper than bad tweets or sensationalist news or expert mistakes and the like. It's in our own thinking, our own behavior, our own vice. "The problem isn't that there are liars," as author Freddie deBoer argues, for "there will always be liars. The problem is that people believe them." Whatever policy progress we can make, we'll never be free of deception, ignorance, error, and confusion in this age, but, as deBoer adds, "you can produce a populace wise and caring enough to reject them. . . . It has to start with the believers, not with the belief."[3]

The resolution of an epistemic crisis requires epistemology. It requires understanding not only that we've believed untrue things but also why they made sense to us and where we went wrong. It requires epistemological self-awareness: noticing how we gain knowledge and form beliefs, observing whether that process is prone to error, and considering how it might be improved. It requires, in the words of the philosopher Alasdair MacIntyre, recognition that our new understanding, just like the old one, might "come to be put in question at any time"[4]— that perhaps we've polished the mirror a bit, but it's still quite dim (1 Cor. 13:12). The aim of this chapter and the next is learning how to polish it habitually.

Stay Practical (or Not)

Suppose you are driving in your car and see a barn. You now have knowledge of that barn, right? At least enough to say, "I know there's a barn over there."

But suppose what you don't know that is you're in a weird pocket of Pennsylvania countryside known as Fake Barn Country, where the locals get a laugh out of building fake barn facades to trick strangers on the highway into believing they have seen a barn. So maybe you don't have knowledge after all; maybe you were wrong to believe you saw a barn.

But then suppose that what you saw actually *was* a barn, the one real barn in all of Fake Barn Country. Still, you had no way of knowing it was real—and good reason to believe it wasn't, given that any other "barn" you could have seen for miles around would have been fake. Supposing all that, do you really *know* about the barn?[5]

This is the sort of story that preoccupies a lot of modern epistemology.[6] And it's . . . fine, I guess. Maybe it's interesting for some. Frankly, I mostly find it tedious, but I concede that teasing out the precise boundaries of knowledge is a perfectly appropriate topic for academic scrutiny. Nevertheless, a puzzle like this isn't directly helpful when you're arguing with a co-worker about QAnon or unsure if you should trust a news outlet or wondering whether there's any truth to the angry, pixelated meme your aunt just posted on Facebook.

Perhaps you're interested in academic epistemology. Do you want to be able to explain the difference between skepticism, rationalism, and empiricism? Or the difference between foundationalism, coherentism, and reliabilism, or between the epistemic thought of Socrates, René Descartes, John Locke, and Michel Foucault? Do you want to explore whether you can be certain you're not dreaming, living in a false reality like that depicted in *The Matrix*, or being constantly deceived by a powerful demon? Great! All of that is worth knowing. Studying the history and current state of epistemological debate can only improve your intellectual rigor and advance your pursuit of truth. (Turn to the endnote attached to the end of this sentence to see what each of those references means, and check other notes nearby for a few books to get you started if you want to learn more.[7])

But that's not the *practical* epistemology I want to share here. What's useful for our purposes, I think, is threefold: first, a few definitions;[8] second, a look at the limits of our ability to know and the humility these limits should generate within us; and third, an inquiry into the intellectual virtues we need "to grasp things correctly and fundamentally."

Definitions

One of the questions I used to introduce the subject of epistemology in chapter 1 was the following: What's the difference between knowledge, opinion, and conjecture? Now I'll finally answer that—and a little more—just to make sure we're on the same page as we talk about epistemic humility and virtue (in this chapter) and the kind of individual (chap. 9) and community (chap. 10) behavior they should produce.

Let's start with truth. Truth is that which accords with reality. We judge a statement true if it corresponds with what we find in reality, whether via sensory or empirical experience, abstract reasoning, the testimony of others, or divine revelation.

Next, knowledge. The classic definition is "justified true belief." It's your acceptance of a statement (belief) based on some evidence (justification) that it accords with reality (is true). You can't have knowledge of something untrue; you can believe it, but you can't *know* it. It's important to note that "justified" is perhaps the trickiest and most-debated piece of this definition. In the barn story, for example, the justification is the part in question.

Opinions are basically beliefs, and they differ from knowledge in that they may or may not be true and may or may not be justified. Conjecture is similar: it's an opinion whose justification is still in doubt or perhaps in process. A conjecture may be on its way from opinion to knowledge, or it may be falsified or simply left uncertain.

Finally, a fact is a piece of verified, true information. It's like knowledge, but not quite the same. A fact is something external to you, while knowledge requires a knower. Facts go in books; knowledge goes in minds.

A Commonsense Humility

Unfortunately, getting knowledge into minds isn't always a straightforward process. If the first seven chapters have demonstrated anything, it should be the fallibility and sinfulness of human thought and public discourse. We are not creatures of pure reason. We mistake opinions for knowledge and anecdotes for data. Too often we are unwittingly ignorant and unjustifiably confident—or we may despair of knowing truth, and occupy ourselves with trolling, tribalism, or empty entertainment. Rather than cultivating humility, we ascend to arrogance or fall into discouraged apathy.

In the eschaton, when Christ returns and dwells among us, when God rights all wrongs and makes all things new, we will know the truth in full. Knowledge, in fact, is a crucial part of God's promises to his people. When God's kingdom is realized, "no longer" will we "say to one another, 'Know the LORD,'" as God said through the prophet Jeremiah, "because [we] will all know [God], from the least of [us] to the greatest" (31:34). The reason God gives Isaiah the vision of the wolf lying down with the lamb (11:6)—peace reigning through the whole of creation—is that "the earth will be filled with the knowledge of the Lord" (11:9). "Then I shall know fully," writes Paul, "even as I am fully known" (1 Cor. 13:12).

But now—well, now we know in part, and often a smaller part than we imagine. Yet we *can* know some things, and we have a responsibility to seek to know aright. Here are a few distinctions I find helpful to that end.

Objective Truth Exists, but Humans Aren't Objective

In chapter 2, discussing the objectivity debate within journalism, I argued reporters should work to be accurate and transparent instead of aiming for objectivity. That's not because I reject objective truth; it's because I don't believe journalists are inhuman or that our brains escaped the effects of the fall.

The same is true of everyone. People are not objective. Our understanding of reality is tinted by our assumptions and biases, our culture and community, even by something as mundane as whether the last meal we ate is sitting well in our stomachs.[9] (Sometimes to be human is horribly embarrassing.)

We can be trustworthy, conscientious, truthful, wise, and fair. But, as biblical scholars E. Randolph Richards and Brandon J. O'Brien write in *Misreading Scripture with Western Eyes*, "There's no way around the fact that our cultural and historical contexts supply us with habits of mind that lead us to read the Bible differently than Christians in other cultural and historical contexts," and the same is true of everything we read—and write and say.[10] To admit our understanding of truth is influenced by our perspective is not to deny that objective truth exists or that we can come to know it. It isn't relativism or subjectivism. It's a humble recognition of our limits as humans who do not yet "know fully," who still must say to one another, "Know the Lord."

Truth Is Knowable, but That Doesn't Mean You Know It

There's a single-panel cartoon that's been floating around Christian corners of the internet for a decade. You may well have seen it. It's a simple stick figure sketch of a church membership class, and charted on the wall is the many-branched tree of Christian history. Schism after schism, split after split, it moves from unity at the start to helter-skelter disagreement in the present. The teacher points to a tiny twig of recent sprout and happily announces, "So this is where our movement came along and finally got the Bible right." One of the attendees replies, "Jesus is so lucky to have us."[11]

I mention that cartoon regularly because it encapsulates the tension of this second distinction. As Christians, we believe truth not only exists but is also knowable for us, here and now, despite our sin and finitude. But at any given moment, in any given belief, you may think you know the truth and be dead wrong. That can be difficult to remember, especially when our theology is concerned, but the cartoon always reminds me of how improbable—not *impossible*, but *improbable*—it is that I am one of a tiny handful of Christians across the whole sweep of history and around the world today who just happened to get everything exactly right.

I mean, I *hope* I have everything right. Obviously, I believe my beliefs are true, because if I didn't believe that, I'd believe different beliefs. I have (what I think are) good justifications for my beliefs and would even go so far as to call them knowledge.

But probability is not on my side here. There are a lot of branches on that tree. The church historic and universal numbers in the billions. Is it really *likely* that I—Bonnie Kristian, resident of Pennsylvania in the Year of Our Lord 2022, unable to read Scripture in its original languages, still inadequately informed of church history, on Twitter too much, not 100 percent certain I could steer clear of well-intended heresy if I tried to explain the interrelation of the Trinity off the top of my head, loitering in a mushy middle in my theology of the sacraments (or maybe they're merely ordinances?)—finally drew together all the threads of truth every saint before and around me failed to connect? C'mon.

Alas, the same goes for you. The likelihood is vanishingly small that everything you believe you know is truly true. This is the case for all of us, all the time. To admit this, as with the distinction about objectivity, is not to deny the existence or knowability of truth. It isn't to say we can never trust our senses, reasoning, or memory, or that we can't receive knowledge through revelation or the testimony of other people. It isn't an argument against confidence in our beliefs. It is simply to say that we are fallible and that truth, as the teacher of Ecclesiastes tells us, is often obscure.[12]

This is why the two rules of free debate I shared in the previous chapter (*no final say* and *no personal authority*) are so important; we make truth claims, and we aren't always right, so every claim we make should be subject to others' review and debate.

In college, I had a professor who insisted on conversation under these rules. He said he would talk religion or politics or philosophy or anything with anyone so long as all parties came to the discussion prepared to end it with different beliefs than they had at the start. This scared me, and I demurred. The idea of entering a conversation with my most significant beliefs held in open hands seemed like a bad idea. *Are Christians allowed to do that?* Could I really have a conversation amid the possibility that at its close I'd leave behind my belief in God?

With the advantage of fifteen years, I think my professor was right and my fear was wrong. I've changed my mind partly because I've seen what happens if we toss out these rules. I'm deeply troubled by the illiberal alternatives to free debate proliferating on left and right alike. Abandon the rules of *no final say* and *no personal authority* and you end up with conspiracism and identitarian deference. You end up in an intellectual war of all against all in which knowledge cannot be established and truth is discarded in favor of reckless rumormongering and sectarian sniping. You end up in an epistemic nightmare.

There are risks and hardships in free debate, granted. To adapt what Winston Churchill said of democratic governance, perhaps free debate is the worst form of conversation—except for all the others. It is the system that broke our bloody addiction to creed wars and made way for the explosion of scientific progress that allows us to live in unprecedented wealth and ease. It can feel unsettling, if not dangerous. It is nevertheless an invaluable inheritance we must conserve.

The other reason I've changed my mind is I have more "confidence in what we hope for and assurance about what we do not see" (Heb. 11:1). I have more trust that the Christian story is true, that it reflects and explains reality, and that it accounts for how incredibly broken our world is and how it can be redeemed.

I don't expect claims of faith will go through free debate and come out the other side as established *public* knowledge in a pluralistic world. Their justification won't persuade the way that justification for knowledge of, say, gravity will. But they are justifiable, and I'm no longer afraid of a conversation that examines whether God exists, because I am persuaded I have knowledge of God through the revelation of Jesus Christ (Col. 1:15; Heb. 1:3). I keep missing my college reunions, but I'm shooting for the twentieth, and I'd be ready to finally have that conversation if my professor is still hanging around the same old halls.

Your Perspective Colors Your Understanding, but You Can Still Understand

We can communicate our understanding, though sometimes we may communicate it badly. Our pursuits of knowledge, though different, aren't irreconcilable.

With illiberal epistemologies on the rise, we "must preserve a faith in imperfect, but nevertheless useful, human communication: language as a site where something real, albeit never something total or complete, can be meaningfully conveyed," argues Episcopalian author Tara Isabella Burton. Identitarian deference and assertions justified only by our own emotions are

> susceptible to . . . a kind of relational nihilism—our experiences are so distinct that we can never really understand one another. . . . Yet, in light of a theology predicated on the Word made flesh, we are called to understand, however humbly, conversation and dialogue as meaningful sites of operation. We may not be able to translate, perfectly, ideas into words into ideas, a liberal vision of neutral dialogue, or a public square, but we can nevertheless render ourselves open to the operation of another, through language, onto our own embodied selves.[13]

The development of intellectual virtues is vital to that task. It is virtue that trains our emotions so we can feel as we ought, virtue that gentles the elephant and wisens the rider, and virtue into which we'll now delve.

Epistemic Virtue

Before epistemology centered around skeptical questions like the barn story, it centered on "the pursuit of intellectual virtue," writes philosopher W. Jay Wood in *Epistemology: Becoming Intellectually Virtuous*. This was philosophers' concern, Wood says, "for the simple reason that your very character, the kind of person you are and are becoming, is at stake. Careful oversight of our intellectual lives is imperative if we are to think well, and thinking well is an indispensable ingredient to living well."[14]

Deliberate development of epistemic virtue is not a formulaic thing. It isn't something you can do once and for all. It doesn't guarantee you'll always be right in your beliefs any more than praying the Aquinas prayer ensured me "a sharp sense of understanding" and a clear path to completing my work every day I wrote this book.

Rather, developing these virtues can make you a *characteristically* trustworthy person. It can equip you to discern truth, gain knowledge, and communicate well what you've come to understand.[15] Responsibility in one moment of belief formation will make it ever so slightly more feasible to be responsible in the next.[16] "Whoever can be trusted with very little can also be trusted with much, and whoever is dishonest with very little will also be dishonest with much" (Luke 16:10). All your small decisions accumulate.

Unlike academic epistemology and its parsing of "-isms" and puzzling through stories, development of epistemic virtue isn't optional for us as Christians who live in a chaotic, complex information environment. "God enjoins us in Scripture to pursue the intellectual virtues," Wood contends. "The Bible is unequivocally clear that Christians are to superintend the life of the mind. 'Do not be conformed to this world, but be transformed by the renewing of your minds' (Rom. 12:3). God cares about *how* you think, not just *what* you think. . . . No walk of life is without the need for insight, discretion, and love of truth."[17]

You have a duty here. We all do. We have a duty to forge these virtues in ourselves—to become, with God's help, the sort of people who are trustworthy now and suited for complete knowledge in the age to come.[18] Without epistemic virtue, "we cannot succeed in the moral life," Wood argues, and we will find it difficult to hold onto even the truths we manage to rightly grasp.[19]

Following Wood, I'll outline three epistemic virtues: studiousness, intellectual honesty, and wisdom. Then I'll bring in two further ideas, one from Anglican theologian N. T. Wright and one from the Anabaptist tradition.

Studiousness

To be studious is to seek knowledge and to seek it rightly. In the classical model of virtues as a happy medium between opposing vices, we find it distinct from vicious curiosity, on the one side, and gullibility and obtuseness, on the other. The studious person wants to know truth, but not by *any* means or at *any* cost. She interrogates herself about why she wants to know something and whether her path to learning it is moral. She considers whether she'll use her knowledge to good ends and whether there is some more worthwhile knowledge she should be pursuing instead.[20]

A studious person is both teachable and willing to share what she knows. She "must not be quarrelsome but must be kind to everyone, able to teach, not resentful" (2 Tim. 2:24). She plays by the rules of free debate and is eager to learn in community. She understands, as *Reading While Black* author Esau Mc-Caulley says, that "truth emerges from considering things from a variety of angles."[21] She seeks out trustworthy authorities and experts and gladly recognizes where their understanding exceeds her own.

Studiousness also entails discipline. This means persistence in acquiring knowledge and, equally, a prudently narrowed focus. A studious person realizes her own limits and knows she cannot be well informed about everything. If she follows the news, she chooses a few stories to follow diligently and many more to follow not at all. That discipline of information input is paired with a discipline of output: the studious person is discreet and understands she does not need to comment on everything. She keeps silent when she is ignorant. "The one who has knowledge uses words with restraint, and whoever has understanding is even-tempered" (Prov. 17:27).

Last, the studious person is attentive to others' thinking and confident—not certain—of her own.[22] She actively strengthens her theory of mind: her capacity to understand that other people have different perspectives, values, information, and goals, and that this will affect their reasoning and moves in perhaps unexpected but still intelligible ways. And she remembers that her own perspective, values, information, and goals may be flawed or misshapen in ways she has yet to notice. She'll cultivate habits of trust and faith and build reliably good practices of belief formation, refusing to settle into a brittle certainty with no room for human finitude.

Intellectual Honesty

While studiousness is largely concerned with how we seek knowledge, intellectual honesty is about our response to the truth we find.[23] It stands apart from the vices of intellectual dishonesty, which knows the truth but denies or suppresses it, and willful naivete, which knows the truth is there but refuses to look.

An intellectually honest person is always sincere and deals in good faith, though he may not be able to expect sincerity and good faith in return (Rom. 12:17–21). He isn't cynical, and he doesn't meet serious argument with trolling. When he's wrong, he holds himself accountable, "put[ting] off falsehood and speak[ing] truthfully to [his] neighbor" (Eph. 4:25). He is always on the lookout for ways his own self-interest could be distorting his thinking. He asks whether he believes something because it is well-justified or because he merely wants it to be true. He is forthright when someone criticizes him correctly; he acknowledges their success even if it means announcing his own failure.

Intellectual honesty demands generosity. An intellectually honest person will be gracious with those who are confused and happy to accept apologies from others who have realized they were wrong. He will practice forbearance with those who know less and does not believe explanation is beneath him.

An intellectually honest person is also courageous. Accountability needs courage, but beyond that, he will defend his best understanding of the truth even when it is unpopular. He never dissembles. This does not make him uncivil, but it does require him to be resolute, to refuse to be dishonest even when dishonesty is the path to acceptance.

Wisdom

After gaining and responding well to knowledge, wisdom should determine how we use it. Wisdom is about good judgment and discernment, and it stands in contrast to folly in its many forms. A wise person's life is "marked by deep and abiding meaningfulness, anchored in beliefs and purposes that offer lasting contentment," Wood says. She is interested in knowledge "of ultimate significance—knowledge that explains the most important features of our world, especially as they bear on human happiness."[24]

The wise person is circumspect and prudent. She resists taking offense (yes, this is a choice; cf. Prov. 12:16). She thinks through her decisions (14:8) and can foresee trouble before it comes (27:12). She acts with humility and restraint, recognizing her own weaknesses and accurately appraising the extent of her own knowledge and power. She does not seek conflict, chaos, or pointless and petty argument.

For Christians, wisdom is something we can foster in ourselves but also something we can request from God in prayer, as Aquinas modeled. "We are not alone in our efforts to cultivate life-characterizing concerns and the virtuous emotions and behavior that stem from them," Wood writes. "God is ready to assist us. We can hardly do better than to recall the words of James: 'If any of you lack wisdom, ask God, who gives to all generously and ungrudgingly, and it will be given you' (James 1:5)."[25]

An Epistemology of Love

"The danger with talking about knowledge," N. T. Wright mused when speaking as a panelist at a university event in 2017, "is that it either tries to get to an unattainable objectivity—where I get out of the picture entirely, and I'm simply telling you objectively what is out there, which is actually unattainable—or it collapses into subjectivity, to which somebody can say, 'Well, you only think that because it suits your interests,' [or] that, 'It may be true for you, but it's not true for anyone else.'" He goes on:

> And I want to say that in many philosophical traditions—and certainly in mine—the notion of love transcends that subject-object divide, because when I genuinely love someone or something, I celebrate what it is or what that person is in themselves, but at the same time this is not in my own interests, [because] if it is, then it isn't love. It's simply manipulation of some sort. And I want to say that actually, when you run an epistemology of love—whether it's scientific knowledge, whether it's artistic

knowledge, whether it's theological knowledge—it then sheds light in both directions on the nature of the ideas we have, which then can get tested out in ordinary, everyday reality, or on the question of how we know what we know which is in front of us. So I would want to put love back into the picture.[26]

I would too. Wright's idea may sound strange in connection to scientific research. What does it mean, for example, for a chemist to "love" the chemical reaction he is exploring? But, as he later elaborated in an article in *First Things*, what Wright means is that when we engage something or someone in love, we try to know them as they are, following our increasing knowledge whither the subject leads. His notion is that an epistemology of love helps us steer between "a cool, detached appraisal of the world" and "a self-indulgent grasping of it" to a "delighted exploration and exposition, in which respect and enjoyment go together."[27] It is of a piece with studiousness and a means to maintain the distinctions outlined above between truth, knowledge, and understanding.

A Hermeneutic of Obedience

I've spent most of my adult Christian life in a Mennonite church. I came to Anabaptism for its theology of nonviolence and its take on the relationship of Christians to the state, but I found much more in the tradition that I hadn't realized my faith was missing. Among those finds is the hermeneutic of obedience.

Anabaptism doesn't much go for academic theology. Early Anabaptists, like Menno Simons (for whom the Mennonites are named), typically didn't write grand, systematic treatises. Their extant writing, a lot of which consists of letters and sermons, tends to be occasional and practical, focused on maintaining faithfulness. And no wonder: faithfulness to their best understanding of biblical truth was no light thing for those early Anabaptists, who faced intense religious persecution by other Christians, Catholic and Protestant alike. Believing God wants Christians to eschew violence, live simply, and practice believer's (not infant) baptism could be a death sentence.

It was in that context that Anabaptists began to speak of the hermeneutic of obedience.[28] The idea is simple but bracing: we gain understanding of Scripture when we are prepared to obey it.[29] Our capacity for knowledge and faithfulness to the truth is determined by the posture of our hearts. If we don't want something to be true, we become less able to perceive its reality.

If we don't want to believe that Jesus calls his followers to nonviolence, for instance, we may find mystifying his commands to love our enemies and turn the other cheek.[30] If we don't want to abandon our materialism and greed, we may be baffled by the New Testament's painfully clear warnings about money. We will struggle to understand the truth if we're unwilling to bend our lives to its authority, and this can be as true of lesser truths as it is of those in Scripture. To revive the metaphor once more, the elephant must be willing to walk toward a destination before the rider will accept it as his aim.

That very need to unite our conscious reasoning with the rest of us is what makes this practical epistemology I've presented inadequate on its own. It needs reinforcement. It needs the strength of habit. It needs a building plan, which is the subject of chapter 9.

A Building Plan

Welcome to the internet! What would you prefer?
Would you like to fight for civil rights or tweet a
    racial slur?
Be happy! Be horny! Be bursting with rage!
We've got a million different ways to engage.

. . . .

Could I interest you in everything all of the time?
A little bit of everything all of the time.
Apathy's a tragedy, and boredom is a crime.
Anything and everything all of the time.

          —Bo Burnham, "Welcome to the Internet"

Around twenty-five minutes into his 2021 Netflix special, *Inside*, performer Bo Burnham takes the pose of a standup comedian and the tone of a Philosophy 101 professor. "Here's a question for you guys," he muses. "Is it necessary that every single person on this planet expresses every single opinion that they have on every single thing that occurs all at the same time? Is that . . . is *that* necessary?"[1]

About five minutes later, Burnham is lying on the floor in the fetal position huddled under a blanket—tired, tentative, earnest. "I don't know about you guys, but uh, you know, I've been thinking recently that, you know, maybe allowing giant digital-media corporations to exploit the neurochemical drama of our children for profit—you know, maybe that was, uh, a bad call by us," he suggests. "Maybe the flattening of the entire subjective human experience into a lifeless exchange of value that benefits nobody except for a handful of bug-eyed sala-manders in Silicon Valley, maybe that as a way of life forever, maybe that's, uh, *not* good."

Another twenty-five minutes on, his critique of the internet takes its most direct turn. With a maniacal laugh and a sinister persona somewhere between carnival barker and *Twilight Zone* villain, Burnham welcomes his audience to the internet: "a little bit of everything all of the time." He careens through disori-enting juxtapositions—"See a man beheaded / Get offended, see a shrink / Show us pictures of your children / Tell us every thought you think / Start a rumor, buy a broom / Or send a death threat to a boomer / Or DM a girl and groom her / Do a Zoom or find a tumor . . ."—but then stops short, shuts off the unsettling swirling lights, and layers over his cynicism the sweet tone of a father reminiscing to a child.

"You know, it wasn't always like this," Burnham sings. "Not very long ago / Just before your time / Right before the towers fell, circa '99 / This was catalogs / Travel blogs / A chat room or two." But then along came "insatiable you," and "mommy let you use her iPad / You were barely two." We "put the world in your hand," he sings in the last line of this wistful bit, but it's no parental triumph to savor. The laugh is back. The lights swirl again. And there's noise, other voices murmuring, laugh-ing, ominous, growing louder as the music accelerates.

"Could I interest you in everything all of the time?" Burnham asks again—only it's not really a question this time, not really a choice, not for you, not anymore. You've had the iPad since you were two. We all know you're not leaving. You like it. Or maybe you hate it, but you *want* it.

You don't know how to want something else.

Why We Need Habits

Burnham knows of what he speaks, because he has been online a long time.[2] So have I.

I didn't have reliable home-internet access until college, though in high school I cycled through AOL dial-up, free-trial CDs trying to maintain my Xanga page. I got Facebook and Gmail accounts in 2004, the year both were founded. I joined Twitter in 2009, as well as Tumblr, where my politics blog amassed a following of 115,000 people (a midsized city!) before the network became the ghost town it is today. I got on Instagram in 2015 and Snapchat around the same time. I've had a smartphone since 2012, and most of my work is done online or with heavy internet use. There are 57,000 emails in my Gmail account as of this writing—and that's with an aggressive deletion regimen.

I didn't grow up with an iPad in hand, but I feel the allure Burnham evokes. I hear that disquieting chatter. I know too well that if my life is to be made up of something better and deeper than "a little bit of everything all of the time," if I want to be able to want differently—heck, if I want to be able to sleep at night, as too much internet gives me insomnia—I must actively foster virtues, buttressed by habits, to keep that choice a real choice.

In the previous chapter we examined those virtues. Now it is time to think about the habits. A metaphor I find helpful here is a gothic cathedral, all spires and stained-glass glow. The virtues are like the windows. They let in light; through them, we gain knowledge and identify truth. But the windows, of course, can't stand on their own. They're held in place by great walls of stone, and this is the function of habit. To form habits conducive to studiousness, intellectual honesty, and wisdom is to create a framework of automatic behavior in which virtue can cast its truthful light.

Without the right habits, we may sometimes chance upon humility or happen to practice an epistemology of love, but it won't be part of our character. That is, it won't be characteristic of us and our unconscious wants. "The habits we adopt form our desires, which drive our beliefs," writes author and professor Alan Noble in *Disruptive Witness: Speaking Truth in a Distracted Age*. "When those habits form desires for immediacy, superficiality, continual engagement, and instant gratification, we should expect our beliefs to reflect those desires."[3]

We tend to think of this relationship the other way around. We try to put up the windows and expect the walls to materialize around them. That's not how it works. A passing fancy for virtue doesn't make you virtuous. Acquiring knowledge is an integral part of Christian maturity, but sanctification doesn't happen by information transfer.[4] We don't think our way to virtue any more than we think our way to liking a new food. Intellectual assent to a truthful proposition is not enough to make that truth evident in your life. Truth must be practiced.[5] "You believe that there is one God. Good! Even the demons believe that—and shudder" (James 2:19). As "faith without deeds is dead" (James 2:26), so virtue without habit is dead.

With our goal of epistemic virtue in mind, we must begin the slow, difficult work of setting stones that can hold these windows in their place.[6] We need to "intentionally recalibrate the unconscious," as philosopher James K. A. Smith argues in *You Are What You Love*, building habits and learning to "worship *well*, to immerse ourselves in liturgies that are indexed to the kingdom of God precisely so that even our unconscious desires and longings—the affective, under-the-hood ways we intend the world—are indexed to God and what God wants for his world."[7] The rider is usually too weak to steer the elephant toward virtue, but God is not, and habits are a crucial part of how we give God access to those reins.

In an information environment as chaotic and overwhelming as our own, much of this habit formation concerns what we do with our attention. Etymologically, "attention" is related to words like "tend" (as in "I tend my garden; I take care of it and give it thought"), "tendency" (a characteristic proclivity), and "tension" (which we experience when we are stretched in more than one direction at once). To "pay attention" to something means stretching ourselves toward it, entering a relationship with it, allowing it to change us into the sort of person who attends to that thing.[8] This is what we do when we practice any new skill. You give an instrument or craft or trade your attention so you can become the kind of person who does that thing well, a cello player or knitter or accountant.

Take an Inventory

Attention has that same formative power, even—or especially—when we aren't so deliberate. Instead of a cello player, you might become something more confused and pathetic: a Twitter obsessive or raging cable-news viewer, or a smartphone addict who can't have a normal conversation without looking at her phone. Instead of constructing towers for virtue, you might build walls for vice, installing not stained glass but fluorescent lights that diminish the cathedral with their dull, twitchy flicker.

The first step in better construction is an inventory, because the misuses of attention each of us needs to guard against will vary. For me, as is probably evident, the chief risk is overuse of the internet, particularly via my phone, at times when I should be attending to something different and better.

I'm not mistaking fake news for real. (I like to think I'm quite good at detecting false or misleading stories, and that my news intake is appropriately thoughtful and varied.) But I'm prone to spending too much time on Twitter and other trivialities. I have sense enough not to tweet too often or too contentiously, but *oh, do I scroll*. I let texted conversations distract me from my work, not only sucking up precious time during childcare hours but breaking up the flow of my thoughts and degrading the quality of my arguments. I sometimes look at my phone in the middle of conversations, though I get peevish when others do the same to me. And I do all this despite being aware of it, aware that if left unchecked these bad habits will rot out the settings of the windows I'm trying to install.

What about you? Is your brain broken? Are you addicted to your phone? Do you *enjoy* cable news? Do you *like* dunking on people on Twitter? Is the content you consume more exciting, more partisan, more vitriolic than it used to be? Is it more video and less text? More memes and fewer books? "Why are you reading so much that does not deserve a serious response?"[9]

Do you flit from cause to cause? Do you have a long stream of profile-picture frames on Facebook touting your stance on whatever was in the news that week? Did you ever take concrete action to fix those problems? Have you spared them a single serious thought in the last month?

Do you indulge in anger or schadenfreude? Are you arguing online or sharing mean-spirited memes? Do you relish seeing your ideological enemies take a loss? Have you been fooled by "satire" that told you what you wanted to hear? Do you do "research" that basically consists of "proving" yourself right? Do you treat watching a YouTube video or reading a Facebook post as research? (It's not.) Do you dip out of arguments you know you're losing and label it "self-care"?

Are you falling into conspiracist thinking? Do you have an unshakable trust and/or a knee-jerk, proud distrust of expertise

and authority? (It's totally possible to have both simultaneously; all you need to do is make yourself the standard of truth
and dole out trust in proportion to others' agreement with you.)
Do you let whims of emotion dictate your beliefs? Do you find
yourself playing by rules of identitarian deference?

Can you still hear yourself think? Are you ever just quiet?
Can you wash the dishes without a podcast? Can you fold the
laundry without TV? Is your mind constantly filled with passing minutiae? Did you *need* to know about that post? Did knowing it make your life better? Are you making anyone's life better
with that knowledge?

Do you ever have time for introspection? Are you doing any
introspection right now, or are you just reading this at a normal
pace, thinking, "Yeah, those are good questions I should ask
myself sometime"?

As you take your inventory, let me suggest two broad lines
of inquiry. One thing to notice is your attention as displayed
in your daily use of time. Notice how you spend your days and
what rituals, technologies, and information sources shape your
existence.[10] You might find something that requires a significant
overhaul of how you live, but it will probably be a litany of
small things. "To live well in a modern world requires constant
reassessment of how our society and technology are shaping
us," Noble says. "We should be open to taking drastic steps to
reject practices and habits that we believe are destructive and
evil. But the vast majority of innovations will not be so clear-
cut, and we will have to weigh benefits, purposes, and damaging
effects individually and in community."[11]

The second thing to notice is your attention as it feels in your
mind. In chapter 2, I quoted Nicholas Carr, author of *The Shallows: What the Internet Is Doing to Our Brains*. Part of what
prompted him to write that book was his interior perception
that his mind was changing.

I feel it most strongly when I'm reading. I used to find it easy to immerse myself in a book or a lengthy article. My mind would get caught up in the twists of the narrative or the turns of the argument, and I'd spend hours strolling through long stretches of prose. That's rarely the case anymore. Now my concentration starts to drift after a page or two. I get fidgety, lose the thread, begin looking for something else to do. I feel like I'm always dragging my wayward brain back to the text.[12]

Is that familiar to you? It's more familiar to me than I like to admit, though one of the best parts of working on this book has been the powerful incentive that research provides for focused reading. I can feel my brain returning to older, better habits. It isn't fun, necessarily, for "no discipline seems pleasant at the time, but painful. Later on, however, it produces a harvest of righteousness and peace for those who have been trained by it" (Heb. 12:11).

The Habits We Need

Depending on the results of your inventory, you may not need every suggestion I'm about to make. You may need different suggestions, and hopefully the resources I suggest at the end will start you on your way toward finding them. You may also find you need help identifying which habits you should change and implementing those changes once decided. That's normal! There's nothing wrong with that need. It's why Christians have historically confessed sin and practiced spiritual disciplines together.

Devices and Desires

There's a passage in Isaiah in which God describes the foolishness of idolatry, going into cringe-inducing detail about the process by which someone would chop down a tree, use part of it for cooking, carve the other part into a statue, and then, somehow, worship the thing he just made (Isa. 44:16–20). "Such a person feeds on ashes; a deluded heart misleads him; he cannot save himself, or say, 'Is not this thing in my right hand a lie?'" (v. 20).

The thing in my right hand isn't always a lie, but it is amply capable of transmitting lies, and it is by design manipulative of me, of knowledge, and of reality. Our devices—phones and computers and televisions alike, as well as the apps we run on them—are made, on purpose, to change our behavior so we'll use them more. Algorithms show us the most engaging content (which is to say, whatever makes us happy, horny, or bursting with rage), and gamification (giving you little rewards and nudges for use) trains our brains to physically enjoy that engagement, including when it's emotionally negative. This means my best interests and the interests of the makers of my devices and the owners of the social media I use are frequently in conflict.

Here's one example. In 2020, the *New York Times* reported that a Facebook team "trained a machine-learning algorithm to predict posts that users would consider 'bad for the world' and demote them in news feeds. In early tests, the new algorithm successfully reduced the visibility of objectionable content." Good, right? People could go on Facebook to see updates from their friends' lives without having to wade through screaming political posts. Ah, but "it also lowered the number of times users opened Facebook, an internal metric known as 'sessions' that executives monitor closely." That reduction "motivated us to try a different approach," said an internal report on the project, which the *Times* reviewed.[13]

Given a choice between making society worse and losing a little traffic, Facebook knowingly chose to make things worse. And Facebook isn't uniquely bad in doing this! It's the nature of the beast—and the beast is humanity. There are alternative social-networking sites that don't have these deleterious features. I can't tell you what they are, though, because they never attract a critical mass of users and often fail altogether. We like the manipulation. We gravitate to the content we know is "bad for the world."

So the first habit is *taking sabbath*, ideally as a daily, weekly, and yearly rhythm.[14] Log out of the site you use most. Turn off your phone altogether. Give your brain a rest from epistemic quandaries. Give virtues a chance to take root. I'm currently focused on building the daily habit, which on my present schedule means my phone is off for an hour in the morning when I'm with my children (from roughly eight to nine o'clock in the morning) and one to two hours in the evening, between the time I finish the bulk of my work for the day and when I either put the kids to bed or say goodnight as they head upstairs to bedtime with their dad while I clean the kitchen.

One daily, conscious hour without devices is a good minimum with which to begin. You'll find that hour (perhaps unwillingly) in your schedule if you look. If you discover you're incapable of keeping this sabbath, ask someone to help you learn. Let them change your Facebook password, perhaps, so they can log you out during your sabbath time, or give them your phone so they can hide it.[15] If you live alone, you can buy a timed lockbox to help you retrain your mind.

The second habit is *Scripture before phone, tablet, laptop, or television*. I owe this idea to Justin Whitmel Earley's excellent book *The Common Rule: Habits of Purpose for an Age of Distraction*.[16] It is what it sounds like: before you use your phone in the morning (or whatever device or medium you favor for taking in information first thing), read the Bible. You don't have to read a lot. You don't have to do an in-depth study. But whatever you do, do not give Twitter or CNN or the *Washington Post* or YouTube the honor of launching your thoughts for the day.

The last habit for this category will be more variable: *eschew distraction*. Habitual distraction "has three major effects on our ability to communicate about matters of faith and ultimate meaning," Noble warns: "(1) it is easier to ignore contradictions and flaws in our basic beliefs, (2) we are less likely to devote time to introspection, and (3) conversations about faith can easily be perceived as just another exercise in superficial identity formation."[17]

You can cut down on distraction by turning off as many notifications on your phone as you can. Uninstall social media and email apps altogether—you can still access most of these sites in your browser (Instagram is an exception), but they won't be able to put popup notifications on your lock screen or interrupt you while you're working on something else. If you have an iPhone, the Screentime app counts where your attention is going and lets you set daily time use limits for apps and websites. Turn off your devices or put them in another room during discrete events like dinner, parties, dates, or important conversations so your attention is undivided.[18] "If I'm not willing to tell someone why I'm asking them to wait [for my attention]," Earley notes, "usually it's because there isn't a good reason to ask."[19]

Space and Subscriptions

This section is straightforward: *arrange your space for virtue*. "Find the room where your family spends the most time," advises Andy Crouch in *The Tech-Wise Family*, "and ruthlessly eliminate the things that ask little of you and develop little in you. Move the TV to a less central location—and ideally a less comfortable one. And begin filling the space that is left over with opportunities for creativity and skill, beauty and risk."[20]

It may also be a good idea to put your phone and tablet chargers somewhere other than your bedroom, so you don't use these devices late into the night or first thing in the morning. If you're finding it difficult to stick to reading the Bible before picking up your phone, you might need to buy an alarm clock. In your workspace, simply placing your phone out of your sightline will make you use and think about it less.

This may seem unnecessary, but we are weaker than we imagine. We're a lot like my dog, Sasha, whose anxious tendencies went into overdrive after we moved. When Sasha felt anxious, she obsessively licked her legs. Left unattended, she'd lick them raw. She couldn't stop herself, which is why, in the four weeks we waited for the specialty behavioral vet appointment, Sasha had to wear the cone of shame. It wasn't a great solution; what she really needed was to be less anxious. But during that period of increased anxiety, it protected her by acting as a limit she couldn't give herself. Arranging our homes for virtue is likewise a limit we need. Don't make yourself constantly fight against your own home.

In a similar vein, *curate your subscriptions* and *cut off cable news* (and its imitators, like *Newsmax* and *The Daily Show*). To begin with the latter, cable news will never make you more studious, intellectually honest, or wise. It does not have that capacity.

Honestly, I'd recommend eliminating *all* television news from your life, because the medium simply is not suited to serious conveyance of nuanced reporting. Research shows the complex multimedia presentation favored in modern cable news inhibits information absorption.[21] The network channels tend to be tamer than their cable counterparts, but they're just as guilty of jerking us from story to story, lurching from one emotion to the next. Television levels topics of vastly different import and implies that you as the viewer can consider yourself well informed if you sit through a four-minute segment. Even without cable's quarrelsomeness, this is epistemic disarray.

As for subscriptions more generally, use the value you place on your money for good. Pay for good content, then consume what you've bought. Support transparent, careful journalism, slow as well as fast.[22] Don't read outlets that never issue corrections; they're probably not perfect, just dishonest. Make sure you're not buying entrance to an ideological echo chamber, though remember hearing a diversity of voices is useless if you never truly listen.[23]

Social Media Use

I've touched on social media a bit already, but now let's address it directly. We may not need to leave these networks entirely, but we do need to sharply interrogate and curtail our use. We should approach each of these habits with a question from Crouch in mind: Does using this social media—and not in theory, but specifically how *you* are using it—"make me the kind of human being who could contribute something of lasting value to my family, my neighbors, my society, and our broken world"?[24]

We should make a point to *take important conversations offline*. Social media is fine for scheduling events or announcing that you had a kid or bought a new house. It is not appropriate for anything that requires intense emotion or extensive explanation.

Relatedly, *be wary of mixing the personal and the political*. I've unsubscribed from many friends' Instagram stories (a separate stream of photo and video posts that disappear after a day) for this reason: they post a lot of politics. It's not that their political content is bad—in many cases, it's thoughtful and good, and I agree with it. But if I'm tapping through stories, going from one friend's new kitten to another's campaign advocacy to a third's day at the fair to a fourth friend's attempt to raise awareness about genocide, it's epistemically disorienting and morally absurd. The joy of the kitten and the fair is dampened; the weight of the campaign and the genocide is lost. All sides suffer, and truth is obscured. As Instagram is, for me, overwhelmingly a personal network I use to see photos of happy moments from distant friends, I chose to cut out all the politics and reserve that for other spaces. A similar culling has proved impossible on Facebook, which is part of why my personal account is near-dormant.

Next, *avoid useless worries*. Social media is a worry-making machine, but some worries are useless. "It is one of the evils of rapid diffusion of news that the sorrows of *all* the world come to us every morning," C. S. Lewis wrote in a letter. He went on:

> I think each village was meant to feel pity for *its own* sick and poor whom it can help, and I doubt if it is the duty of any private person to fix his mind on ills which he cannot help. (This may even become an *escape* from the works of charity we really *can* do to those we know.) A great many people (not you) do now seem to think that the mere state of being *worried* is in itself meritorious. I don't think it is. We must, if it so happens, give our lives for others; but even while we're doing it, I think we're meant to enjoy Our Lord and, in Him, our friends, our food, our sleep, our jokes, and the birds song and the frosty sunrise.[25]

Lewis penned these words in 1946, just after the end of World War II. He wasn't naive about the sorrows of the world; he was realistic about his own ability to affect the great bulk of them and the temptation to devote more attention to distant worries that lay no obligation on us than near ones involving people we may actually serve. We should practice that same realism.

These three practices will be easier when combined with the next five, most of which are derived from Earley's *Common Rule*.[26] *Only log on for a specific purpose*, like making a post you already have in mind or responding to a message you already know is there. If your specific purpose is more open-ended—for example, I sometimes find article ideas by browsing Twitter, because lots of other writers post their work there—*only log on for a specific time*. Keep your sabbath, and expand it whenever you can. (That Screentime app I mentioned can be a handy reminder for this.) Also, *avoid random scrolling.* Don't use social media to fill every moment of boredom, and be wary of plunging into unknown content streams. There's a big difference between scrolling through posts from accounts you've deliberately followed and browsing a hashtag full of content from users you've never vetted.

Whether engaging with users you know or those you don't, *do not argue.* If you're talking with a friend or family member and the tone turns argumentative, either graciously agree to disagree or, if it's an important conversation, move it offline. If a conversation with a stranger becomes argumentative, mute it and leave. The chances that you will change their mind are vanishingly few; the chances you will sin in your anger are many (Eph. 4:26, Ps. 4:4). If people attack you on social media, *love your enemies and pray for those who persecute you* (see Matt. 5:44). Don't respond in kind. Log off, and take the opportunity to evaluate whether the time has come to delete your account.[27]

News Consumption

Moving from social to traditional media, my suggestions are all oriented around depth and curation of knowledge. To that end, *avoid passive consumption* and *limit rapid consumption.* Passive consumption is what happens when we scan headlines, idly scroll through newsfeeds, drift from one YouTube clip to the next, or get our news from television. It's when we're not looking to learn anything in particular, just aimlessly trawling for "the news," which is, functionally, politics-themed entertainment. Passive consumption lowers our epistemic standards and puts us off our guard against deception.[28] It is not studious.

Rapid consumption is endlessly possible in our twenty-four-hour news cycle, but it's rarely wise. In matters of great significance, the earliest reports are frequently the least accurate. More and better information will emerge with time, completing a partial picture. More-measured opinions will be given. Historical context will be found. Initial emotional reactions will calm. For most of us, most of the time, waiting a day or two or longer to read up on a major event will only improve the quality of the news we consume, and our delay will change exactly nothing about how that event unfolds.[29] (If you find yourself protesting that you'll no longer care about the topic tomorrow so you need to look now—well, you have your answer already.)

Maybe the single most important habit of news consumption, though, is this: *choose to know only a few stories well.* You do not need to be informed about every story. You *cannot* be well informed about every story. Even as a journalist at a general-interest outlet, I don't follow every story, and following the news is my job. It likely isn't yours.

If you want to keep abreast of the news of the day, use a short-form summary, preferably one composed by humans, not an algorithm. At *The Week*, for example, we publish a daily email newsletter with the ten most significant stories of the day, each told in about a hundred words. It's free, and you can read it in five minutes or less. Something like that is all the average person actually *needs* for general news.

Beyond, that, however, you could choose up to half a dozen news stories of interest to you. I don't mean a story like "The president signed a tax bill on Monday" or "The police shot an unarmed black man." I mean a story like "federal tax policy" or "policing reform." Something you can follow for years or decades, not hours or days. Something you care about enough to read legal filings and white papers, to learn a new vocabulary and cast of characters, to truly (even sympathetically) understand the reasoning of people with whom you disagree. Something you can come to understand with a degree of expertise.

If you follow more stories than you can follow well, you're not better-informed. You're distracted. Your attention is divided, and your epistemic judgment will suffer.[30] You'll attend to trivialities and fail to give weighty stories their due.[31] You'll follow "a little bit of everything all of the time."

Strengthen the Rider

Deep, curated consumption of good journalism is one way to strengthen the rider, but it isn't itself enough. Author Dorothy L. Sayers, whom you may recall from chap. 2, writes:

> We let our young men and women go out unarmed in a day when armor was never so necessary. By teaching them all to read, we have left them at the mercy of the printed word. By the invention of the film and the radio, we have made certain that no aversion to reading shall secure them from the incessant battery of words, words, words. They do not know what the words mean; they do not know how to ward them off or blunt their edge or fling them back; they are a prey to words in their emotions instead of being the masters of them in their intellects.[32]

If we don't deliberately strengthen the rider, we send ourselves out unarmed too. That means we *abide by the rules of free debate*, applying *no final say* and *no personal authority* rules to ourselves as well as our ideological opponents. It means *read good books,* including fiction, and especially old books, works that have stood the test of time and can give us a vantage from an era other than our own. *Have challenging conversations.* Being reasonable is a skill built by practice, and we practice best with a partner.

You may find it worthwhile to read up on common logical fallacies, like red herrings, bandwagoning, and ad hominem, so you can spot them in your own thinking and that of others. It might also be helpful to familiarize yourself with types of distorted, automatic thought that cognitive-behavioral therapists use, like dichotomous thinking, overgeneralizing, and unfair comparisons.[33]

Notice the Elephant

The elephant doesn't need strengthening, but it does need notice and care. My best habits all start to decay when I'm tired, sick, frustrated, angry, or overly busy. My daily phone use will grow by *hours* precisely when I have no time to spare. I'll respond to exhaustion by aimlessly scrolling an hour after I should have been asleep. Caring for the elephant means keeping to my bedtime, getting in some exercise and leisure, and engaging rider and elephant together in productive activities like home improvement. (After I file this manuscript, I'm painting my powder-blue dining room a lush, dark teal.)

In the context of content consumption, whether news or entertainment, to notice the elephant is to *pay attention to your emotional responses*. Does a story easily enrage or alarm you? Sometimes, with stories of great tragedy or injustice, that degree of emotional upheaval is the right reaction—but sometimes it's the result of deliberate manipulation.

Evoking strong negative emotion attracts eyeballs in any media format, and that creates at least an incentive for sensationalism if not a temptation to be deceitful. If you have an extreme emotional response to a story, it's wise to take a pause before you react or share it. Examine it more closely to make sure it's not fabricated or misleadingly framed. Check whether and how it was reported elsewhere. Look at the details. Wait an hour or a day to see if any further information emerges and whether the story still makes you scared or angry. Maybe fill that pause with prayer and Scripture, where God tells us over and over, "Be not afraid."[34]

Better Things

After your inventory, making all this space—whether literal space in the living room or sabbath space in the schedule or mental space where screeching of the squawk box used to be—is the second step in the building plan. The third step is filling that space with better things. "When an impure spirit comes out of a person," Jesus warned, "it goes through arid places seeking rest and does not find it. Then it says, 'I will return to the house I left.' When it arrives, it finds the house swept clean and put in order. Then it goes and takes seven other spirits more wicked than itself, and they go in and live there. And the final condition of that person is worse than the first" (Luke 11:24–26).

I've pointed to a few better things already: good journalism and books, real-life conversation with loved ones, and undistracted dinners, parties, and dates. These will help build your habits and change your tastes. They'll help make your brain less broken and transform the detritus of our information environment from a temptation to be resisted into garbage eagerly tossed away. They'll help you become "as shrewd as snakes and as innocent as doves" (Matt. 10:16). They'll help build the walls through which epistemic virtues illuminate the proper objects of your trust.

But they are all supplements to a higher priority: *worship* "in the Spirit and in truth" (John 4:24), in God's Word and in the community of God's people. It is "through Spirited worship [that] the grace of God captivates and orients even our unconscious," James K. A. Smith explains.[35] "Jesus Christ is the very embodiment of what we're made for, of the end to which we are called," and we move toward him by "being regularly immersed in the drama of God in Christ reconciling the world to himself, which is precisely the point of Christian worship—to invite us into that story over and over again, 'character-izing' us as we rehearse the gospel drama over and over."[36]

It is in worship—through song, study, liturgy, prayer, communion, contemplation, and every other way we offer ourselves "as a living sacrifice, holy and pleasing to God" (Rom. 12:1)—that we encounter the God of truth and slowly learn to recognize truth wherever we may find it. In worship, we are "transformed by the renewing of [our] mind[s]" (Rom. 12:2).

That transformation is long and difficult and changes much more than our media habits and epistemology. God doesn't hand down a foolproof fact-checking rubric with which we can always tell truth from error and lies. Rather, we aim to become the sort of people who love the truth and seek it well, people who cultivate epistemic virtue to push back on epistemic crisis, people who can offer a breath.

RESOURCES

Because of the primacy of worship in this building plan, the single most important resource is active membership in a church that worships well. If you have struggled to find a good church or are not sure where to begin, my first book, *A Flexible Faith: Rethinking What It Means to Follow Jesus Today,* may be a useful resource to you, particularly the chapter titled, "What's with All These Churches?"

If you want to read more than this brief overview of the importance that habit and desire have for character, virtue, and sanctification, I recommend Alan Noble's *Disruptive Witness* and James K. A. Smith's *You Are What You Love.* Nicholas Carr's *The Shallows* and Jeffrey Bilbro's *Reading the Times: A Literary and Theological Inquiry into the News* look more specifically at the effects of media use on our minds and lives, Carr from a historical and social science standpoint and Bilbro with an eye to discipleship.

Justin Earley's *The Common Rule* and Andy Crouch's *The Tech-Wise Family* go into greater detail about formative habits and practices than I have here. Earley presents a daily and weekly rhythm of life, while Crouch focuses more on one-time decisions and on children, to whom we have an enormous responsibility to keep *their* brains unbroken by the internet and other distracting media.

Finally, in addition to lists of logical fallacies and kinds of distorted automatic thought (from cognitive-behavioral therapy), I recommend "The Questions Concerning Technology" from L. M. Sacasas, a Christian tech critic with a philosophical bent. Pause with the kind of considerations he raises before you introduce any new communication technology into your life or your child's life—or maybe use them alongside your inventory of technologies you've already adopted. There are forty-one questions on the list, so I'll only list a few:

- What sort of person will the use of this technology make of me?
- What will the use of this technology encourage me to ignore?
- Can I imagine living without this technology? Why, or why not?
- Does using this technology require me to think more or less?
- Does my use of this technology make it easier to live as if I had no responsibilities toward my neighbor?
- Can I be held responsible for the actions which this technology empowers? Would I feel better if I couldn't?*

* L. M. Sacasas, "The Questions Concerning Technology," *Convivial Society* (newsletter), Substack, June 4, 2021, https://theconvivialsociety.substack.com/p/the-questions-concerning-technology.

A Breath

Forgetful, you neglect your shrines and churches;
The men you are in these times deride
What has been done of good, you find explanations
To satisfy the rational and enlightened mind.

Second, you neglect and belittle the desert.
The desert is not remote in southern tropics,
The desert is not only around the corner,
The desert is squeezed in the tube-train next to you,
The desert is in the heart of your brother.

—T. S. Eliot, *The Rock*

When I began writing about epistemic crisis, I found my-self turning over and over to the book of 1 Peter. This surprised me, because 1 Peter was not a book I knew well. Galatians, 1 Corinthians, Philippians, Luke—those are the mainstays of my New Testament knowledge. I don't think I'd ever given 1 Peter more than a casual read.

But I kept coming back to it because 1 Peter is deeply concerned with truth, belief, knowledge, hope, holiness, love, and the virtuous life. Peter counsels his readers to "be alert and of sober mind" (5:8), to be unfailingly reasonable and respectful (3:15—probably a hard-earned lesson for the notoriously indiscreet disciple), to reject "all malice and all deceit, hypocrisy, envy, and slander of every kind" (2:1), and to love those who wrong us and those who are wrong about us (3:8–16; 4:8).

We tend to see acquiring knowledge, becoming virtuous, and living in love as significantly distinct projects; knowledge especially is carved out from the other two. But Peter's brief missive tangles them all together: "As obedient children, do not conform to the evil desires you had when you lived in ignorance. But just as he who called you is holy, so be holy in all you do. . . . [And] now that you have purified yourselves by obeying the truth so that you have sincere love for each other, love one another deeply, from the heart" (1 Pet. 1:14–15, 22).

This is an entanglement I think we need. It's how "we demonstrate allegiance to Jesus in a way that contradicts worldly expectations when we face the challenges of the world," Dennis R. Edwards told me during a phone interview—including challenges like epistemic crisis.[1]

Edwards, a longtime pastor, was a professor of mine at Bethel Seminary in St. Paul before he began teaching New Testament at North Park Theological Seminary in Chicago, and as I was reading over 1 Peter with epistemology in mind, I was thrilled to remember I know a 1 Peter scholar: Edwards published a lay-level commentary on the letter in 2017, and he was working on a more technical commentary when we spoke. I reached out to him to learn more about what Peter has to say of our belief and behavior in a time of contested truth.

Our conversation left me even more convinced of the importance of this little book for pushing back on epistemic confusion in ourselves and our communities. Some scholars think "Peter's audience was largely Jewish because he references the Old Testament so much," Edwards told me, "but it may very well be that the majority of his audience are gentile people who were living like the rest of their neighbors until they came to know Christ." They likely weren't suffering severe state persecution—though that was soon to come—but they were dealing with resentment, Edwards said, from family and friends from whom they were suddenly divided by belief, suddenly in disagreement about what truth is and how to know it, suddenly irreconcilable in their convictions about the nature of reality itself.

A Better Way

That divide—and that resentment—is uncomfortably familiar to me, but not only to me. In late 2020, I wrote an article for *The Week* about the brain-breaking effects of the internet, especially political content on social media and with the accelerant of cable news.[2] I pitched the story because I was regularly talking with friends who were worried their loved ones had screen-broken brains, but the outpouring of response to the article still surprised me.

Reader after reader told me they had the same worries, the same frustration, the same feeling of helplessness, and the same sense that their loved ones resented it when they did try to help. "What do you do when you feel you're losing the people you love to a false reality?" as *Christianity Today*'s president, Timothy Dalrymple, would ask a few months later. "What do you do with the humbling truth that they have precisely the same fear about you?"[3]

My instinct, as I wrote in the introduction of this book, is to argue. I want to take the advice of Proverbs 26:5: "Answer a fool according to his folly, or he will be wise in his own eyes." I want to craft a persuasive case for why I'm right and he's wrong and thus he should drop all his nonsense and concede all my self-evidently correct and compelling points.

Argument has its place, unquestionably. It makes up the bulk of my writing and the bulk of this book. But what I've found in research and life alike is that argument is a tool of limited uses. It's also a tool I'm only sometimes prepared to wield well. I don't have the time or wherewithal to rebut every illogical argument that comes my way, to discover and detail what's wrong with every misleading story or deceptive documentary or inane meme a relative sends me. I can't fact check every three-thousand-word chain email my cousin forwards, and I don't think he'd change his conspiracist mindset if I did. An hour's conversation with me will never beat twenty hours of talk radio or Twitter spats a week. I'm happy to have a congenial argument in the right time and place and ideally over good food and drink, but I no longer expect to argue people out of epistemic crisis. I'm trying to change my instinct.

Often, I've learned, the better proverb to heed is found one verse prior: "Do not answer a fool according to his folly, or you yourself will be just like him" (Prov. 26:4). The better way is to stop "find[ing] explanations / To satisfy the rational and enlightened mind," as T. S. Eliot wrote in his pageant play *The Rock*, to stop "neglect[ing] and belittl[ing] the desert . . . in the heart of your brother."[4] It is, as G. K. Chesterton advised in the *Orthodoxy* passage I've quoted several times, to supply "air" instead of arguments, to give a reminder that there's "something cleaner and cooler outside the suffocation" of confusion or delusion.[5] This final chapter is about how we offer that breath.

Giving Air

The foundation for all that follows is a relationship, ordinary and grounded in love.

We can offer a breath only to people we know, not to strangers, and especially not to strangers on the internet. This is about our family, friendships, and churches, people who know and trust us and whom we know and trust in turn.

If we want any hope of being "like-minded," as Peter exhorts us to be in 1 Peter 3:8, we first must follow the rest of the verse: "Be sympathetic, love one another, be compassionate and humble." That mutual care and faithfulness isn't possible without a preexisting relationship. There's value in public discussion of our knowledge crisis, the sort of thing I often do in my journalism—but that is typically not the same as giving air, and bickering in the comments section is even less likely to fit the bill.

Likewise, to give someone air will almost never mean sitting them down for a dramatic, epistemic intervention. That moment may come, but more often it will steer clear of contentious topics, the subjects on which each thinks the other most mistaken.

Talk about the mundane: kids, pets, church, work, school, hobbies, vacations. Keep your tongue from evil; seek peace and pursue it (1 Pet. 3:10–11). Never initiate a debunking, but welcome sincere questions if they come (1 Pet. 3:15). Don't dissemble in the face of disagreement, but never disdain (Prov. 30:11–13). "Do not repay evil with evil or insult with insult. On the contrary, repay evil with blessing" and keep the relationship intact insofar as it depends on you (1 Pet. 3:9; Rom. 12:17–18).

Your aim, again, is not victory in a debate. It's to strengthen your relationship so that if—hopefully, *when*—your loved one begins to wonder if there is something amiss in his thinking, he knows he can come to you. He knows he'll be met with grace rather than belittlement, with aid rather than I-told-you-so.

None of this comes naturally to most of us. I remember seeing lots of articles a decade ago on how to win political arguments with relatives (usually "your crazy Republican uncle") at Thanksgiving. Now it seems the standard impulse across the political spectrum is to cut those relatives out of your life entirely. They're too far gone, the thinking goes. Maintaining relationships where it is clear you will never see eye to eye will just cause you pain and aggravation.

It might well cause you pain and aggravation. I'd be lying if I said I've never wanted to take that counsel, but I'd equally be lying if I said I can square it with the love Jesus modeled and commanded of us as his followers.[6] "Rather than withdrawing into communities of common loathing, the church should be offering a community of common love, a sanctuary from the fragmentation and polarization, from the loneliness and isolation of the present moment," Dalrymple says. "The church should model what it means to care for one another in spite of our differences on social and political matters and affirm the incomparably deeper rootedness of our identity in Christ."[7]

Remembering that our beliefs and habits of thought undoubtedly have unrecognized errors—that the confused minds, sometimes and on some questions, may be our own—it's our difficult duty to pair grace for confusion in our communities with commitment to the truth as best we know it.

Ask for Help

In 1736 Benjamin Franklin was chosen to be the clerk of the Pennsylvania legislature, a selection he said no one opposed. The next year, however, a new legislator "made a long speech against me," Franklin wrote in his autobiography, proposing another candidate for the job. Franklin prevailed in the vote, but he "did not like the opposition of this new member, who was a gentleman of fortune and education, with talents that were likely to give him, in time, great influence."[8] Franklin determined to win the lawmaker over to his side. His method was counterintuitive: instead of trying to ingratiate himself by doing his enemy a favor, he asked his enemy to do a favor for him.

Having heard that he had in his library a certain very scarce and curious book, I wrote a note to him, expressing my desire of perusing that book, and requesting he would do me the favour of lending it to me for a few days. He sent it immediately, and I return'd it in about a week with another note, expressing strongly my sense of the favour. When we next met in the House, he spoke to me (which he had never done before), and with great civility; and he ever after manifested a readiness to serve me on all occasions, so that we became great friends, and our friendship continued to his death. This is another instance of the truth of an old maxim I had learned, which says, *"He that has once done you a kindness will be more ready to do you another, than he whom you yourself have obliged."*[9]

Psychologists have dubbed that closing maxim the "Ben Franklin effect," and it probably works for a handful of reasons. One is that we do favors for people we like, so if we find ourselves doing a favor for someone, well, it must mean we like them. Our brains are manipulable this way; acting as if we love our enemies can move us toward actually loving them. Another reason is that getting someone to do you a favor can give them a sense of investment in your well-being. They come to want a relationship with you so they can see how their investment fares. And, of course, the request itself is flattering. Asking someone for help signals respect for them or at least acknowledges they have something—some skill, insight, or resource—we lack.

So, if you have a loved one who you believe is in the throes of a knowledge crisis, you could try asking them for help. Instead of trying to fix their epistemic confusion, seek their support to address your own. Instead of offering unsolicited input about what's wrong with *their* beliefs or media use or whatever, ask them to keep *you* accountable as you build good habits in pursuit of intellectual virtue. Maybe propose a weekly screen-time check-in over coffee or ask them to help you take your inventory.

If they agree, you may get some Ben Franklin effect benefits, strengthening your relationship. You'll also have a natural way to raise issues around media habits and epistemology without plunging into conflict. They may even ask you for the same favor in return.

But this can't purely be a calculated move. It's not *just* a strategy. If you ask for this help, you must be truly ready to receive it. You must be truly prepared to learn about the log in your own eye (Matt. 7:3–5), to discover some hypocrisy in your own intellectual life or excess in your own behavior. The very differences in the relationship may make your friend uniquely suited to identify your unnoticed foibles and vice, even if he's utterly oblivious to his own.

That doesn't mean accepting every suggestion without question. (You shouldn't drop a trustworthy media outlet, for example, simply because your friend expresses personal distaste—yet if she presents a reasoned, well-supported case for using it less or not at all, take that seriously.) But there should be truth to the respect you signal, a real willingness to accept your friend's advice just as you're hoping she'll accept yours. Anything less will corrupt you before it corrects your friend.

To Each His Task

Perhaps the most difficult part of all of this, for me, is the uncertainty. The slowness. The total absence of a quick fix.

I can't win one big, come-to-Jesus argument and put everything right. I can't cut off another adult's cable-news subscription or close her Facebook account. I can't keep my more impressionable relatives from reading sketchy websites, nor can I teach them all the ineffable intricacies and evolving whims of internet culture that would enable them to recognize the sketchiness for themselves. I can't build someone else's habits or pursue intellectual virtue on their behalf. Sometimes, I can't even do it for myself.

"Keep the relationship going" is by far the most common recommendation for dealing with crises among friends and family. It was a through line in my research, the closing recommendation of one writer and thinker after another, Christian and secular alike. And I don't think it's *bad*. Quite the contrary: it's vital.

But it's not *sufficient*. Read accounts by people whose family members have plunged into conspiracism, for instance, and you'll notice they rarely end with a return to normalcy. "I wish I could offer some evidence showing that the gulf between us might be narrowing, that my love, persistence, and collection of facts might be enough to draw her back into a reality we share, and that . . . she'll realize that the voices she trusts have been lying to her," concludes one such essay by a man whose mother went all-in on QAnon. "But I don't think that will happen," he says. "I think new voices will emerge, new theories will replace the old ones, and new leaders will take up the fight with new deceptions to weaponize. What can I do but try to limit the damage?"[10]

I've asked the same question myself. I feel a duty here, but I don't seem to be able to reliably fulfill it. I want to be effective. I want the quick fix. I particularly wanted it for the end of this book—how great, right, to conclude with a 100 percent guaranteed solution to your loved one's epistemic mess? Just tell them to do X, Y, and Z, and watch the clarity dawn upon their grateful faces.

I was talking through my discontent with Edwards when I realized the two ways I'd gone wrong. I'd been circling one of them already but hadn't quite gotten it into words: my longing to fix other people's epistemic confusion left no room for the Spirit to act.

"I think about the son who left in Luke 5—we call him 'prodigal'—and how he had to go through some things before he was humiliated and came to himself," Edwards told me. "And I often think it's a spiritual work that has to be done" to get someone out of epistemic crisis. "I think of it as a delusion, and I think of delusion as a spiritual thing. I think of it

as a demonic thing, and I'm not exaggerating in that regard."
He continued:

> I know people, for example, who twenty years ago minimized
> my voice on racism and Christian complicity in it. And now
> . . . they're champions for racial justice. Something happened
> along the way. God works mysteriously, and so I will trust that
> the Spirit was at work, and that this could be a longer process
> than I am prepared to undergo, or longer than I even think it
> might be. We've placed a premium on rational arguments and
> convincing people, [but] I honestly think it's a spiritual work that
> has to be done that can't easily be accomplished with our words.

Sometimes our witness will be wordless (Edwards pointed
to 1 Pet. 3:1–2), or at least wordless where epistemology is concerned. We won't win arguments, but the Spirit will still be on
the move.

Edwards's comment about time pointed to my other error:
my assumption that *I'd* be the one to see the process through—
that if I offered someone air, I'd get to see them take a breath.
His words reminded me of the apostle Paul's rebuke to the
church at Corinth, chastising them for dividing into different
camps according to which teacher they prefer. In service to a
larger point about Christian unity and loyalty to Christ, Paul
observes that "the Lord has assigned to each his task. I planted
the seed, Apollos watered it, but God has been making it grow"
(1 Cor. 3: 5–6).

That "building and strengthening," as Edwards mused, is
"slow work" in the individual Christian as much as the church
communities Paul originally addressed. It is work done largely
by the Spirit and certainly not entirely by me. My instinct to
argue is an instinct to plant and water and grow everything
myself—but "neither the one who plants nor the one who waters
is anything, but only God, who makes things grow" (1 Cor. 3: 7).

I won't pretend to be wholly content with that truth, for my instinct isn't wholly changed. But truth I believe it to be.

Build What Is Good

I've written at length of repairing an epistemic crisis, but better than repairing a problem is forestalling it before it begins. It is better to build a home with windows to let in air than to knock holes in the walls of a suffocating box. Perpetual repair may be the only option for ourselves, our peers, and our elders, but it is not the only option for our children and their children yet to come.

The Eliot poem in this chapter's opening epigraph is a chorus from *The Rock*, which he wrote in 1934 as a fundraiser to support the construction of forty-five new churches in the suburbs of London.[11] Suitably for the purpose at hand, Eliot's theme was the Christian responsibility to build amid the bleak alienation of the modern world. We are heirs to the faith of our forebears and beneficiaries of their love and labor, Eliot remarked, but their work won't last forever. We must love and labor too, for "the Church must be forever building, and always decaying, and always being restored."[12]

"You, have you built well, that you now sit helpless in a ruined house?" Eliot's chorus asks—a question that deserves our answer. "What life have you if you have not life together? / There is no life that is not in community / And no community not lived in praise of GOD."[13] Building that community, a community (among its other attributes) into which epistemic crisis can't slink, is the work of the church universal, and it is our individual work as followers of Jesus. The lines I shared above begin to sketch its shape, first in negation. This passage is a bracing forward call:

> Forgetful, you neglect your shrines and churches;
> The men you are in these times deride

What has been done of good, you find explanations
To satisfy the rational and enlightened mind.
Second, you neglect and belittle the desert.
The desert is not remote in southern tropics,
The desert is not only around the corner,
The desert is squeezed in the tube-train next to you,
The desert is in the heart of your brother.
The good man is the builder, if he build what is good.
I will show you the things that are now being done,
And some of the things that were long ago done,
That you may take heart. Make perfect your will.
Let me show you the work of the humble. Listen.[14]

There are three parts to Eliot's admonition here. First, we cannot neglect the local church and become the people our pastors complain are being discipled more by our favorite media than by Scripture, sacrament, and service. That neglect makes a space in our lives that won't be filled by something better. It makes the desert in us.

Second, we must be sincere in love and truth (1 Pet. 1:22), rejecting scorn toward goodness and determining that our duty here will involve more than composition of a tidy, rational argument. That sort of self-justification can be very satisfying (and entirely correct!), but rarely does it form a community. Rarely does it help us take heart.

It also precludes the third part: to see the desert in the heart of our brother—the loneliness and disaffection media consumption purports to cure—and more than simply seeing, to respond to it in love as Christ loved us and gave himself for us.

To respond in love is to build, and there is "much to cast down, much to build, much to restore," as Eliot wrote. "Let the work not delay, time and the arm not waste,"[15] for American society has a knowledge crisis, and the American church is no exception. If we are to overcome it, we must build what is good.

NOTES

Introduction

1. I was primarily a contributing editor at *The Week* during that time but was promoted to deputy editor while working on this book. The difference is that earlier I was a freelancer and did little editing of other writers' work; now I'm on staff and oversee all the opinion writers in addition to writing my own stuff.

2. G. K. Chesterton, *Orthodoxy* (New York: John Lane, 1908), 30–31.

3. Chesterton, *Orthodoxy*, 32.

Chapter 1 Naming the Crisis

1. The root of these terms is a Greek word, *epistēmē*, often used to mean theoretical knowledge more than skill knowledge.

2. Bonnie Kristian, "The Epistemic Crisis of Political Polling," *The Week*, September 11, 2020, https://theweek.com/articles/936589/epistemic-crisis -political-polling.

3. Mike Wendling, "The (Almost) Complete History of 'Fake News,'" BBC News, January 22, 2018, https://www.bbc.com/news/blogs-trending -42724320.

4. Bonnie Kristian, "Kellyanne Conway Says the White House Used 'Alternative Facts' about the Inaugural Crowd Size," *The Week*, January 22, 2017, https://theweek.com/speedreads/675071/kellyanne-conway-says-white-house -used-alternative-facts-about-inaugural-crowd-size.

5. Bonnie Kristian, "Rudy Giuliani Says 'Truth Isn't Truth,'" *The Week*, August 19, 2018, https://theweek.com/speedreads/791160/rudy-giuliani-says -truth-isnt-truth.

6. Mark Lilla, *The Once and Future Liberal: After Identity Politics* (New York: HarperCollins, 2017), 90.

7. "Confidence in Institutions," Gallup, 2022, https://news.gallup.com /poll/1597/confidence-institutions.aspx.

8. Hannah Arendt, *The Origins of Totalitarianism* (1951; repr. New York: Harcourt Brace Jovanovich, 1973), 382.

9. Arendt, *Origins of Totalitarianism*, 382.

10. Philip Bump, "Trump on Twitter: Playing Three-Dimensional Chess, or Just Saying Stuff?," *Sydney Morning Herald*, August 2, 2019, https://www .smh.com.au/world/north-america/trump-on-twitter-playing-three-dimen sional-chess-or-just-saying-stuff-20190802-p52d4q.html.

11. "*The Economist* / YouGov Poll Toplines," 2018, https://d25d2506sfb94s .cloudfront.net/cumulus_uploads/document/u1o7azwdvf/econToplines.pdf.

12. Robby Soave, "A Year Ago, the Media Mangled the Covington Catholic Story. What Happened Next Was Even Worse," *Reason*, January 21, 2020, https://reason.com/2020/01/21/covington-catholic-media-nick-sandmann -lincoln-memorial/.

13. C. S. Lewis, *Mere Christianity* (New York: Macmillan, 1952), 106.

14. Julie Irwin Zimmerman, "I Failed the Covington Catholic Test," *The Atlantic*, January 21, 2019, https://www.theatlantic.com/ideas/archive/2019 /01/julie-irwin-zimmerman-i-failed-covington-catholic-test/580897/.

15. Alan Abramowitz and Steven Webster, "'Negative Partisanship' Explains Everything," *Politico*, September/October 2017, https://www.politico .com/magazine/story/2017/09/05/negative-partisanship-explains-everything -215534/.

16. Bonnie Kristian, "America's New Yard Sign Discourse," *The Week*, July 31, 2020, https://theweek.com/articles/928379/americas-new-yard-sign -discourse.

17. John Eggerton, "Howard Dean: Scream 'Never Happened,'" Broadcasting+Cable, June 14, 2004, https://www.nexttv.com/news/howard-dean -scream-never-happened-103490.

18. "The Perception Gap," More in Common, 2019, https://perceptiongap .us/.

19. Bonnie Kristian, "There's a Perfect German Word for America's Perpetually Enraged Culture," *The Week*, November 15, 2018, https://theweek .com/articles/807478/theres-perfect-german-word-americas-perpetually-en raged-culture.

20. Arendt, *Origins of Totalitarianism*, 382, 478.

21. Charles Taylor, *A Secular Age* (Cambridge, MA: Belknap, 2007), 380.

22. "Loneliness in America: How the Pandemic Has Deepened an Epidemic of Loneliness and What We Can Do about It," Making Caring Common Project, February 2021, https://mcc.gse.harvard.edu/reports/loneliness -in-america.

23. Brian Resnick, "22 Percent of Millennials Say They Have 'No Friends,'" Vox, August 1, 2019, https://www.vox.com/science-and-health/2019/8/1 /20750047/millennials-poll-loneliness.

24. Arendt, *Origins of Totalitarianism*, 477–78.

25. Bonnie Kristian, "Dispelling the Smog of Falsehood and 'Fake News,'" *Christianity Today*, February 21, 2021, https://www.christianitytoday.com/ct /2021/february-web-only/dispelling-smog-of-falsehood-and-fake-news.html.

26. Justin Martyr, *The First Apology*, in *The First and Second Apologies*, trans. Leslie William Barnard (Mahwah, NJ: Paulist Press, 1997), 77.

27. Justin Martyr, *First Apology*, 55.

28. Kristian, "Dispelling the Smog."

29. Aaron Earls, "Half of U.S. Protestant Pastors Hear Conspiracy Theories in Their Churches," Lifeway Newsroom, January 26, 2021, https://blog .lifeway.com/newsroom/2021/01/26/half-of-u-s-protestant-pastors-hear-con spiracy-theories-in-their-churches/.

30. Kristian, "Dispelling the Smog."

31. W. H. Auden, "September 1, 1939," *The Collected Poetry of W. H. Auden* (New York: Random House, 1945), 57–59.

Chapter 2 Media

1. Bonnie Kristian, "Liberty University Is Staying Open because Jerry Falwell Jr. Wants to Own the Libs," *The Week*, March 24, 2020, https:// theweek.com/articles/902715/liberty-university-staying-open-because-jerry -falwell-jr-wants-libs.

2. The term "evangelical" has become a political signifier in the last few years. That is not the sense in which I am using it here. Though I often hesitate to use the term publicly because of the political connotation, I am an evangelical in the older, more theological sense. I can check all four boxes, e.g., in the "Bebbington Quadrilateral," a schema of British historian David Bebbington, which characterizes evangelicalism as emphasizing conversion, biblical authority, activism, and crucicentrism. See Mark A. Noll, *The Scandal of the Evangelical Mind* (Grand Rapids: Eerdmans, 1994), 8.

3. "Confidence in Institutions," Gallup, 2022, https://news.gallup.com /poll/1597/confidence-institutions.aspx.

4. Jack Jenkins, "Survey: Faith Groups Showcase Media Divide," Religion News Service, May 14, 2021, https://religionnews.com/2021/05/14/survey -white-evangelicals-trust-fox-news-black-protestants-look-to-mainstream -networks/.

5. Sarah Pulliam Bailey, "Evangelicals, Your Attacks on 'The Media' Are Getting Dangerous," *Washington Post*, December 8, 2016, https://www.wash ingtonpost.com/news/acts-of-faith/wp/2016/12/08/evangelicals-your-attacks -on-the-media-are-getting-dangerous/.

6. John Sands, "Americans Are Losing Faith in an Objective Media. A New Gallup/Knight Study Explores Why," Knight Foundation, August 4, 2020, https://knightfoundation.org/articles/americans-are-losing-faith-in-an -objective-media-a-new-gallup-knight-study-explores-why/.

7. Mason Walker and Jeffrey Gottfried, "Americans Blame Unfair News Coverage on Media Outlets, Not the Journalists Who Work for Them," Pew

Research Center, October 28, 2020, https://www.pewresearch.org/fact-tank /2020/10/28/americans-blame-unfair-news-coverage-on-media-outlets-not -the-journalists-who-work-for-them/.

8. Hadas Gold, "Survey: 7 Percent of Reporters Identify as Republican," *Politico*, May 6, 2014, https://www.politico.com/blogs/media/2014/05/survey -7-percent-of-reporters-identify-as-republican-188053.

9. Amée LaTour, "Fact Check: Do 97 Percent of Journalist Donations Go to Democrats?," BallotPedia, August 16, 2017, https://ballotpedia.org /Fact_check/Do_97_percent_of_journalist_donations_go_to_Democrats.

10. Hugh Hewitt, "*The New York Times'* Jane Coaston on Whether Legacy Media Is 'Left, Left, Left—An Extension of the Democratic Party,'" *Hugh Hewitt* website, May 21, 2021, https://hughhewitt.com/the-new-york -times-jane-coaston-on-whether-legacy-media-is-left-left-left-an-extension -of-the-democratic-party/.

11. Matt Taibbi, *Hate Inc.: Why Today's Media Makes Us Despise One Another* (New York: OR Books, 2021), 162.

12. Taibbi, *Hate Inc.*, 162.

13. Walker and Gottfried, "Americans Blame Unfair News Coverage on Media Outlets."

14. Bonnie Kristian, "2020 Democrats' Shallow Media Criticism," *The Week*, August 14, 2019, https://theweek.com/articles/858934/2020-democrats -shallow-media-criticism.

15. Taibbi, *Hate Inc.*, 20.

16. Jesse Singal (@jessesingal), "For paid subscribers: Watching an LGBT organization celebrate some deeply homophobic, stiflingly patriarchal cultures for their supposed wokeness," Twitter, April 16, 2021, 11:49 a.m., https://twitter.com/jessesingal/status/1383085190940098560.

17. Taibbi, *Hate Inc.*, 154.

18. Tom Rachman, "America's Is–Ought Problem," *The Atlantic*, May 11, 2021, https://www.theatlantic.com/ideas/archive/2021/05/journalists-media -trust-impartiality-rachman/618844/.

19. Taibbi, *Hate Inc.*, 39.

20. Bonnie Kristian, "The Coming End of Christian America," *The Week*, October 20, 2019, https://theweek.com/articles/872709/coming-end-christian -america.

21. Nicole Winfield and Colleen Barry, "Tourist Mecca Notre Dame Also Revered as Place of Worship," Associated Press News, April 17, 2019, https:// www.apnews.com/f309ea14c9b346acb1d3b72c2564c56b.

22. Cailin O'Connor and James Owen Weatherall, *The Misinformation Age: How False Beliefs Spread* (New Haven: Yale University Press, 2019), 152.

23. Kathleen Ann Ruane, "Fairness Doctrine: History and Constitutional Issues," Congressional Research Service, July 13, 2011, https://fas.org/sgp /crs/misc/R40009.pdf.

24. O'Connor and Weatherall, *Misinformation Age*, 166–67.

25. Wesley Lowery, "A Reckoning over Objectivity, Led by Black Journalists," *New York Times*, June 23, 2020, https://www.nytimes.com/2020/06/23/opinion/objectivity-black-journalists-coronavirus.html.

26. Rachman, "America's Is–Ought Problem."

27. Jesse Singal, "Why the Media Is Melting Down," *Spectator World*, May 18, 2021, https://spectator.us/topic/media-moral-madness-journalism/amp/?__twitter_impression=true.

28. Andrey Mir, "Postjournalism: From the World-as-It-Is to the World-as-It-Should-Be," Human as Media, November 11, 2020, https://human-as-media.com/2020/11/11/postjournalism-from-the-world-as-it-is-to-the-world-as-it-should-be/.

29. Andrew Sullivan, "When the Narrative Replaces the News," *The Weekly Dish* (newsletter), Substack, March 19, 2021, https://andrewsullivan.substack.com/p/when-the-narrative-replaces-the-news-9ea.

30. Richard Fausset, Nicholas Bogel-Burroughs, Ruth Graham, and Jack Healy, "Accused Gunman Had Visited Massage Parlors He Targeted, Police Say," *New York Times*, March 18, 2021, https://www.nytimes.com/2021/03/18/us/robert-aaron-long-atlanta-spa-shooting.html.

31. Nicholas Bogel-Burroughs, "The Suspect Had Sought Treatment for Sex Addiction, a Former Roommate Says," *New York Times*, March 18, 2021, https://www.nytimes.com/2021/03/18/us/robert-long-halfway-house.html.

32. Kate Brumback, "Atlanta Spa-Shooting Suspect Pleads Not Guilty in 4 Killings," *Associated Press*, September 28, 2021, https://abcnews.go.com/US/wireStory/atlanta-spa-shooting-suspect-enter-plea-killings-80272807.

33. Joe Walsh, "FBI Director Says Atlanta Shooting 'Does Not Appear' Racially Motivated," *Forbes*, March 18, 2021, https://www.forbes.com/sites/joewalsh/2021/03/18/fbi-director-says-atlanta-shooting-does-not-appear-racially-motivated/?sh=5d43c7031a0d.

34. Jonathan Krohn, "Atlanta Shooter's Ex-Roommate Describes Him as Guilt-Ridden about Pornography and His Spa Visits," *Washington Post*, March 18, 2021, https://www.washingtonpost.com/nation/2021/03/18/atlanta-shooting-live-updates/#link-NDHHS3PMJNG6HNFZ25NRAAXTI4.

35. Taibbi, *Hate Inc.*, 5.

36. Kristian, "2020 Democrats' Shallow Media Criticism."

37. Timothy P. Carney, "What a Columnist Is, and How to Be One," Intercollegiate Studies Institute, January 18, 2016, https://isi.org/intercollegiate-review/what-a-columnist-is-and-how-to-be-one/.

38. Lowery, "A Reckoning over Objectivity."

39. Mike Wendling, "The (Almost) Complete History of 'Fake News,'" BBC News, January 22, 2018, https://www.bbc.com/news/blogs-trending-42724320.

40. Sydney Schaedel, "Did the Pope Endorse Trump?" FactCheck.org, October 24, 2016, https://www.factcheck.org/2016/10/did-the-pope-endorse-trump/.

41. O'Connor and Weatherall, *Misinformation Age*, 3–5.

42. Peter Dizikes, "Study: On Twitter, False News Travels Faster than True Stories," MIT News, March 8, 2018, https://news.mit.edu/2018/study-twitter-false-news-travels-faster-true-stories-0308.

43. Taibbi, *Hate Inc.*, 154–56.

44. Susan B. Glasser, "Covering Politics in a 'Post-truth' America," Brookings Institution, December 2, 2016, https://www.brookings.edu/essay/covering-politics-in-a-post-truth-america/.

45. Glasser, "Covering Politics in a 'Post-truth' America."

46. Jeffrey Bilbro, *Reading the Times: A Literary and Theological Inquiry into the News* (Downers Grove, IL: InterVarsity, 2021), 24–25.

47. Bonnie Kristian, "Our Parents Warned Us the Internet Would Break Our Brains. It Broke Theirs Instead," *The Week*, November 25, 2020, https://theweek.com/articles/951759/parents-warned-internet-break-brains-broke-theirs-instead.

48. Nicholas Carr, *The Shallows: What the Internet Is Doing to Our Brains*, rev. ed. (New York: Norton, 2020), 5–6.

49. Nicholas Carr, "Is Google Making Us Stupid? What the Internet Is Doing to Our Brains," *The Atlantic*, July/August 2008, https://www.theatlantic.com/magazine/archive/2008/07/is-google-making-us-stupid/306868/.

50. Carr, *The Shallows*, 3.

51. Bilbro, *Reading the Times*, 4.

52. Nicholas A. Christakis and James H. Fowler, *Connected: How Your Friends' Friends' Friends Affect Everything You Feel, Think, and Do* (New York: Back Bay Books, 2009).

53. O'Connor and Weatherall, *Misinformation Age*, 172.

54. Nic Newman, Richard Fletcher, Antonis Kalogeropoulos, David A. L. Levy, and Rasmus Kleis Nielsen, "Reuters Institute Digital News Report 2018," Reuters Institute, https://reutersinstitute.politics.ox.ac.uk/sites/default/files/digital-news-report-2018.pdf.

55. Bonnie Kristian, "Facebook Is Unfixable," *The Week*, January 29, 2021, https://theweek.com/articles/963649/facebook-unfixable.

56. Charles Baudelaire, *The Flowers of Evil*, trans. Robert Lowell, ed. Marthiel and Jackson Matthews (New York: New Directions, 1963).

57. Christakis and Fowler, *Connected*, 275.

58. Douglas S. Bursch, *Posting Peace: Why Social Media Divides Us and What We Can Do about It* (Downers Grove, IL: InterVarsity, 2021), chap. 1.

59. Bonnie Kristian, "How the Very Act of Tweeting Makes Your Opinions Worse," *The Week*, January 29, 2020, https://theweek.com/articles/891221/how-act-tweeting-makes-opinions-worse.

60. On the connection between these verses, see Peter H. Davids, *The Epistle of James* (Grand Rapids: Eerdmans, 1982), 137.

61. Thomas à Kempis, *The Imitation of Christ*, trans. Aloysius Croft and Harold Bolton (Milwaukee: Bruce Publishing, 1940), book 1, chap. 1.

62. Dorothy L. Sayers, *Letters to a Diminished Church* (Nashville: W Publishing Group, 2004), 46.

63. Sayers, *Letters to a Diminished Church*, 46–47.

64. Sayers, *Letters to a Diminished Church*, 47.

65. Bonnie Kristian, "The Loaded Gun of Language," *The Week*, August 4, 2020, https://theweek.com/articles/929215/loaded-gun-language.

Chapter 3 Mob

1. Kashmir Hill, "Justine Sacco's Nightmare before Christmas, Twitter-Version," *Forbes*, December 21, 2013, https://www.forbes.com/sites/kashmirhill /2013/12/21/justine-saccos-nightmare-before-christmas-twitter-version/?sh =17beaa4314a2.

2. See, e.g., comments from writer Roxane Gay on the subject in early 2021, where she rejects the phrase but essentially accepts its common meaning as descriptive of a real phenomenon: "Cancel culture is this boogeyman that people have come up with to explain away bad behavior and when their faves experience consequences. I like to think of it as consequence culture, where when you make a mistake—and we all do, by the way—there should be consequences. The problem is that we haven't figured out what consequences should be, so it's all or nothing. Either there are no consequences, or people lose their jobs, or other sort of sweeping grand gestures that don't actually solve the problem at hand." Molly Schwartz, "Roxane Gay Says Cancel Culture Does Not Exist," *Mother Jones*, March 5, 2021, https://www.mother jones.com/media/2021/03/roxane-gay-says-cancel-culture-does-not-exist/.

3. "Compare: 'Online Shaming' 'Cancel Culture,'" Google Trends, https:// trends.google.com/trends/explore?date=all&geo=US&q=%2Fg%2F11f_kn _f1z,cancel%20culture.

4. Ross Douthat, "10 Theses about Cancel Culture," *New York Times*, July 14, 2020, https://www.nytimes.com/2020/07/14/opinion/cancel-culture .html.

5. Douthat, "10 Theses about Cancel Culture."

6. Douthat, "10 Theses about Cancel Culture."

7. Bonnie Kristian, "What Cancel Culture Has in Common with Medieval Outlawry," *Reason*, July 28, 2020, https://reason.com/2020/07/28/what-cancel -culture-has-in-common-with-medieval-outlawry/.

8. Melissa Sartore, *Outlawry, Governance, and Law in Medieval England* (New York: Peter Lang, 2013), 11.

9. Douthat, "10 Theses about Cancel Culture."

10. That your history of cancellation would be discovered when a potential employer googles you points to the class dynamic of cancel culture: it is primarily a phenomenon of the professional-managerial class, and it is most likely to affect people early in their careers. Blue-collar and service-industry employers typically do not exercise the same social scrutiny, while a very wealthy, famous, or professionally established person may be relatively

immune to cancellation because their reputation is already determined, and they have the funds to survive firing. The main threat of cancellation is expulsion from the professional-managerial class; it is the loss of your white collar.

11. Graeme Wood, "The Cancellation of Nikole Hannah-Jones," *The Atlantic*, May 21, 2021, https://www.theatlantic.com/ideas/archive/2021/05/cancellation-unc-nikole-hannah-jones/618951/.

12. Kat Rosenfield, "Someone Is Wrong on the Internet," Arc Digital, March 2, 2021, https://medium.com/arc-digital/someone-is-wrong-on-the-internet-8bb8ce537ac3.

13. Jon Ronson, *So You've Been Publicly Shamed* (New York: Riverhead Books, 2015), 10, 53–56, 82–86.

14. This is where I think the argument fails in Christopher Schelin's article, "Cancel Culture Looks a Lot Like Old-Fashioned Church Discipline," The Conversation, April 28, 2021, https://theconversation.com/cancel-culture-looks-a-lot-like-old-fashioned-church-discipline-158685. Schelin, a theology professor at Starr King School for the Ministry, is correct that cancel culture has some points in common with church discipline, but he gives far too little attention to the fact that members of a congregation typically have voluntarily placed themselves under the authority of whatever ecclesial body or figure is administering the discipline. We have not comparably placed ourselves under the authority of a Twitter mob.

15. Russell Moore, "Does Cancel Culture Exist?," Moore to the Point, March 8, 2021, http://createsend.com/t/r-22F4FBF5BBB039EC2540EF23F30FEDED.

16. Wendell Berry, "Do Not Be Ashamed," in *The Selected Poems of Wendell Berry* (Berkeley: Counterpoint, 1998), 32.

17. Ronson, *So You've Been Publicly Shamed*, 31, 282.

18. Emily Ekins, "Poll: 62% of Americans Say They Have Political Views They're Afraid to Share," CATO Institute, July 22, 2020, https://www.cato.org/survey-reports/poll-62-americans-say-they-have-political-views-theyre-afraid-share.

19. Damon Linker, "Why Political Correctness Fails," *The Week*, May 28, 2021, https://theweek.com/politics/1000894/political-correctness-fails.

20. Miroslav Volf, *Exclusion and Embrace: A Theological Exploration of Identity, Otherness, and Reconciliation*, rev. updated ed. (Nashville: Abingdon, 2019), 44.

21. "The Overton Window," Mackinac Center for Public Policy, 2019, https://www.mackinac.org/OvertonWindow.

22. Alan Jacobs, "The New Heretics," *Snakes and Ladders* (blog), March 15, 2021, https://blog.ayjay.org/the-new-heretics/.

23. Moore, "Does Cancel Culture Exist?"

24. Ronson, *So You've Been Publicly Shamed*, 282.

25. Jonathan Rauch, *Kindly Inquisitors: The New Attacks on Free Thought*, expanded ed. (Chicago: University of Chicago Press, 2013), 6–13.

26. Moore, "Does Cancel Culture Exist?"

27. Leigh Stein, "Matt and Rachael's Breakup on *The Bachelor* Is a Symbol of a Broken America," *Newsweek*, March 16, 2021, https://www.news week.com/matt-rachaels-breakup-bachelor-symbol-broken-america-opinion -1576640.

28. Bonnie Kristian, "Shaming Can't Fix Racism. But Guilt Can," *Christianity Today*, July 22, 2020, https://www.christianitytoday.com/ct/2020/july -web-only/shaming-cant-fix-racism-but-guilt-can.html.

29. Andy Crouch, "The Return of Shame," *Christianity Today*, March 10, 2015, https://www.christianitytoday.com/ct/2015/march/andy-crouch-gospel -in-age-of-public-shame.html?share=TpXih9BTOZ5XVTIN6sRVlVusVW9 KGY0n.

30. Bonnie Kristian, "Our Political Obsession with Shame," *The Week*, February 26, 2019, https://theweek.com/articles/821655/political-obsession -shame.

31. Samuel D. James, "'I'm Beginning to Think I've Been Duped,'" *Letter & Liturgy*, February 1, 2021, https://letterandliturgy.wordpress.com/2021/02 /01/im-beginning-to-think-ive-been-duped/.

32. Kristian, "Shaming Can't Fix Racism."

33. Alan Jacobs, "Race at Baylor," *Snakes and Ladders* (blog), July 28, 2020, https://blog.ayjay.org/race-at-baylor/.

34. Volf, *Exclusion and Embrace*, 13.

35. Thomas Aquinas, *The Summa Theologiae*, trans. Fathers of the English Dominican Province (London: Burns, Oates & Washbourne, 1920), II-II, Q. 130.

36. Alan Jacobs, "Vengeance," *Snakes and Ladders* (blog), June 26, 2017, https://blog.ayjay.org/vengeance/.

37. Leah Libresco Sargeant, "Penance and Public Shaming," *The Bulwark*, May 29, 2021, https://thebulwark.com/penance-and-public-shaming/.

38. Volf, *Exclusion and Embrace*, 18.

39. See the first half of Joseph Bottum, *An Anxious Age: The Post-Protestant Ethic and Spirit of America* (New York: Crown, 2014).

40. Sargeant, "Penance and Public Shaming."

41. "How Many American Children Have Cut Contact with Their Parents?," *The Economist*, May 22, 2021, https://www.economist.com/united -states/2021/05/22/how-many-american-children-have-cut-contact-with-their -parents.

42. Joseph Bottum writes in "The Spiritual Shape of Political Ideas":
To shun these days is to take away from sinners any access to the forums of public life. And the result, curiously, is to turn the effect of shunning in on the congregation: What once concerned primarily the disciplining of the erring brother, keeping him outside the temple until repentance, now seems to concern mostly the disciplining of the community itself by making sure no one dares join him in his sinful opinions. . . . And so we expel the guilty and close our eyes in holy dread. But what then? With the idea of shunning now entirely free

from its old theological context, we offer no clear path back for the shunned sinner. (*Washington Examiner*, December 1, 2014, https://www.washingtonexaminer.com/weekly-standard/the-spiritual-shape-of-political-ideas)

43. Sargeant, "Penance and Public Shaming."
44. G. K. Chesterton, *The Secret of Father Brown* (1927; repr. West Valley City, UT: Waking Lion, 2006), 165.
45. Sargeant, "Penance and Public Shaming."
46. Volf, *Exclusion and Embrace*, 47.

Chapter 4 Schemes

1. Posts with the unique ID "BQ7V3bcW" and in ascending order, Archives: /pol/—Politically Incorrect, https://archive.4plebs.org/pol/search/uid/BQ7V3bcW%20/order/asc/.

2. For example, do you ask about QAnon by name, or do you describe its tenets and ask people if they agree? If you do the former, you risk missing people who believe the theory without knowing its name; if you do the latter, you risk overcounting people who believe similar but distinct conspiracy theories. Likewise, how should pollsters account for the possibility of the "shy" Q believer? That's someone who will lie about their acceptance of QAnon, perhaps because they don't trust the media or fear retaliation by the cabal if they identify themselves as adherents. See, for instance, Kaleigh Rogers, "Why It's So Hard to Gauge Support for QAnon," *FiveThirtyEight*, June 11, 2021, https://fivethirtyeight.com/features/why-its-so-hard-to-gauge-support-for-qanon/.

3. James Shanahan, "Support for QAnon Is Hard to Measure—and Polls May Overestimate It," The Conversation, March 5, 2021, https://theconversation.com/support-for-qanon-is-hard-to-measure-and-polls-may-overestimate-it-156020.

4. Giovanni Russonello, "QAnon Is Now as Popular in US as Some Major Religions, Poll Suggests," *Chicago Tribune*, May 28, 2021, https://www.chicagotribune.com/nation-world/ct-aud-nw-qanon-popularity-poll-20210528-lpm6ik5mrjevdbifaikmcmdnta-story.html.

5. Bonnie Kristian, "QAnon Is a Wolf in Wolf's Clothing," *Christianity Today*, August 26, 2020, https://www.christianitytoday.com/ct/2020/august-web-only/qanon-is-wolf-in-wolfs-clothing.html.

6. "Disinformation is real. Distractions are necessary," said an early Q drop. "Focus was US today while real happening in [Saudi Arabia] under same context (military control, martial law, missile strike (rogue) etc). Necessary." Adherents took this as license to ignore any Q drop they wanted, chalking it up as a distraction to confuse the cabal. "Intel Drop #88," QAlerts, November 5, 2017, https://qalerts.app/?n=88.

7. Bonnie Kristian, "The Biden Inauguration Breaks QAnon," *The Week*, January 20, 2021, https://theweek.com/articles/962128/biden-inauguration-breaks-qanon.

8. Ben Collins, "QAnon's New 'Plan'? Run for School Board," NBC News, July 7, 2021, https://www.nbcnews.com/tech/tech-news/qanon-new-plan-run-school-board-rcna1352.

9. Richard Hofstadter, "The Paranoid Style in American Politics," *Harper's Magazine*, November 1964, https://harpers.org/archive/1964/11/the-paranoid-style-in-american-politics/.

10. Jesse Walker, *The United States of Paranoia: A Conspiracy Theory* (New York: Harper Perennial, 2013), 11.

11. Walker, *United States of Paranoia*, 42, 287.

12. Walker, *United States of Paranoia*, 283.

13. James Deutsch and Levi Bochantin, "The Folkloric Roots of the QAnon Conspiracy," Folklife, December 7, 2020, https://folklife.si.edu/magazine/folkloric-roots-of-qanon-conspiracy.

14. Walker, *United States of Paranoia*, 16.

15. Adrienne LaFrance, "The Prophecies of Q," *The Atlantic*, June 2020, https://www.theatlantic.com/magazine/archive/2020/06/qanon-nothing-can-stop-what-is-coming/610567/.

16. Walker, *United States of Paranoia*, 162.

17. Walker, *United States of Paranoia*, 160–66.

18. Nancy L. Rosenblum and Russell Muirhead, *A Lot of People Are Saying: The New Conspiracism and the Assault on Democracy* (Princeton: Princeton University Press, 2019), 2–3.

19. Walker, *United States of Paranoia*, 15.

20. David Hume, *The Natural History of Religion* (London: Bradlaugh Bonner, 1889), 12.

21. Walker, *United States of Paranoia*, 333–38.

22. Hofstadter, "Paranoid Style in American Politics."

23. Jack Jenkins, "Survey: More Than a Quarter of White Evangelicals Believe Core QAnon Conspiracy Theory," Religion News Service, February 11, 2021, https://religionnews.com/2021/02/11/survey-more-than-a-quarter-of-white-evangelicals-believe-core-qanon-conspiracy-theory/.

24. Kaleigh Rogers, "Why QAnon Has Attracted So Many White Evangelicals," *FiveThirtyEight*, March 4, 2021, https://fivethirtyeight.com/features/why-qanon-has-attracted-so-many-white-evangelicals/.

25. Aaron Earls, "Half of U.S. Protestant Pastors Hear Conspiracy Theories in Their Churches," *Lifeway Newsroom*, January 26, 2021, https://blog.lifeway.com/newsroom/2021/01/26/half-of-u-s-protestant-pastors-hear-conspiracy-theories-in-their-churches/.

26. Zeynep Tufekci, "How Social Media Took Us from Tahrir Square to Donald Trump," *MIT Technology Review*, August 14, 2018, https://www.technologyreview.com/2018/08/14/240325/how-social-media-took-us-from-tahrir-square-to-donald-trump/.

27. Tufekci, "How Social Media Took Us from Tahrir Square to Donald Trump."

28. C. S. Lewis, "The Inner Ring," in *The Weight of Glory* (1949; repr. New York: HarperSanFrancisco, 1980), 145–47.

29. W. B. Yeats, "The Second Coming," in *The Collected Poems of W. B. Yeats* (Ware, Hertfordshire: Wordsworth Editions, 1994), 158–59.

30. Hofstadter, "Paranoid Style in American Politics."

31. Daniel Bessner and Amber A'Lee Frost, "How the QAnon Cult Stormed the Capitol," *Jacobin*, January 19, 2021, https://jacobinmag.com/2021/01 /q-anon-cult-capitol-hill-riot-trump.

32. Rogers, "Why QAnon Has Attracted So Many White Evangelicals."

33. I offer my thanks to two Twitter threads from researchers associated with The Q Origins Project for guidance here: G. Fox (@QOrigins), "Q has used Christian language since the first canonical drops," Twitter, March 15, 2021, 7:27 a.m., https://twitter.com/ResearchFQX/status/1371422854324105218; The Q Origins Project (@QOrigins), "This is an incredible find," Twitter, March 14, 2021, 4:05 a.m., https://twitter.com/QOrigins/status/137100966 4754794500.

34. Ray Walters, "Ten Years of Best Sellers," *New York Times*, December 30, 1979, https://www.nytimes.com/1979/12/30/archives/ten-years-of-best -sellers-best-sellers.html.

35. Hal Lindsey, with Carole C. Carlson, *The Late Great Planet Earth* (Grand Rapids: Zondervan, 1970), 1–2.

36. *The Late Great Planet Earth* (product page), Zondervan, 2022, https:// www.zondervan.com/9780310277712/the-late-great-planet-earth/.

37. Joel Lawrence, "Faith, Apocalypse, and Nationalism: Why Evangelicals Are Vulnerable to Conspiracy Theories," Center for Pastor Theologians, January 25, 2021, https://www.pastortheologians.com/articles/2021 /1/25/faith-apocalypse-and-nationalism-why-evangelicals-are-vulnerable-to -conspiracy-theories.

38. Mark A. Noll, in his book *The Scandal of the Evangelical Mind* (Grand Rapids: Eerdmans, 1994), says,

> Christian fascination with the end of the world has existed for a very long time, but . . . recent evangelical fixation on such matters—where contemporary events are labeled with great self-confidence as the ful- fillment of biblical prophecies heralding the End of Time—has been particularly intense. For those who doubt the continuing domination of this way of thinking among evangelicals, it is worth remembering the Gulf War of 1991. Within weeks of the outbreak of this conflict, evan- gelical publishers provided a spate of books featuring efforts to read this latest Middle East crisis as a direct fulfillment of biblical prophecy heralding the end of the world. The books came to various conclusions, but they all shared the disconcerting conviction that the best way to provide moral judgment about what has been happening in the Middle East was *not* to study carefully what was going on in the Middle East. Rather, they featured a kind of Bible study that drew attention away from careful analysis of the complexities of Middle Eastern culture

or the tangled twentieth-century history of the region toward speculation about some of the most esoteric and widely debated passages of
the Bible. Moreover, that speculation was carried on with only slight
attention to the central themes of the Bible (like the divine standard
of justice applied in all human situations), which are crystal clear and
about which there is wide agreement among evangelicals and other
theologically conservative Christians. How did the evangelical public
respond to these books? It responded by immediately vaulting several
of these titles to the top of religious best-seller lists. (13–14)

39. Quotations attributed to Derek Kubilus (pastor, Uniontown United
Methodist Church, Uniontown, OH) in this chapter are drawn from an interview via an email exchange between Kubilus and Bonnie Kristian, June
18–July 23, 2021.

40. Quotations attributed to Ben Marsh (pastor, First Alliance Church,
Winston-Salem, NC) in this chapter are drawn from an interview via an email
exchange with Bonnie Kristian, June 17–29, 2021.

41. Quotations attributed to James Kendall (pastor, Grace Community
Church, Madera, CA) in this chapter are drawn from an interview via an
email exchange between Kendall and Bonnie Kristian, June 17–July 8, 2021.

42. Mike Rothschild, "Liberals Obsessed with QAnon Are Ignoring a
Burgeoning Conspiratorial Movement of Their Own," Daily Dot, March
17, 2021, https://www.dailydot.com/debug/conspiracy-theories-true-false/.

43. I owe the image to Jacob Ludwig Karl Grimm and Wilhelm Carl Grimm,
"The True Bride," in *Grimm's Complete Fairy Tales* (Garden City, NY: Double-
day, 1960), 218–23.

44. G. K. Chesterton, *Orthodoxy* (New York: John Lane Company, 1908),
32–33.

45. Chesterton, *Orthodoxy*, 34, 36.

46. See, e.g., Greg Jaffe and Jose A. Del Real, "Life amid the Ruins of
QAnon: 'I Wanted My Family Back,'" *Washington Post*, February 23, 2021,
https://www.washingtonpost.com/nation/interactive/2021/conspiracy-theo
ries-qanon-family-members/. See also Jesselyn Cook, "'I Miss My Mom':
Children of QAnon Believers Are Desperately Trying to Deradicalize Their
Own Parents," HuffPost, February 11, 2021, https://www.huffpost.com/entry
/children-of-qanon-believers_n_601078e9c5b6c5586aa49077.

47. Mack Lamoureux, "QAnons Are Harassing People at the Whim of
a Woman They Say Is Canada's Queen," Vice News, June 17, 2021, https://
www.vice.com/en/article/3aqvkw/qanons-are-harassing-people-at-the-whim
-of-a-woman-they-say-is-canadas-queen-romana-didulo.

48. BurritoSorceress (Reddit user), "Mole Children Theory Escalation,"
Reddit, June 15, 2021, https://www.reddit.com/r/QAnonCasualties/com
ments/o0o282/mole_children_theory_escalation/.

49. Sophia Ankel, "Pastors Are Leaving Their Congregations after Losing
Their Churchgoers to QAnon," Business Insider Australia, March 14, 2021,

https://www.businessinsider.com.au/pastors-quit-after-qanon-radicalize-congregation-2021-3.

50. Bonnie Kristian, "The World Is Too Stupid for Your Conspiracy Theories," *The Week*, August 13, 2019, https://theweek.com/articles/858593/world-stupid-conspiracy-theories.

51. Ed Stetzer, "Evangelicals Need to Address the QAnoners in Our Midst," *USA Today*, September 4, 2020, https://www.usatoday.com/story/opinion/2020/09/04/qanon-and-evangelicals-its-time-address-qanoners-column/3446756001/.

52. John Piper, "How Should We Respond to Christian Conspiracy Theories?," Desiring God, April 23, 2021, https://www.desiringgod.org/interviews/how-should-we-respond-to-christian-conspiracy-theories.

Chapter 5 Skepticism

1. Bonnie Kristian, "Orthodox Jews Say They're Being Targeted by New NYC Lockdowns," *Reason*, October 8, 2020, https://reason.com/2020/10/08/orthodox-jews-say-theyre-being-targeted-by-new-nyc-lockdowns/.

2. Reuvain Borchardt, "De Blasio: Only Protest Gatherings OK, Due to '400 Years of American Racism,'" *Hamodia*, June 2, 2020, https://hamodia.com/2020/06/02/de-blasio-allowing-protesters-defy-social-distancing-due-angst-400-years-american-racism/.

3. Tom Nichols, *The Death of Expertise: The Campaign against Established Knowledge and Why It Matters* (New York: Oxford University Press, 2017), 5.

4. Nichols, *Death of Expertise*, 30.

5. Nichols, *Death of Expertise*, 3.

6. Alex Kaufman, "Prepare to Be Shocked!" Slate, July 30, 2013, https://slate.com/business/2013/07/how-one-weird-trick-conquered-the-internet-what-happens-when-you-click-on-those-omnipresent-ads.html.

7. Nichols, *Death of Expertise*, 5.

8. Nichols, *Death of Expertise*, xix, 15.

9. Martin Gurri, *The Revolt of the Public and the Crisis of Authority in the New Millennium* (San Francisco: Stripe, 2018), 420.

10. Derek Thompson (@DKThomp), "Life and knowledge really are getting more complex," Twitter, April 2, 2021, 8:23 a.m., https://twitter.com/DKThomp/status/1377959907991941120.

11. Gurri, *Revolt of the Public*, 101–2.

12. Nichols, *Death of Expertise*, 82–83.

13. Jonathan Rauch, *Kindly Inquisitors: The New Attacks on Free Thought*, expanded ed. (Chicago: University of Chicago Press, 2013), 67–69.

14. Charles Warzel, "Extremely Isolated, and Yet Never Alone," interview with Julia Marcus, *Galaxy Brain* (newsletter), Substack, May 27, 2021, https://warzel.substack.com/p/extremely-isolated-and-yet-never.

15. Gurri, *Revolt of the Public*, 175.

16. Gurri, *Revolt of the Public*, 24.

17. Nichols, *Death of Expertise*, 178–88.

18. Michael B. Hancock (@MayorHancock), "Pass the potatoes, not COVID." Twitter, November 25, 2020, 10:43 a.m., https://twitter.com/Mayor Hancock/status/1331624516267589634?s=20.

19. Andrea Salcedo, "Denver's Mayor Urged Residents to Avoid Thanksgiving Travel. Then He Flew Cross-country to See Family," *Washington Post*, November 26, 2020, https://www.washingtonpost.com/nation/2020/11/26 /denver-mayor-hancock-thanksgiving-covid/.

20. Matt Cannon, "Every Mayor, Governor Accused of Breaking COVID Restrictions—and Why," *Newsweek*, December 3, 2020, https://www.news week.com/every-mayor-governor-caught-breaking-covid-restrictions-155 2033.

21. Angelina Weld Grimké, "The Puppet-Player," Academy of American Poets, July 26, 2020, https://poets.org/poem/puppet-player.

22. Plato, *The Republic,* trans. Allan Bloom (New York: Basic Books, 1991), 415a–d.

23. Alex Nowrasteh, "Against the 'Noble Lie'—COVID-19 Edition," *CATO at Liberty* (blog), CATO Institute, March 25, 2020, https://www.cato .org/blog/against-noble-lie-covid-19-edition.

24. T. A. Frank, "'I Was Looking at Them in the Wrong Way': Mask Misinformation and the Failure of the Elites," *Vanity Fair*, April 8, 2020, https://www.vanityfair.com/news/2020/04/mask-misinformation-and-the -failure-of-the-elites.

25. This tweet no longer exists, but see Miriam Fauzia, "Fact Check: Trump Surgeon General Initially Dismissed Mask-Wearing, but Then Endorsed," *USA Today*, February 17, 2021, https://www.usatoday.com/story /news/factcheck/2021/02/17/fact-check-ex-surgeon-general-jerome-adams -reversed-position-masks/6765301002/.

26. Huo Jingnan, "Why There Are So Many Different Guidelines for Face Masks for the Public," NPR, April 10, 2020, https://www.npr.org/sections /goatsandsoda/2020/04/10/829890635/why-there-so-many-different-guide lines-for-face-masks-for-the-public.

27. Kerrington Powell and Vinay Prasad, "The Noble Lies of COVID-19," Slate, July 28, 2021, https://slate.com/technology/2021/07/noble-lies-covid -fauci-cdc-masks.html.

28. Donald G. McNeil Jr., "How Much Herd Immunity Is Enough?," *New York Times*, December 24, 2020, https://www.nytimes.com/2020/12 /24/health/herd-immunity-covid-coronavirus.html.

29. Bonnie Kristian, "The Harm Reduction Phase of the Pandemic," *The Week*, June 19, 2020, https://theweek.com/articles/920513/harm-reduction -phase-pandemic.

30. Michael Powell, "Are Protests Dangerous? What Experts Say May Depend on Who's Protesting What," *New York Times*, July 6, 2020, https:// www.nytimes.com/2020/07/06/us/Epidemiologists-coronavirus-protests -quarantine.html.

31. Jennifer Frey, "Political Wisdom and the Limits of Expertise," Breaking Ground, July 20, 2020, https://breakingground.us/political-wisdom-and-the-limits-of-expertise/.

32. Powell, "Are Protests Dangerous?"

33. Norman Doidge, "Hydroxychloroquine: A Morality Tale," Tablet, August 14, 2020, https://www.tabletmag.com/sections/science/articles/hydroxychloroquine-morality-tale.

34. Bonnie Kristian, "The COVID Lab-Leak Debate Is Asking the Wrong Question," *The Week*, May 19, 2021, https://theweek.com/articles/983265/covid-lableak-debate-asking-wrong-question.

35. Paul Basken, "How Academia Shunned the Science behind the Covid Vaccine," *Times Higher Education*, February 8, 2021, https://www.timeshighereducation.com/news/how-academia-shunned-science-behind-covid-vaccine.

36. Basken, "How Academia Shunned the Science behind the Covid Vaccine."

37. Matthew Yglesias, "The Media's Lab Leak Fiasco," *Slow Boring* (newsletter), Substack, May 26, 2021, https://www.slowboring.com/p/the-medias-lab-leak-fiasco.

38. Earthley Wellness New, "If science was never questioned you'd still be drinking cocaine," Facebook, https://www.facebook.com/EarthleyWellnessNew/posts/135425391992912.

39. Gurri, *Revolt of the Public*, 187.

40. Mark A. Noll, *The Scandal of the Evangelical Mind* (Grand Rapids: Eerdmans, 1994), 193.

41. Noll, *Scandal of the Evangelical Mind*, 245.

42. Nichols, *Death of Expertise*, 23.

43. Bertrand Russell, "On the Value of Scepticism," 1928, available at http://personal.kent.edu/~rmuhamma/Philosophy/RBwritings/valueSceptism.htm.

44. Noah Smith, "Yes, Experts Will Lie to You Sometimes," *Noahpinion* (newsletter), Substack, March 28, 2021, https://noahpinion.substack.com/p/yes-experts-will-lie-to-you-sometimes.

45. Joseph M. Keegin, "The Cop-Out of 'Follow the Science,'" *New Atlantis,* Spring 2021, https://www.thenewatlantis.com/publications/the-cop-out-of-follow-the-science.

46. Gurri, *Revolt of the Public*, 422, 424–25.

47. Kevin Breuninger, "Fauci Blasts 'Preposterous' Covid Conspiracies, Accuses His Critics of 'Attacks on Science,'" CNBC, June 9, 2021, https://www.cnbc.com/2021/06/09/fauci-blasts-preposterous-covid-conspiracies-accuses-critics-of-attacks-on-science.html.

48. Bonnie Kristian, "It's Almost Time for Pandemic Apologies," *The Week*, May 16, 2020, https://theweek.com/articles/914427/almost-time-pandemic-apologies.

49. Samuel D. James, "The Death of Expertise," *Letter & Liturgy* (blog), April 20, 2017, https://letterandliturgy.wordpress.com/2017/04/20/the-death -of-expertise/.

Chapter 6 Emotion

1. I quote the King James Version because it was the preferred version of the churches I attended up through middle school. The NIV rendering, interestingly, is actually harsher than the KJV: "The heart is deceitful above all things and beyond cure."

2. "Strong's H3820—*lēb*," *Blue Letter Bible*, https://www.blueletterbible .org/lexicon/h3820/kjv/wlc/0-1/.

3. James Swan, "Luther: For Feelings Come and Feelings Go, and Feelings Are Deceiving; My Warrant Is the Word of God, Nought Else Is Worth Believing," *Beggars All: Reformation & Apologetics*, June 28, 2015, https:// beggarsallreformation.blogspot.com/2015/06/luther-for-feelings-come-and -feelings.html.

4. I have very lightly modernized (e.g., "feelest" changed to "feels," "thee" to "you," "forgivest" to "forgives") the translation presented in Martin Luther, *The Familiar Discourses of Dr. Martin Luther*, trans. Henry Bell and Joseph Kerby (London: Sussex, 1818), 144.

5. If you're ever tempted to think Luther eschewed emotion, look up his insults.

6. Ben Shapiro (@benshapiro), "Facts don't care about your feelings," Twitter, February 5, 2016, 11:03 a.m., https://twitter.com/benshapiro/status /695638866993115136.

7. Kevin D. Williamson, "The Civil War of Wishful Thinking," *National Review*, March 7, 2021, https://www.nationalreview.com/2021/03/the-civil -war-of-wishful-thinking/.

8. Bonnie Kristian, "The Right Is Hooked on a Feeling," *The Week*, January 6, 2021, https://theweek.com/articles/958732/right-hooked-feeling.

9. Derek Robertson, "How 'Owning the Libs' Became the GOP's Core Belief," *Politico*, March 21, 2021, https://www.politico.com/news/magazine /2021/03/21/owning-the-libs-history-trump-politics-pop-culture-477203.

10. Kristian, "The Right Is Hooked on a Feeling."

11. Media Matters staff, "Fox Host Defends 'Skepticism' of Election Results because 'It Certainly Feels Like Society Is Rigged,'" Media Matters for America, January 5, 2021, https://www.mediamatters.org/fox-friends/fox -host-defends-skepticism-election-results-because-it-certainly-feels-society -rigged.

12. Jackson Elliott, "Some Christians Express Concerns over 'Bizarre' Pro-Trump Jericho March," *Christian Post*, December 15, 2020, https://www .christianpost.com/news/some-christians-concerned-over-bizarre-pro-trump -jericho-march.html.

13. The Eric Metaxas Radio Show channel has since been removed from YouTube. Video and a transcript of this portion of the interview can be found at https://www.mediamatters.org/charlie-kirk/right-wing-radio-host -eric-metaxas-we-need-fight-death-last-drop-blood. These quotations are copied from my transcription of the original video for Kristian, "The Right Is Hooked on a Feeling."

14. David Brooks got this right in a perceptive *New York Times* piece on the subject:

> Today many of us feel that America is suffering an epistemic crisis. We don't see the same reality. People say that they often assume the problem is intellectual. Our system of producing propositional knowledge is breaking down. Why can't those people fact-check themselves? But Donald Trump doesn't get away with lies because his followers flunked Epistemology 101. He gets away with his lies because he tells stories of dispossession that feel true to many of them. Some students at elite schools aren't censorious and intolerant because they lack analytic skills. They feel entrapped by a moral order that feels unsafe and unjust. The collapse of trust, the rise of animosity—these are emotional, not intellectual problems. ("How to Destroy Truth," *New York Times,* July 1, 2021, https://www.nytimes.com/2021/07/01 /opinion/patriotism-misinformation.html)

15. Alison M. Jaggar, "Love and Knowledge: Emotion in Feminist Epistemology," *Inquiry* 32, no. 2 (1989): 151.

16. Plato, *Timaeus,* trans. Benjamin Jowett, The Internet Classics Archive, 2009, http://classics.mit.edu/Plato/timaeus.html.

17. Jaggar, "Love and Knowledge," 151–52.

18. My thanks to David French for directing my attention to Haidt's metaphor.

19. Jonathan Haidt, *The Happiness Hypothesis: Finding Modern Truth in Ancient Wisdom* (New York: Basic Books, 2006), 4, 17.

20. Haidt, *The Happiness Hypothesis,* 22.

21. Jonathan Haidt, *The Righteous Mind: Why Good People Are Divided by Politics and Religion* (New York: Vintage Books, 2012), 39–41.

22. Jaggar, "Love and Knowledge," 164.

23. See, in its entirety, Mark A. Noll, *The Scandal of the Evangelical Mind* (Grand Rapids: Eerdmans, 1994).

24. Quotations attributed to David French in this chapter are drawn from a phone interview with Bonnie Kristian on August 9, 2021.

25. For a fascinating example of this, see the discussion about former New Jersey governor Chris Christie in Ira Glass (host), "The Herd," *This American Life* (radio show), April 23, 2021, https://www.thisamericanlife .org/736/transcript. The section related to Christie comes near the end of the conversation.

26. Zeynep Tufekci, "How Social Media Took Us from Tahrir Square to Donald Trump," *MIT Technology Review,* August 14, 2018, https://www

.technologyreview.com/2018/08/14/240325/how-social-media-took-us-from
-tahrir-square-to-donald-trump/.

27. Michael Brendan Dougherty, "Good Friday for Backsliders," *National Review*, April 2, 2021, https://www.nationalreview.com/2021/04/good-friday
-for-backsliders/.

Chapter 7 Experience

1. Katie Herzog, "The Detransitioners: They Were Transgender, Until They Weren't," *The Stranger*, June 28, 2017, https://www.thestranger.com
/features/2017/06/28/25252342/the-detransitioners-they-were-transgender
-until-they-werent.

2. Katie Herzog, "A Response to the Uproar over My Piece, 'The Detransitioners,'" *The Stranger*, July 3, 2017, https://www.thestranger.com/slog
/2017/07/03/25262759/a-response-to-the-uproar-over-my-piece-the-detransi
tioners.

3. John McDermott, "Those People We Tried to Cancel? They're All Hanging Out Together," *New York Times*, November 2, 2019, https://www
.nytimes.com/2019/11/02/style/what-is-cancel-culture.html.

4. Jason Rantz, "Former *Stranger* Writer on Rise of Cancel Culture in Seattle and across the US," KTTH talk radio, June 11, 2020, https://mynorth
west.com/1935924/cancel-culture-seattle-herzog/?.

5. Hallie Lieberman, "Why Is Reporting on Trans Issues So Fraught?" News to Table, May 3, 2019, https://medium.com/news-to-table/https
-medium-com-news-to-table-why-is-reporting-on-trans-issues-so-fraught
-c3b52b4b97c4.

6. Katie Herzog, interview with Bonnie Kristian, August 19, 2021. Unless otherwise indicated, all quotations from Herzog are from this interview.

7. Herzog, "A Response to the Uproar."

8. Carl R. Trueman, *The Rise and Triumph of the Modern Self: Cultural Amnesia, Expressive Individualism, and the Road to Sexual Revolution* (Wheaton: Crossway, 2020), 115, 325, 402–3.

9. Matt Bruenig, "What Does Identitarian Deference Require?," *Matt Bruenig Dot Com*, February 26, 2013, https://mattbruenig.com/2013/02/26
/what-does-identitarian-deference-require/.

10. Bruenig, "What Does Identitarian Deference Require?"

11. Herzog, "A Response to the Uproar."

12. Bruenig, "What Does Identitarian Deference Require?"

13. Matt Bruenig, "Identitarian Deference Continues to Roil Liberalism," July 17, 2020, https://mattbruenig.medium.com/identitarian-deference-con
tinues-to-roil-liberalism-6a1fc88e7f34.

14. Jesse Singal, "On Chimamanda Ngozi Adichie, Invisible Identities, and Weaponized Fragility," *Singal-Minded* (newsletter), Substack, June 17, 2021, https://jessesingal.substack.com/p/on-chimamanda-ngozi-adichie-invisible.

15. Chimamanda Ngozi Adichie, "It Is Obscene, A True Reflection in Three Parts," June 15, 2021, https://www.chimamanda.com/news_items/it-is-obscene-a-true-reflection-in-three-parts/.

16. Bruenig, "Identitarian Deference Continues to Roil Liberalism."

17. Mark Lilla, *The Once and Future Liberal: After Identity Politics* (New York: HarperCollins, 2017), 90–91.

18. Jesse Singal, "Why Trump's Lived Experience as a Covid Victim Matters Less Than He Thinks," *Singal-Minded* (newsletter), Substack, October 6, 2020, https://jessesingal.substack.com/p/why-trumps-lived-experience-as-a.

19. Jonathan Rauch captures well the way in which this power play cloaks itself in humanitarian garb:

> The [free/scientific discourse] process often rules against someone whose cause seems sympathetic. So be it. All other paths to knowledge lead to creed wars. And the attempt to intimidate would-be debunkers by calling them "racist" or "sexist" or whatever is nothing but an attempt to replace science with political muscle. Further, only after an idea has survived checking is it deserving of respect. Not long ago, I heard an activist say at a public meeting that her opinion at least deserved respect. The audience gave her a big round of applause. But she and they had it backwards. Respect was the most, not the least, that she could have demanded for her opinion. Except insofar as an opinion earns its stripes in the science game, it is entitled to no respect whatsoever. (*Kindly Inquisitors: The New Attacks on Free Thought*, expanded ed. [Chicago: University of Chicago Press, 2013], 119)

20. Justin Brierley (chair), "NT Wright & Douglas Murray: Identity, Myth & Miracles; How Do We Live in a Post-Christian World?," *Unbelievable?*, (YouTube video), May 13, 2021, https://www.youtube.com/watch?v=VN8OUi9MF7w.

21. Rauch, *Kindly Inquisitors*, 48–49. See also his follow-up book, *The Constitution of Knowledge: A Defense of Truth* (Washington, DC: Brookings Institution Press, 2020).

22. Rauch, *Kindly Inquisitors*, 145–46.

23. Rauch, *Constitution of Knowledge*, 89–91, 113.

24. Rauch, *Constitution of Knowledge*, 113.

25. Esau McCaulley, *Reading While Black: African American Biblical Interpretation as an Exercise in Hope* (Downers Grove, IL: InterVarsity, 2020), 9–15.

26. McCaulley, *Reading While Black*, 22.

27. "Esau McCaulley on *Reading While Black*," interview by Dru Johnson, *OnScript* (podcast), December 25, 2020, https://hebraicthought.org/podcast/esau-mccaulley-reading-while-black-onscript/.

28. "Esau McCaulley on *Reading While Black*."

Chapter 8 A Practical Epistemology

1. What I've quoted in the epigraph above is a modernized and slightly abbreviated version of the prayer as it appears in Pope Pius XI, "Studiorum Ducem on St. Thomas Aquinas," Papal Encyclicals Online, https://www.pa palencyclicals.net/pius11/p11studi.htm.

2. Tish Harrison Warren, *Prayer in the Night: For Those Who Work or Watch or Weep* (Downers Grove, IL: InterVarsity, 2021), 7–9.

3. Freddie DeBoer, "Nitro Edition: None of This Is New," *Freddie De-Boer* (newsletter), Substack, April 5, 2021, https://freddiedeboer.substack .com/p/nitro-edition-none-of-this-is-new.

4. Alasdair MacIntyre, "Epistemological Crises, Dramatic Narrative and the Philosophy of Science," *The Monist* (1977): 456.

5. Jennifer Nagel, *Knowledge: A Very Short Introduction* (Oxford: Oxford University Press, 2014), 52–53.

6. W. Jay Wood, *Epistemology: Becoming Intellectually Virtuous* (Downers Grove, IL: IVP Academic, 1998), 7–8.

7. The first three terms identify major views of the attainability of knowledge. Skepticism says some or all knowledge is impossible for humans to attain. Rationalism says we can attain knowledge through logical reasoning. Empiricism says we can attain it through empirical observation of the world, as with the scientific method. The next three terms are about the justification of knowledge. Foundationalism says we start with a few self-evident—i.e., self-justifying—beliefs and build from there. Coherentism says what matters is that all our beliefs are consistent (or coherent) with one another. Reliabilism advises we look instead to how we formed our beliefs and ask whether the process was reliable. Socrates was fairly skeptical, as we see especially clearly in Plato's *Theaetetus*. Descartes was a rationalist and Locke an empiricist. Foucault has been influential in his linking of truth to the exercise of power. The dreams, *The Matrix*, and the demon are simply three versions of a classic question of skepticism that asks us to consider whether we can trust our most basic sense perceptions. The demon version comes from Descartes, the dream version predates him, and *The Matrix*, of course, is much more recent.

8. The whole definition section is informed by James K. Dew and Mark W. Foreman, *How Do We Know? An Introduction to Epistemology* (Downers Grove, IL: IVP Academic, 2014), 20–25, 56.

9. Miroslav Volf, *Exclusion and Embrace: A Theological Exploration of Identity, Otherness, and Reconciliation*, rev. and updated ed. (Nashville: Abingdon, 2019), 232.

10. E. Randolph Richards and Brandon J. O'Brien, *Misreading Scripture with Western Eyes: Removing Cultural Blinders to Better Understand the Bible* (Downers Grove, IL: InterVarsity, 2012), 12.

11. I'm not fully confident about this attribution, but I believe the original source to be Saji George (@S_A_J_I), "The cartoon Tom's Doubts, #14,"

Twitter, September 3, 2011, 1:22 p.m., https://twitter.com/S_A_J_I/status
/110040087445782528.

   12. Many scholars now believe the word traditionally translated "meaningless"—as in "'Meaningless! Meaningless!' says the Teacher. 'Utterly meaningless! Everything is meaningless'" (Eccles. 1:2)—is better rendered "obscure." See Ryan P. O'Dowd, "A Chord of Three Strands: Epistemology in Job, Proverbs, and Ecclesiastes," in *The Bible and Epistemology: Biblical Soundings on the Knowledge of God*, ed. Mary Healy and Robin Parry, 65–87, (Colorado Springs: Paternoster, 2007), 80.

   13. Tara Isabella Burton, "Postliberal Epistemology," *Comment*, June 16, 2020, https://www.cardus.ca/comment/article/postliberal-epistemology/.

   14. Wood, *Epistemology*, 16–17.

   15. Wood, *Epistemology*, 47.

   16. Wood, *Epistemology*, 26.

   17. Wood, *Epistemology*, 18, 31.

   18. Wood, *Epistemology*, 19.

   19. Wood, *Epistemology*, 19.

   20. Wood, *Epistemology*, 55–61.

   21. "Esau McCaulley on *Reading While Black*," interview by Dru Johnson, *OnScript* (podcast), December 25, 2020, https://hebraicthought.org/podcast/esau-mccaulley-reading-while-black-onscript/.

   22. Dew and Foreman, *How Do We Know?*, 160.

   23. Wood, *Epistemology*, 61–66.

   24. Wood, *Epistemology*, 66. For a fuller discussion in Wood, see 66–74.

   25. Wood, *Epistemology*, 196.

   26. N. T. Wright, "How Do We Know What We Know?," The Veritas Forum, (YouTube video), July 24, 2017, https://www.youtube.com/watch?v=Nr-yoty_cHw.

   27. N. T. Wright, "Loving to Know," *First Things*, February 2020, https://www.firstthings.com/article/2020/02/loving-to-know.

   28. The Anabaptist tradition is not the only place in Christianity where we find this or a very similar idea; it's merely where I encountered it. See Volf, *Exclusion and Embrace*, 246–48.

   29. Ben C. Ollenburger, "The Hermeneutics of Obedience: A Study of Anabaptist Hermeneutics," *Direction* 6, no. 2 (1977): 19–31.

   30. Greg Boyd speaks to Anabaptist commitment to nonviolence in "Early Anabaptists and the Centrality of Christ" (*ReKnew*, May 16, 2017, https://reknew.org/2017/05/early-anabaptists-centrality-christ):

> This conviction . . . was by no means an Anabaptist innovation. It's deeply rooted in Scripture, and one finds it reflected in a variety of ways throughout the Church tradition. What was distinctive about the Anabaptists' use of this insight, however—and what set them at odds with their Protestant and Catholic contemporaries—was that this insight was fused with their distinctive emphasis on the importance of obeying the teachings and example of Jesus. Some Anabaptists

thus insinuated that the reason magisterial church leaders failed to see the centrality of non-violence in Jesus' teaching and example was not because it is objectively ambiguous but because it's impossible to correctly interpret Scripture unless one is willing to obey it.

Chapter 9 A Building Plan

1. Bo Burnham, *Inside*, produced by Josh Senior, Netflix, released May 30, 2021.
2. Early in his fame, Burnham showed awareness of the destructive potential of the internet generally and social media specifically, but *Inside* was a newly adamant critique. His own social media accounts, once the mainstay of his celebrity, are nearly inactive. See Bo Burnham, "Welcome to Youtube," Bo Burnham (YouTube video), November 25, 2008, https://www.youtube.com/watch?v=W0quDfpfRUQ.
3. Alan Noble, *Disruptive Witness: Speaking Truth in a Distracted Age* (Downers Grove, IL: InterVarsity, 2018), 30.
4. James K. A. Smith, *You Are What You Love: The Spiritual Power of Habit* (Grand Rapids: Brazos, 2016), 4–7.
5. Justin Whitmel Earley, *The Common Rule: Habits of Purpose for an Age of Distraction* (Downers Grove, IL: IVP Books, 2019), 15–16.
6. Andy Crouch, *The Tech-Wise Family: Everyday Steps for Putting Technology in Its Proper Place* (Grand Rapids: Baker Books, 2017), 160.
7. Smith, *You Are What You Love*, 24.
8. Jeffrey Bilbro, *Reading the Times: A Literary and Theological Inquiry into the News* (Downers Grove, IL: InterVarsity, 2021), 15–16.
9. Alan Jacobs, "Attending to Technology," *New Atlantis*, Winter 2016, https://www.thenewatlantis.com/publications/attending-to-technology-theses-for-disputation.
10. Smith, *You Are What You Love*, 40.
11. Noble, *Disruptive Witness*, 20.
12. Nicholas Carr, *The Shallows: What the Internet Is Doing to Our Brains*, rev. ed. (New York: Norton, 2020), 5–6.
13. Kevin Roose, Mike Isaac, and Sheera Frenkel, "Facebook Struggles to Balance Civility and Growth," *New York Times*, November 24, 2020, https://www.nytimes.com/2020/11/24/technology/facebook-election-misinformation.html.
14. Crouch, *Tech-Wise Family*, 98.
15. Caitlin Flanagan, "You Really Need to Quit Twitter," *The Atlantic*, July 5, 2021, https://www.theatlantic.com/ideas/archive/2021/07/twitter-addict-realizes-she-needs-rehab/619343.
16. Earley, *Common Rule*, 90.
17. Noble, *Disruptive Witness*, 25.
18. Earley, *Common Rule*, 64–65.
19. Earley, *Common Rule*, 70.

20. Crouch, *Tech-Wise Family*, 79–80.

21. Carr, *Shallows*, 131.

22. Lawrence M. Eppard, "Healthy News Diets Help Guard against Dangers of Misinformation," *Pittsburgh Post-Gazette*, June 13, 2021, https://www.post-gazette.com/news/insight/2021/06/13/Healthy-news-diets-help-guard-against-dangers-of-misinformation/stories/202106130037.

23. The risk with careless subscription selection isn't only that you'll find yourself in an echo chamber but that you'll land in a state of "epistemic closure." Cato Institute scholar Julian Sanchez, who coined that term, distinguishes between the two this way: "An 'echo chamber' just means you never hear any contrary information. The idea of 'epistemic closure' was that you WOULD hear new and contrary information, but you have mechanisms in your belief system that reject anything that might force you to update your beliefs." Julian Sanchez (@normative), "So an 'echo chamber' just means you never hear any contrary information," Twitter, August 26, 2020, 5:51 p.m., https://twitter.com/normative/status/1298739917770625026.

24. Crouch, *Tech-Wise Family*, 66.

25. C. S. Lewis, *Yours, Jack: Spiritual Direction from C. S. Lewis* (New York: HarperOne, 2008), 119.

26. Earley, *Common Rule*, 88–89.

27. "Delete your account" is a common Twitter insult but, honestly, maybe for the sake of your own growth in Christ you *should* delete your account. Your account likely isn't worse than anyone else's. It might even be better than the account of the person attacking you. That still doesn't mean it's a good thing that moves you closer to Christ.

28. Bilbro, *Reading the Times*, 24–25.

29. Alan Jacobs, "The Year of Hypomone," *Snakes and Ladders* (blog), January 11, 2021, https://blog.ayjay.org/the-year-of-hypomone/.

30. On this point, Sanchez says, "I think a lot of disinfo flourishes by hitting a sweet spot: Too complicated to shoot down in a couple sentences, too obviously absurd to people with real expertise to be worth wasting time on, but superficially persuasive to people with no relevant background." Julian Sanchez (@normative), "I think a lot of disinfo flourishes by hitting a sweet spot," Twitter, May 8, 2021, 10:28 a.m., https://mobile.twitter.com/normative/status/1391037174213222403.

31. Earley, *Common Rule*, 122.

32. Dorothy L. Sayers, "Lost Tools of Learning," paper read at Oxford University, 1947, https://www.pccs.org/wp-content/uploads/2016/06/LostToolsOfLearning-DorothySayers.pdf.

33. For a list of seventeen types of distorted automatic thought, see Robert L. Leahy, Stephen J. F. Holland, and Lata K. McGinn, *Treatment Plans and Interventions for Depression and Anxiety Disorders* (New York: Guilford, 2012), 702.

34. Joseph M. Keegin, "Be Not Afraid," Breaking Ground, May 5, 2021, https://breakingground.us/be-not-afraid/.

35. Smith, *You Are What You Love*, 24–25.

36. Smith, *You Are What You Love*, 90.

Chapter 10 A Breath

1. All quotes attributed to Dennis R. Edwards in this chapter are drawn from a phone interview with Bonnie Kristian, September 21, 2021.

2. Bonnie Kristian, "Our Parents Warned Us the Internet Would Break Our Brains. It Broke Theirs Instead," *The Week*, November 25, 2020, https://theweek.com/articles/951759/parents-warned-internet-break-brains-broke-theirs-instead.

3. Timothy Dalrymple, "The Splintering of the Evangelical Soul," *Christianity Today*, April 16, 2021, https://www.christianitytoday.com/ct/2021/april-web-only/splintering-of-evangelical-soul.html.

4. T. S. Eliot, *The Rock: A Pageant Play* (New York: Harcourt, Brace, 1934), 9.

5. G. K. Chesterton, *Orthodoxy* (New York: Lane, 1908), 32–34.

6. Just to be clear, I am talking about decisions to cut ties solely based on differences in viewpoint, not a refusal to maintain relationships that are manipulative and unhealthy at their core.

7. Dalrymple, "The Splintering of the Evangelical Soul."

8. Benjamin Franklin, *Autobiography of Benjamin Franklin* (New York: Holt, 1916), https://www.gutenberg.org/files/20203/20203-h/20203-h.htm.

9. Franklin, *Autobiography*.

10. Albert Samaha, "My Mom Believes in QAnon. I've Been Trying to Get Her Out," BuzzFeed News, March 12, 2021, https://www.buzzfeednews.com/article/albertsamaha/qanon-parents-millennial-children.

11. Hazel Atkins, "Raising 'The Rock': The Importance of T. S. Eliot's Pageant-Play," *Christianity and Literature* 62, no. 2 (Winter 2013): 261–82.

12. Eliot, *The Rock*, 21.

13. Eliot, *The Rock*, 21.

14. Eliot, *The Rock*, 9.

15. Eliot, *The Rock*, 21–22.